Island in Trust
Culture Change and Dependence in a Micronesian Economy

Westview Special Studies

The concept of Westview Special Studies is a response to the continuing crisis in academic and informational publishing. Library budgets are being diverted from the purchase of books and used for data banks, computers, micromedia, and other methods of information retrieval. Interlibrary loan structures further reduce the edition sizes required to satisfy the needs of the scholarly community. Economic pressures on university presses and the few private scholarly publishing companies have greatly limited the capacity of the industry to properly serve the academic and research communities. As a result, many manuscripts dealing with important subjects, often representing the highest level of scholarship, are no longer economically viable publishing projects--or, if accepted for publication, are typically subject to lead times ranging from one to three years.

Westview Special Studies are our practical solution to the problem. As always, the selection criteria include the importance of the subject, the works contribution to scholarship, and its insight, originality of thought, and excellence of exposition. We accept manuscripts in camera-ready form, typed, set or word processed according to specifications laid out in our comprehensive manual, which contains straightforward instructions and sample pages. The responsibility for editing and proofreading lies with the author or sponsoring institution, but our editorial staff is always available to answer questions and provide guidance.

The result is a book printed on acid-free paper and bound in sturdy library-quality soft covers. We manufacture these books ourselves using equipment that does not require a lengthy make-ready process and that allows us to publish first editions of 300 to 1000 copies and to reprint even smaller quantities as needed. Thus, we can produce Special Studies quickly and can keep even very specialized books in print as long as there is a demand for them.

About the Book and Author

Many small-scale economies depend on or are
affected significantly by subsidies granted by foreign
powers. An especially interesting example of this form
of financial dependence is Micronesia, a Pacific archipelago that has been a trust territory of the United
States since 1947. During the 1970s, appropriations from
the U.S. government to Micronesia amounted to more than
$1000 per capita. The appropriations provided social
services and capital improvement projects, along with
employment opportunities for many local people.

This book describes the impact of externally
funded, public sector employment on the economy of
Micronesia in general and of one island (Kosrae) in
particular. Dr. Peoples shows how government employment
affects the agricultural sector, consumption patterns,
investment decisions by private businesses, allocation
of labor, and the economies of individual households. He
also shows how the island's indigenous economic organization and cultural practices interact with U.S. policy
to influence the pattern of economic change. Comparisons
with other dependent areas examine the relevance of the
Micronesian case to development studies in general.

James G. Peoples is visiting assistant professor
of anthropology at the University of Tulsa.

Island in Trust
Culture Change and Dependence in a Micronesian Economy

James G. Peoples

Westview Press / Boulder and London

A Westview Special Study

Copyright © 1985 by Westview Press, Inc.

Published in 1985 in the United States of America by Westview Press, Inc.;
Frederick A. Praeger, Publisher; 5500 Central Avenue, Boulder, Colorado 80301

Library of Congress Cataloging in Publication Data
 Peoples, James.
   Island in Trust.
   (A Westview special study)
   Includes index.
   1. Kosrae (Micronesia)--Economic conditions.
2. Economic assistance, American--Micronesia--Kosrae.
3. Kosrae (Micronesia)--Dependency on the United
States.   4. Economic assistance, American--Micronesia.
5. Micronesia--Dependency on the United States.
I. Title.
HC681.5.Z7K677 1985   330.996'6   84-25685
ISBN: 0-8133-7034-5

Composition for this book was provided by the author
Printed and bound in the United States of America

10 9 8 7 6 5 4 3 2 1

Contents

Tables, Figures, and Maps

TABLES

ix

FIGURES

MAPS

Acknowledgments

The field data for this monograph was gathered between January, 1975, and February, 1976, with the aid of a Grant for the Improvement of Doctoral Dissertation Research in the Social Sciences from the National Science Foundation, SOC74-21426. In addition to the eleven month period spent on Kosrae, I spent two weeks in Honolulu, two weeks in Agaña, Guam, and five weeks in Kolonia, Ponape, perusing documents that have been of invaluable aid in the historical portions of this study. The late Walter Scott Wilson and his wife Eleanora were extremely gracious hosts in Guam. E.O. Bryan of the Pacific Science Information Center allowed me to make use of aerial photographs taken by the American armed forces during World War II.

I owe thanks to Henry Rutz, William Davis, and the late Martin Baumhoff, who served on my dissertation committee, for their thoughtful comments. Mark N. Cohen and Garrick Bailey read portions of the manuscript. Over the years, I have profitted from discussions with Glenn Petersen, Philip Ritter, and Lynn Takata Ritter. Thanks are due to Donna Humphreys for a professional job on the final version. The Office of the Dean of the College of Arts and Sciences at the University of Tulsa financed the word processing; Warren Jones in the Dean's office was particularly helpful. Dean Birkenkamp and the staff at Westview Press were always prompt and courteous. My wife Deborah Carter Peoples has had saintly patience over the years of my job-hunting attempts.

Any anthropologist's primary debt is to those who made the research enterprise successful, his or her informants and hosts. I thank especially Bingham Palik and his wife Rensilina and all of their children for the hospitality they gave me in their home. Gratitude is also due to the following men who contributed selflessly of their time and knowledge: Boas Abraham, Nana Sigrah, Simeon Skilling, Elaijah Tosie, Franklin James, Kun Jerry, Norman Skilling, Walton Palik, Kilafwa Sikain, Kotaro Palik, and Renny Palik. I also thank Moses

Aliksa, Fred S. Skilling, and all other young men who befriended me. Rollence Weilbacher and Hibson, Aren, and Heinrich Palik did fine jobs as research assistants. Dedicating this book to the people of Lelu village is the only means I have of reciprocating their kindness.

James G. Peoples

1
Perspectives

This book is a case study of economic change on a small Pacific island. The island, called Kosrae by the inhabitants, lies in the eastern Caroline Islands, which are part of the geographic and culture area known popularly as Micronesia. My major aim is to show how economic change in one of the island's four villages is affected by the recent policies of the United States government, which has administered the widely scattered islands of Micronesia since 1947. In particular, I analyze how the American subsidization of Micronesia since the 1960s affects the patterning of change in certain economic variables, such as production, consumption, business expansion, and the allocation of labor time across its alternative uses.

Presumably, these economic patterns develop as a result of the interaction between two sets of forces. On the one hand are the present-day environmental, economic, social, and cultural conditions of Kosrae. On the other hand are the historic and present external inputs to which the island has been and is being subjected. In the short term, these "endogenous" and "exogenous" forces confront villagers as objective circumstances to which their behavior must adapt. The pace and form of change, in Kosrae and elsewhere, is determined by how individuals and groups perceive these circumstances and adjust their lives to them.

If a claim that the pattern of change is determined by the interaction between inputs into the economy "from the outside" and local-level conditions already "in place" seems like a truism, consider the modernization literature. In their effort to understand development, and the lack of it, from a holistic perspective, modernization theorists constructed an ideal type of social form called the "traditional society" and attributed to it certain features that distinguished it from the "modern society." The two societal forms thus opposed, it was argued that the defining characteristics of the traditional type impeded its transformation into the

1

modern type. (Hagen 1962; Hoselitz 1960; Levy 1966). Thus we read of "institutional and cultural barriers to modernization," such as the following. Extended family structures oblige those with surplus income to distribute their wealth among a wide range of distant relatives, to the detriment of accumulation (Bauer and Yamey 1957:66; Lambert 1966:122; Lewis 1955). Culturally obligatory ceremonial expenditures also promote the wasteful consumption of resources that otherwise could be saved or invested (Lambert and Hoselitz 1963:397; Smelser 1963:104). World views (Kunkel 1970:218-40) or unconscious cognitive orientations (Foster 1965) of many peasants stifle incentive. Even child-rearing practices and resulting personality types are seen as "obstacles" to the transformation of traditional society (Hagen 1962; McClelland 1970).

It is true that family organizations, ceremonial expenditures, egalitarian ideologies, and other internal social forces can impede change or channel it into undesirable directions. But these negative impacts occur only under certain conditions; under other conditions these same endogenous structures and cultural practices can be positive forces for change. Good examples of such positive effects occur in several regions of Melanesia studied by Belshaw (1964), Finney (1968; 1973), Epstein (1964; 1968), and Salisbury (1970). One common element in these studies is their documentation of economic growth in the context of non-Western, "traditional," social institutions and cultural values. For example, in some societies indigenous leaders maintained their familial and ceremonial obligations to extended kin and political clients. These social and economic debts later were called in for purposes of investment in novel economic activities. Relations originating in a "traditional" society thus became important resources that aided accumulation of land, labor, and capital. In other regions, traditional family forms have provided a ready-made organizational framework for the development of specialized economic groupings (Benedict 1968).

These case studies remind us of two facts that social scientists familiar with non-Western sociocultural systems already should know. First, the diagnostic features ascribed to "traditional society" in order to form a historical contrast to "modern society" drastically understates the diversity that exists in non-Western societies. Ethnographic research surely has demonstrated that there is no empirical basis for dichotomizing societies into only two abstract forms. Certainly it is useful for some purposes to construct ideal types, even if they are mere caricatures of reality. But to construct such caricatures and then argue that the features of the one impede its transformation into the other is to reify an abstraction. Second, because of this diversity, there is no a priori reason to expect that the institutions and ideologies found in non-Western societies will hinder the growth of their economies. "Sociocultural factors" may affect economic growth positively, negatively, or not at all, depending both on their specific characteristics and on the nature of external inputs.

Equally important for the present study, the modernization approach gave insufficient attention to those forces that originate from outside the so-called "traditional" society, that had an important role in creating it, and that continue to affect it. There was an assumption that the present-day characteristics of these societies, if not entirely representative of their aboriginal state, at least are remnants of it. The centuries of colonial pressures that affected most of Latin America, Asia, and Africa seemingly had no role in generating the form that these societies have today. The people of these regions therefore were denied the history that would show that their present is the historical product of their interaction with the agents of the colonizing nations. Thus, in his worldwide study of "the people without a history," Wolf writes of modernization theory:

> By equating tradition with stasis and lack of development, it denied societies marked off as traditional any significant history of their own. Above all, by dividing the world into modern, transitional, and traditional societies, it blocked effective understanding of relationships among them. (Wolf 1982:13)

This history need not produce a society with the characteristics ascribed to "modernity"; nor should the variety of societies in the world today be viewed simplistically as stages in the transition from "traditionalism." (Amin 1972:520; Hutton and Cohen 1975)

Thus, by collapsing non-Western societies into a single ideal type, modernization theory gave insufficient attention to the diversity of these societies and to the potentially variable impact that this diversity has on development. Further, lacking an historical perspective on societies lumped into the traditional category, it mistakenly equated their contemporary institutions and cultural practices with their original state. However, an even more serious weakness of modernization theory did not become apparent until the late 1960s and 1970s, with the emergence of an alternative approach that became known as dependency. Dependency "takes as its central premise that it is impossible to

4

comprehend the processes and problems of development in
the Third World without treating this within the wider
socio-historical context of the expansion of Western
Europe mercantile and industrial capitalism and the
colonization of the Third World by these advanced
economies" (Long 1977:71). It is not "what's inside"
the society that blocks its transformation, but rather
the way in which it was and is incorporated into the
worldwide political and economic system (Frank 1966;
Wallerstein 1974, 1979). Contrary to the popular conception, poverty was not the original state of those
regions that today are underdeveloped. Rather, in
China, India, and parts of Southeast Asia, Latin
America, and Africa, the colonizing nations encountered
civilizations that themselves were developing rapidly.
European powers extracted their natural resources, en-
slaved or otherwise exploited their labor, and appropriated their surplus, all for the purpose of developing
Europe's own capitalistic economy.

According to the dependency approach, just as the
rich nations owe their rapid rates of growth and industrialization to the exploitation of their colonies in
the past, so today do they continue to develop at the
expense of their satellites in the Third World. But the
process by which the wealthy nations "extract" economic
surplus from underdeveloped regions by "penetrating"
their economies has altered as the world system has
evolved. Expropriation of natural resources, labor,
talent, and so forth now occur through the agency of the
multinational corporation and financial institutions
(Barnet and Muller 1974; Muller 1973). Development and
underdevelopment thus are part of the same worldwide
process, namely the global expansion of the capitalist
economic system, which underdevelops the rest of the
world as it develops itself.

I do not wish to debate the empirical merits of the
dependency literature, which has been criticized from
a variety of political and scientific perspectives
(Dannhaeuser 1983; Foster-Carter 1978; Laclau 1971;
O'Brien 1975; Taylor 1979). Despite its deficiencies,
one contribution of the approach that is likely to survive is its most general point: Third World peoples are
today and have been for centuries part of a worldwide
economic and political system that affects their possi-
bilities for improving their lives more strongly than
any institutional or cultural characteristics internal
to their societies. Dependency thus corrected modernization theory's overemphasis on the internal characteristics attributed to a traditional type of society that
itself was imaginary.

The dependency approach is useful to the description and analysis of this book for two reasons. First,
its historical perspective is required to understand the

present economic and cultural state of the island. As shown in chapter 3, the interaction of the Kosraen people with early traders and missionaries gave rise to novel organizational forms and cultural practices. These forms and practices themselves now are critical influences on the pattern of response of the islanders to recent external inputs. Second, regardless of the relative adequacy of dependency as a theory of development and underdevelopment, it does have the merit of focussing our attention beyond the boundaries of specific research sites (and academic disciplines) to determine the global-level forces that affect the societies we study. Indeed, even if dependency is weak as a generalized "theory" of underdevelopment, it still might be useful as a "methodology" for the investigation of concrete cases (Palma 1978), a point discussed further in the concluding chapter.

I also hope to make two substantive contributions to the dependency literature. First, although Micronesia is a dependent area in almost any sense of the term, the way in which it is dependent scarcely is described in the existing literature on the subject. Chapter 2 documents the existence of this seldom-described form of dependency and describes its economic implications for a little-known area of the world. Second, through this case study I hope to make an anthropological contribution to the dependency approach. In my view, we ethnographers usually do our best work in villages with populations of a few hundred to a few thousand. In their effort to overcome the excesses of the modernization approach, some dependency writers leave the impression that the constraints imposed on the small villages of the world are so severe that "what's inside" them organizationally and culturally is of little consequence for understanding their reactions. Yet, within these constraints, villagers make choices about how to allocate the resources at their disposal. Most anthropologists believe that the resulting strategies vary with local-level environmental, economic, and sociocultural conditions, as well as with world-system inputs. A major theme of this study, and I hope a correction to dependency's tendency to underestimate the significance of these conditions, is that the economic patterns in the village studied result from the interaction between endogenous and exogenous forces. I describe the specific local-level conditions that interact most strongly with external inputs, analyze how they interact, and show the economic patterns that result from the interaction. This analysis appears throughout the book, but is most explicit in chapters 5 through 10.

2
Dependence in Micronesia

The islands known popularly as Micronesia are located between 1 to 22 degrees north latitude and 130 to
172 degrees east longitude (Map 2.1). So defined, the
total area encompassed is around three million square
miles, or roughly the size of the continental United
States. Over 2,000 islands are located within this
expanse, of which less than 100 are settled permanently.
Most of the islands are so tiny that the total area of
land is only a little over 700 square miles, and most of
this land mass is comprised by the six largest islands.
The larger islands are called "high" or "volcanic,"
because geologically they are the tips of ancient volca-
noes. The other islands, called "low" or "coralline,"
have a bedrock of limestone built up through the mille-
nia by secretions of the coral organism. A few of the
high islands have elevations of over 2,000 feet, but
most of the low extend only to about 10 feet above sea
level.
Micronesia is composed of three extensive archi-
pelagos: the Northern Mariana Islands, the Caroline
Islands, and the Marshall Islands. The westernmost
islands of Kiribati (formerly the Gilbert Islands) sometimes are considered part of Micronesia, based on certain linguistic and cultural affinities. However,
because they have been separated politically by a different colonial history since 1892, and today are part
of an independent nation, they are excluded from further
consideration in this study. Two other islands also are
excluded by their present political status: Guam has
been an American territory since 1898, and Nauru became
an independent nation in 1969. As used today, the term
Micronesia thus refers not to islands that share a relatively uniform culture, but rather denotes three archi-
pelagos united mainly by a common history of colonialism
since the late nineteenth century.
The United States has administered these widely
scattered islands since the end of World War II, when
the American Navy seized the islands by force from the

7

8

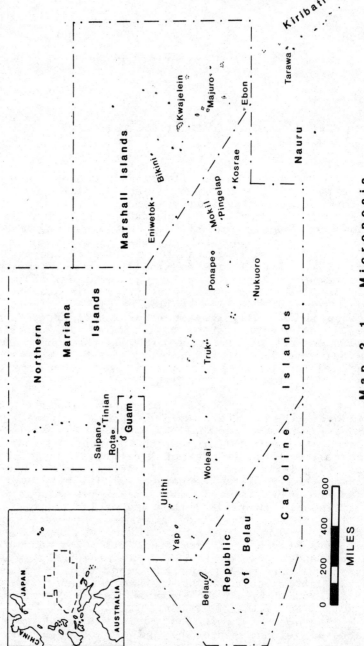

Map 2.1. Micronesia

Japanese military. In 1947, the United Nations desig-
nated America as the Administering Authority for the
newly created United States Trust Territory of the
Pacific Islands, which became the official name for the
islands comprising Micronesia. For administrative purposes, the islands were subdivided into six districts:
the Northern Marianas, Palau, Yap, Truk, Ponape, and the
Marshalls. In 1977, the island called Kosrae (formerly
Kusaie) separated administratively from Ponape to form
its own district. Under the terms of the Trusteeship
Agreement signed in 1947, the United Nations empowered
the Administering Authority to use the islands for certain military purposes and charged it with developing
the islands socially, educationally, politically, and
economically. These rights and obligations of the
United States in the region are covered in a later section. Here I wish to describe, in a preliminary
fashion, the economic problems of the islands in the
late 1970s.

These problems are explained partly by Micronesia's
geographic features. The region has lots of ocean but
very little land on which an export-oriented agricultural economy could be based. The islands are widely
scattered, which allegedly makes internal transportation
and communication difficult. Many low islands of the
Carolines and Marshalls are so small and isolated that
high transportation costs make the production of land
and sea resources for export uneconomic. Finally, the
whole area is relatively distant from major markets in
the industrial countries. These characteristics have
led most observers to conclude that Micronesia has
little to develop or "no resources" or that the economic potential of the area is "pitifully small" (Nevin
1977:24, 36, 141).

This "nothing to develop" view of Micronesian
natural resources probably has been overstated. If it
means merely that multinational corporations from the
developed countries generally find the islands relatively unattractive as a region in which to invest, then
it may be justified, a point to which I return in the
conclusion. It almost certainly is incorrect if it
is taken to mean that the land and sea resources of
Micronesia are inadequate to supply the indigenous
inhabitants with the necessities of existence. It is
important to understand that Micronesians do not suffer
from the severe poverty familiar from most of Africa,
Asia, and Latin America. Until the 1960s, the economies
of the various islands were subsistence-oriented, but
they were largely self-sufficient. The most important
cultigens are tropical root crops such as taro and yams
and tree crops such as bananas, breadfruit, coconut, and
pandanus. The cultivation of these using traditional
methods requires only a few tools, of which the most

important are the bush knife and the digging stick, and
no Micronesian lacks access to this simple technology.
Land obviously is limited, but cultivation methods, land
tenure practices, and social organization have been
adapting to this reality for hundreds of years, and few
Micronesian families are unable to feed themselves
because they lack adequate land. As will be documented
for one island in chapter 5, the major cultigens do not
require long hours of drudgery for subsistence purposes,
so in general caloric returns to agricultural labor are
high. Micronesians have developed sophisticated tech-
nologies and methods to acquire fish, which is supple-
mented on most islands by domestic animals such as the
pig, chicken, dog, and goat. Finally, consumption of
imported durables such as motor vehicles, household
goods, and building materials for new houses, and of
nonmaterial services such as education and health care,
has risen dramatically since the 1960s, as documented
later in this chapter. In short, compared to most other
regions considered underdeveloped, Micronesians generally are well-nourished and healthy, and in fact their
consumption of goods and services of many kinds is increasing at an astounding rate.

In spite of these facts, most observers agree that
the economy of the islands is in a sorry state. Numerous facts and figures support this judgment. One index
is the balance of trade. In 1977, Micronesians imported
about $7 worth of goods for every $1 worth of goods
exported. This ratio represents a deterioration compared to the 1950s and early 1960s, when the figure was
more on the order of $2 of imports for every $1 of
exports. A disturbing statistic is the level of imports
of food, which alone were about two and one-half times
the value of all exported commodities in 1977. Again,
this is a serious change for the worse: the dollar
value of imported foodstuffs in 1977 was almost six
times that of 1963. Another index is the level of production of agricultural commodities, both for subsistence uses and for export to foreign markets. There is
no doubt that the production of agricultural, fish, and
animal husbandry products for household uses has not
nearly kept pace with population growth since 1960.
Indeed, it is likely, but cannot be documented, that
production of foodstuffs for subsistence purposes has
declined absolutely, not just relatively to population
increase. Nor have agricultural exports increased. For
the past 30 years, since the Americans have administered
the islands, the only agricultural commodity produced in
significant quantities for export is copra, the dried
meat of the coconut. It almost always is produced on
private land using household labor. In 1977, an average
Micronesian earned only about $15 from copra production,
again a decline over most of the previous 15 years.

(Numerical data documenting this and most of the following discussion are taken from the Annual Reports to
United Nations on the Administration of the Trust Territory of the Pacific Islands, which the U.S. Department
of State has published every year since it acquired control over the islands.)

An apparent economic paradox of Micronesia is that
material standards of living have risen rapidly since
the middle 1960s even while production of local commodities both for subsistence uses and market sale have
declined. As shown in later sections, this situation is
possible because the United States government has sub-
sidized the area with hundreds of millions of dollars
since the early 1960s.

COLONIAL HISTORY

The United States is the fourth world power to
acquire control over Micronesia. Spain held the islands
of the Marianas and Carolines from 1888-1899, but outside of the Mariana Islands did little in the way of
either administration or development. Several German
companies had established trading stations in the
Marshalls and Carolines by the 1870s, before the islands
became official colonies of any foreign power. Two
German firms active in the copra trade in the Marshalls
appealed to their government to annex these tiny islands
in 1885; the Carolines and Marianas were purchased from
Spain in 1899, also largely to promote the commercial
interests of German nationals. Micronesians were encouraged, and sometimes forced, to extend coconut plantings for the copra trade. Companies such as the Jaluit-
Gesellschaft, Godeffroy and Sons, Capelle and Company,
and Robertson and Hernsheim established trading stations
to purchase copra and sell trade goods to the islanders
in the late nineteenth and early twentieth centuries.
According to S. Firth (1973:28), Germany's Pacific colonies (which included parts of Melanesia and Western
Polynesia as well as the Caroline and Marshall Islands)
were not as profitable as the early enthusiasts had
hoped, but "what must not be overlooked . . . is that
some individuals benefited enormously from their investment in the Pacific Islands." Further, "German
firms made their greatest profits not in Samoa or New
Guinea but in the scattered atolls of Micronesia" (S.
Firth 1973:24).

At the outbreak of World War I, the Japanese navy
took possession of the whole of Micronesia. Their de
facto control was confirmed legally in 1921, when the
League of Nations granted Japan a Class C Mandate,
applying to territories not expected to attain independence in the forseeable future. In 1922, the mandated

area was placed under the civil administration called the South Seas Bureau, with headquarters at Koror, Palau.

More than any colonial power before or since, between 1914 and 1945 the Japanese found it in their own interest to exploit the natural resources of Micronesia. Japan continued the mining of phosphate begun by the Germans on Angaur (in the Palau group) and on three other islands in the western Carolines, using both indigenous and imported laborers. In the 1920s and 1930s, the South Seas Bureau undertook a land survey and title registration program on most of the major islands. The result of this "survey" was that most of the land not actually under cultivation was declared the property of the Japanese government. (Purcell 1976:198) Subsequently, much of this alienated land was leased or otherwise utilized by the South Seas Development Company, a private corporation that by 1937 had organized the planting of 30,000 acres of sugar cane in the Northern Marianas. Most of the land was worked by imported Japanese or Okinawan families under a lease arrangement (Purcell 1976:200-202). By 1935, so many immigrants had poured into the Northern Marianas that there were more Japanese residents than Micronesians in the whole territory (Yanaihara 1940). The Japanese also exploited the ocean resources of the territory: in 1939, 674 vessels exported over 21,000 tons of tuna to the home country (Purcell 1976:206-7). Altogether, 48.5 million yen of tropical products were exported from Micronesia to Japan in 1940 (Oliver 1971:34).

Increases in production of this magnitude require an expansion of infrastructure and of social services. New roads, harbor facilities, water systems, and power generating plants were constructed on most of the major islands, which also became linked to one another and to Japan by regular shipping and communication lines. Micronesian standards of living did improve as a result of such developments, although clearly most of the profits went to Japanese residents and to their resource-hungry homeland. Copra production by Micronesians expanded threefold between 1922 and 1935 (Purcell 1976:203), and the indigenous population received wages from stevedoring, mining, land clearing, and services.

Many elderly Micronesians of today remember the rule of Japan with ambivalent emotions. Their economic accomplishments are admired and the infrastructure and social services they provided were unmatched until the late 1960s. On the other hand, during World War II many of the islands were fortified with military equipment and many thousands of personnel. Towards the end of the war, the American naval blockade cut off supplies to the large Japanese garrisons in the Marianas, Marshalls, and

some of the Carolines. As supplies ran low, mistreat-
ment of islanders by Japanese servicemen grew extreme in
some areas. When, island by island, the Japanese sur-
rendered, the Americans generally were viewed as a
rescuing force; on Kosrae, for example, the day of the
Japanese surrender still is celebrated with games and
feasts.

After the war, the United States decided that, due
to its fortuitous proximity to Asia, Micronesia was so
vital to international peace and to American security
that a special arrangement was needed to ensure that the
islands did not fall into the hands of nations judged to
be a threat to world peace. The Americans proposed, and
in 1947 the United Nations accepted, that the area
become a "strategic" trust territory administered by the
United States. Of the 11 trust territories established
after World War II, Micronesia was the only one to receive the designation of "strategic trusteeship." This
title gave the Administering Authority the right to
establish military fortifications and to station military personnel in the islands. It also allowed the
United States to close off part or all of the area to
international inspection for security reasons. Finally,
international supervision of the islands was placed
under the control of the Security Council, where the
Americans have a veto, rather than the Trusteeship
Council (McHenry 1975:33-4).

However, the Trusteeship Agreement signed in 1947
was not meant to imply that the Americans remain in permanent political control. Indeed, Article 6 of the
Trusteeship Agreement requires the Administering
Authority to

> Foster the development of such political institu-
> tions as are suited to the trust territory and ...
> promote the development of the inhabitants of the
> trust territory toward self-government or indepen-
> dence as may be appropriate to the particular cir-
> cumstances of the trust territory and its peoples
> and the freely expressed wishes of the peoples con-
> cerned ... (U.S. Department of State 1977:155)

Although the Agreement specified no date for the termi-
nation of the trusteeship, clearly the United States was
obligated in the future to take steps towards a restruc-
turing of its unique relationship with the islands. The
phrases "particular circumstances" and "freely expressed
wishes," however, left considerable room for later political maneuver by the Administering Authority. Other
portions of the Agreement specify additional obligations
of the United States to Micronesians, one of which is to
"promote the economic advancement and self-sufficiency
of the inhabitants" by improving infrastructure,

encouraging the development of land and sea resources, and protecting the inhabitants against loss of their land and other resources (U.S. Department of State 1977: 155).

The interests of the United States in Micronesia were in 1947, and continue to be today, almost entirely strategic/military rather than economic, unlike the Japanese whose motives apparently were a mixture of both. Historically, the Defense Department has been most concerned to prevent other nations from having military access to the islands, i.e., with "strategic denial" rather than with actual "strategic use." However, the United States has exercised its rights to establish fortifications and to use the area for military purposes. From 1951-62, a C.I.A. installation on Saipan was established to train the Chinese supporters of Chiang Kai-shek, explaining why Saipan and Tinian were under tight military security during the 1950s (McHenry 1975:57). In the 1950s an Army missile-tracking facility was constructed on Kwajelein atoll in the Marshall Islands. Still operational, it is by far the most important use of the islands by the military today. Most famous of all military operations in Micronesia are the nuclear tests conducted on Bikini and Eniwetok atolls in the Marshalls during the 1940s and 1950s. The indigenous populations were removed to other islands, and only in the late 1970s were Bikini and Eniwetok judged marginally safe for human habitation. To public knowledge, these activities are the only significant military uses made by the United States of the islands to date. In other respects, the American government has been content to deny other nations access to Micronesia and, equally important, to hold onto the area in case changes in world politics should require the active use of the area in the future (McHenry 1975).

How well did the United States live up to its commitments to promote the political, economic, social, and educational development of Micronesia after 1945? The productive enterprises and infrastructural improvements set up by the Japanese largely were destroyed by wartime bombing and fighting. The Navy was the governmental department charged with the administration and rebuilding of the islands from 1945-51. Some attempt was made to improve physical infrastructure, to provide shipping and communications, and to promote commerce and external trade. In 1946, the Navy commissioned a team of scientists to carry out a four-month long survey of the economic resources of the islands and to make recommendations for future economic policy. The final report, edited by anthropologist Douglas Oliver (1971; original 1951), recognized the economic achievements of the Japanese and contrasted the high living standards of Micronesians in the 1930s with their stagnant economy at

the time of the survey (Oliver 1971:24). The major recommendation that runs throughout the report is that "the
United States Administration should establish a level of
income for residents of the islands at least equal to
that existing under the Japanese prior to the war."
(Oliver 1971:28)

During the 1950s, this recommendation was unheeded
by Washington policy makers. Responsibility for the
administration of the Caroline and Marshall Islands was
transferred from the Navy to the Department of the
Interior in 1951, where it remains until the present.
Under Interior, the area's economy received little external support. Shipping was irregular, there was
almost no improvement of physical infrastructure, no
reliable markets were established for Micronesian products, and few wage labor opportunities existed.
Micronesians retrenched back into subsistence cultivation and fishing, acquiring minimum cash income from
copra, handicrafts, and a small amount of wage labor
working for the Trust Territory government as teachers
or unskilled laborers. During this decade, Micronesia
was called "America's Paradise Lost," "The Forgotten
Islands," "Showcase of Neglect," and the "Rust
Territory," in various publications (McHenry 1975:14).
Later critics charged the administration with main-
taining an "anthropological zoo" or a "cultural museum."
These may be overstatements, but everyone agrees that
the United States made little attempt to carry out its
obligations under the Trusteeship Agreement of 1947. To
my knowledge, the rationale for the official inaction
during these years has not been analyzed. It may have
been due to humanitarian concerns about the adverse consequences of "too much acculturation too quickly," which
some anthropologists continually intoned to colonial
governments during this period. More likely, lack of
pressure from the United Nations and from Micronesians
themselves, combined with Defense's satisfaction with
"strategic denial," rendered the territory low on the
list of American priorities. Certainly, it was mainly
because of pressure from the United Nations that the
United States reversed its policy in the 1960s and
1970s.

THE POLITICS OF MICRONESIAN DEPENDENCE

In 1961, the Trusteeship Council of the United
nations sent a Visiting Mission to Micronesia to inves-
tigate American policy. Anticolonial sentiment in the
United Nations was sufficiently strong that a critical
report was issued, stunning many in the Kennedy administration. Among other deficiencies, the Administering
Authority was claimed to have failed to provide adequate

transportation, to have neglected economic development, to have been remiss in providing education and adequate health care, and to have taken no steps to end the trusteeship (McHenry 1975:13). Also disturbing to Washington was the "considerable dissatisfaction and discontent" with the administration that the Mission reported among Micronesians (Nevin 1977:103). The issuance of this report, and subsequent actions taken by the Kennedy and future administrations, mark the major turning point in United States policy in Micronesia.

Washington policy makers were faced with a dilemma. National security was believed to require that the United States retain political control over the region indefinitely, if only to deny military access to other foreign powers. At the same time, anticolonial feelings in the United Nations made the continuation of the status quo somewhat embarrassing, if not politically intolerable. A way had to be found to reconcile "indefinite control" with the principle of "self-determination" for Micronesians. The obvious solution was to satisfy the United Nations' legitimate demands for economic development and political self-determination while at the same time giving the Micronesians every reason to desire permanent affiliation with the United States.

Donald F. McHenry (1975), in his important book Micronesia: Trust Betrayed, has summarized the events that led up to the eventual policy adopted. National Security Action Memorandum (NSAM) 145 was issued on April 18, 1962. It recognized the American objective to bring Micronesia into some kind of permanent political relationship with the United States. It also "called for accelerated development of the area to bring its political, economic, and social standards into line with an eventual permanent association" (McHenry 1975:17). One year later, in May, 1963, NSAM 243 directed that a survey mission headed by Anthony N. Solomon be sent to Micronesia to review conditions and make recommendations. The infamous Solomon Report, in three volumes, was issued in late summer, 1963. Its contents later were classified, because the Department of State "did not wish to make public the political policy objectives which were referred to throughout Volumes II and III" (McHenry 1975:16). The entire document still is unavailable for public scrutiny, but a portion of its contents are reprinted in McHenry (1975:Appendix I).

The Solomon Report reiterated the strategic/military goals of the United States. It accepted as a political necessity that Micronesia should remain in some kind of a "permanent relationship" with the American government, even while acknowledging that the area would be the only trust territory to affiliate with the administering power. The report recommended that a plebiscite be held in Micronesia in 1968 in which the people

would choose between independence and permanent affiliation with the United States. It went further to
suggest possible actions that Washington officials could
take to "insure a favorable vote in the plebiscite." In
the portions of the report available, these actions
included:

1. "An effective capital investment program before
   the plebiscite to give Micronesians a sense of
   progress";
2. "Introduction in the school system of US-
   oriented curriculum changes and patriotic
   rituals";
3. "Increasing the number of college scholarships
   offered to Micronesians";
4. The introduction of 60 Peace Corps Volunteers
   into the area;
5. The promise that Micronesian pay scales would
   be equivalent to that of U.S. citizens employed
   by the Trust Territory government after a vote
   for affiliation;
6. The imposition of a governmental structure that
   gives "a reasonable appearance of self-govern-
   ment through an elected Micronesian legislature
   and a Micronesian Chief Executive"; and,
7. "The formulation of programs and policies for
   an accelerated rate of development" (McHenry
   1975:Appendix I).

It was recognized in the report that such policies
necessarily would be expensive, but that the subsidy
could be justified as a "strategic rental" amounting to
more than $300 annually per Micronesian through 1968.
As further insurance that the United States interests
would be protected in the plebiscite, the report recommended that the ballot alternatives be limited to two:

(a) Are you in favor of becoming an independent
    nation?
(b) Are you in favor of a permanent affiliation
    with the US of America? (McHenry 1975:237)

Because, in 1963, the mission detected little desire for
independence, it estimated that about 95% of the voters
would choose option (b). If some countries at the
United Nations perceived that option (a) would not be a
viable alternative by 1968, than a third possibility
could be included: the maintenance of the status quo.
This would reduce the size of the vote for (b), but it
still would win by a majority.

National Security Action Memorandum 268, issued
in late 1963, directed that the task force's recommendations be implemented as policy. Kennedy was

assasinated in November, and there is some doubt about
whether the document had any major influence subsequently. Young Micronesian political activists
reprinted the report in two newspapers in 1971, one of
which described it as "a ruthless five-year plan to
systematically Americanize Micronesia into a permanent
association in clear and conscious defiance of [the
United States'] trusteeship obligations" (quoted in
McHenry 1975:19). However, Nevin (1977:124-8) downplays
its significance for subsequent American actions,
arguing that the policy already was formulated before
the report was issued. Whether this specific document
was the major determinant of future American programs
thus is arguable, but it is clear that enough Washington
officials agreed with the general objective of permanent
affiliation for this goal to have dominated U.S. concerns. Further, subsequent American actions reveal with
equal clarity that the policy means recommended in the
report actually were implemented.

In 1963, the U.S. Congress began to pour in money.
Funds for administration, education, medical services,
infrastructural development, capital improvement projects, and governmental services always had come mainly
from two sources: appropriations made annually by the
U.S. Congress, and tax revenues and reimbursements for
government services paid by Micronesians. The Congressional appropriations increased unsteadily until 1962,
reaching a maximum of $6.8 million in 1960. In 1963,
the appropriated funds suddenly more than doubled, to
$15 million; by 1969, they increased to $30 million; by
1975, to $69.7 million; by 1978, to $96.6 million. (U.S.
Department of State 1949-78) Despite the high rate of
population growth in Micronesia, the amount appropriated
per capita by the U.S. Congress increased about eight-
fold between 1960 and 1978. Even these figures do not
express the full magnitude of the increase. The Trust
Territory government also is eligible to compete for
additional federal grants. In 1970, the area received
an additional $2.4 million through this channel; by
1978, $33.9 million in federal grants were received.
The real magnitude of American assistance for 1978 was
$130.5 million, or an appropriation per Micronesian of
over $1,000 (U.S. Department of State 1978: Statistical
Table 32c).

These funds are spent in a variety of ways. Quantitatively, education, public works, and health care
consistently receive the largest share of funds. New
school buildings, electricity generating plants, roads,
docks, and hospitals have been constructed in all districts. By 1977, there were 234 public elementary
schools and 18 public high schools with a total enroll-
ment of over 18,000 students in the Trust Territory.
Every district now has its own modern hospital. In

1977, there were 78 electric power generating facilities. (U.S. Department of State 1977:Statistical Tables 20, 36a, 37, and 41). Other governmental services, such as police, transportation, communication, administration, and community development, also have been improved.

The obvious result of this monetary investment by the United States to achieve its own political goals in the area has been an increase in the standards of living of almost all Micronesians. In part, this improvement appears as an increased volume of available social services and capital improvements. Equally important, Micronesian cash incomes and material consumption levels have risen dramatically. This is because roughly one-third of the funds appropriated annually by the U.S. Congress have been paid as wages to Micronesians who have found employment with one or another externally funded governmental agency. In 1962, before the budget expansion began, the government employed only about 2,200 Micronesians; in 1970, there were almost 5,000 government employees; by 1977, there were over 10,000. Because of increases in government wage rates, mainly in the 1970s, the amount of income earned through government employment rose even faster (Table 2.1). Using total wage income from both governmental and private sources as a rough measure of consumption levels, and taking population increase into account, between 1962 and 1977 consumption increased about 1,000%!

ECONOMIC CONSEQUENCES

In succeeding chapters, I discuss in detail the far-reaching economic effects of the United States' "big bucks" policy on one island. The political effects are equally profound, but are outside the scope of this work (see McHenry 1975, Nevin 1977, Nufer 1978, and Gale 1979 for extended discussions). In the remainder of this chapter, I wish to show, in general terms, how the actions taken by the United States to achieve its own political goals in Micronesia have affected several economic variables. These include employment, business opportunity, and external trade.

Governmental Employment

Micronesians earn cash income from several sources, of which the most important are employment with the Trust Territory administration or some other governmental agency, jobs with private businesses, profits of local businesses, copra production, and small-scale sale of handicrafts, fish, pork, and agricultural

TABLE 2.1
Trust Territory government employment and wage statistics, 1962-1977

Year	Number of Employees	Government Sources ($ million)	Private Sources ($ million)	Total ($ million)	Total Wages Per Capita	Government/Total Wages Ratio
1962	2,191	$ 2.69	$ .82	$ 3.51	$ 39	.77
1963	2,483	3.50	.93	4.43	52	.79
1964	2,831	4.44	1.14	5.58	63	.80
1965	3,530	5.74	1.37	7.10	78	.81
1966	3,530	5.88	1.86	7.74	84	.76
1967	3,908	6.84	2.21	9.95	109	.76
1968	N/A	9.55	2.37	11.92	126	.80
1969	4,415	11.56	3.18	14.74	150	.78
1970	4,960	15.57	4.99	20.55	203	.76
1971	6,024	18.12	6.09	24.21	233	.75
1972	5,785	23.13	5.79	28.47	266	.80
1973	6,718	23.21	7.25	30.47	277	.76
1974	6,611	N/A	N/A	N/A	N/A	N/A
1975	7,146	30.06	10.37	40.43	346	.74
1976	10,591	39.39	11.24	50.63	418	.78
1977	10,753	42.15	13.18	55.33	444	.76

N/A=Not Available

Source: U.S. Department of State (1962-1977)

commodities. By far the most significant of these
sources are wages earned directly from employment with
some U.S.-funded governmental agency, which accounted
for roughly one-half of all cash income in 1977 (calculated from data given in U.S. Department of State 1977:
Statistical Table 35). Of course, this income is transferred from American taxpayers through Congressional
appropriations.

Private Employment

This figure of about 50% of all cash income earned
directly from employment with, in effect, a foreign government is disturbing enough, but even this statistic
understates the actual level of Micronesia's dependence
on the United States. This is because wages and profits
in the private sector represent a form of "indirect
dependence." The income earned from government jobs
creates demand, thus providing new opportunities for
Micronesian businesses. Since the 1960s, new private
enterprises developed in direct proportion to the amount
of wages earned through government employment. This is
documented in the Government/Total Wages Ratio column of
Table 2.1. Between 1962 and 1977, this ratio varied
only between .74 and .81, a clear indication that the
expansion of Micronesian-owned businesses during this
period is made possible by the increasing demand generated from government employment. This ratio also
reveals that the expansion of jobs in the public sector
creates new opportunities even for persons not employed
by the government. As an estimate, perhaps one-third of
all cash income is earned from profits of private businesses or employment in the private sector. Almost all
this income exists only because of wages earned through
working for the Trust Territory administration.

Nature of Business Expansion

It is thus apparent that expenditures by the U.S.
government in Micronesia stimulate the territory's economy. But the stimulation is unevenly distributed
across sectors: it is the service sector that has
expanded, not the productive sector. In 1971, for
example, the largest sources of private employment in
Micronesia were: general merchandise (mostly retail
outlets), construction companies (most of which were on
contract with the government), transportation, and
stevedoring. These kinds of businesses, which depend on
the presence of government wages among the population
or, in many cases, directly on contracts with the government, accounted for $4.3 million of the $6.1 million

earned from private sources (U.S. Department of State 1971: Statistical Appendix 18). More recently, in 1977, about $7.8 million of the $13.2 million earned from employment in the private sector came from the same four activities. By contrast, in 1977, only $0.6 million were earned from business activities listed as "Manufacturing and Handicrafts" and "Agricultural and Fisheries" in the Annual Reports; significantly, these are the only two categories of tabulated activities that produce some local resource for monetary profit (U.S. Department of State 1978:Statistical Table 10). Clearly, production (as opposed to import) for resale purposes has received only a slight, if any, boost from the expansion of government employment. I have attempted to explain why Micronesian businesses "cluster" in service industries elsewhere (Peoples 1978).

Balance of Trade

The direct and indirect dependence of Micronesians on the U.S. government for cash income and the dependence of local service industries on the demand resulting from government employment do not exhaust the dependency relationship of the area on the outside. Micronesians rely on foreign producers (mainly in the United States, Japan, the Philippines, and Australia) for almost all their manufactured commodities and for an ever-increasing portion of their food supply. The dollar value of imports in 1977 was eight times the value for 1963 (Table 2.2). Most alarming is the six-fold increase in imports of food over this period. It shows that Micronesians have increasingly substituted rice, tinned fish and meats, sugar, flour, and other imported foodstuffs for their traditional breadfruit, taro, yams, bananas, pork, fish, and other locally produced agricultural goods. What this has done to their formerly self-sufficient subsistence economies is obvious: from once having produced their own food on their own land, employed Micronesians (and many unemployed as well) now purchase much of their food from the world market. Subsistence cultivation for most wage earners has become a spare-time activity.

Increases in exports have not nearly kept pace with the rise in the consumption of imported commodities, as Table 2.3 reveals. Excluding tourism, which became significant on a few islands outside the Marianas only in the 1970s, the ratio of imports to exports of goods worsened from 2.33 in 1963 to 7.16 in 1977. Like other figures, these are discouraging enough, but $3.52 of the $5.62 total commodity exports in 1977 were from a foreign firm that exported tuna from Palau. If this amount is excluded from 1977 export figures, only $2.1 million

TABLE 2.2
Value of imports in millions of dollars, 1963-77

Year	Rice	Total Food[a]	Building Materials[b]	Other Non-Food[c]	Grand Total
1963	.469	2.281	.350	2.398	5.029
1965	.733	3.399	.647	3.045	7.091
1967	1.149	4.811	1.268	3.740	9.819
1969	1.153	5.767	1.623	6.522	13.942
1971	2.005	7.978	3.498	14.691	26.167
1973	1.568	8.917	2.883	14.228	26.028
1975	3.200	12.635	2.143	23.434	38.212
1977[d]	N/S	13.018	N/S	27.209	40.227

N/S=not specified in U.S. Department of State 1978: Statistical Table 23b

[a]Other than rice, the main food imports are tinned meats and fish, sugar, and flour.

[b]This category includes lumber and plywood, tin, cement, and glass. Most of these materials are used to construct private dwellings.

[c]In the Annual Reports, these include: beverages, petroleum products, tobacco, clothing and textile products, machinery, boat parts, and "others."

[d]The figures for this year do not include the Mariana Islands, which came under separate administration from the districts in the Marshalls and Carolines in 1977. Further, the grand total for this year excludes $4.5 million worth of copra imported for processing and export to the United States by the copra mill owned by the Micronesian Industrial Corporation in Palau.

Source: U.S. Department of State (1963-1977)

TABLE 2.3
Value of exports in millions of dollars, 1963-77

Year	Copra[a]	Total Commodity Exports[b]	Tourism Income[c]	Total Value, All Exports	Ratio of Imports/ All Exports	Ratio of Imports/ Commodity Exports
1963	1.92	2.16	—	2.16	2.33	2.33
1965	2.53	3.15	—	3.15	2.25	2.25
1967	1.69	2.32	—	2.32	4.23	4.23
1969	2.20	2.86	—	2.86	4.87	4.87
1971	1.65	3.00	2.40	5.40	4.85	8.72
1973	.95	1.89	3.53	5.42	4.80	13.77
1975	3.27	6.83	4.95	11.78	3.24	5.59
1977[d]	1.77	5.62	1.98	7.61	5.28	7.16

[a]Until recently, copra produced by private households and exported unprocessed was by far the largest commodity export. World prices reached their highest level in history in 1975, explaining the large dollar value in that year. By 1976, its value ($1.62 million) approximated normal levels.

[b]Includes the value of copra plus all other exported commodities, including scrap metal (left from World War II), handicrafts, and fish (exported from a cannery operated by Van Camp's in Palau).

[c]Estimates of the amounts earned by Micronesians from the expenditures of tourists begin to appear in the Annual Reports in 1970. Prior to that year, tourism was insignificant, due partly to shortage of hotels and inadequate transportation. Consistently, the bulk of tourism has been in the Mariana Islands.

[d]Figures for 1977 do not include the Northern Mariana Islands (see note d, Table 2.2). If the $3.64 million earned from tourist expenditures in the Northern Marianas were included, total tourism revenue would be increased to $5.62 million. Also not included in the 1977 figures are the $4.5 million of raw copra imported for processing at the copra mill in Palau (see note d of Table 2.2). To have included this sum would convey the wrong impression that production of copra by Micronesian households increased in that year.

Source: U.S. Department of State (1963-1977)

were exported in goods, and the ratio of imports to
exports worsens to 19.2!

STRUCTURE AND DEPENDENCE

The economic situation of Micronesia may be summarized in the following way. In the form of annual
Congressional appropriations and other federal grants,
the American government subsidizes the economy by over
$1,000 per capita annually. These monies are expended
in developing public capital and infrastructure, and in
improving education, health care, and other government
services. In providing these public goods and services,
the Trust Territory administration creates jobs for over
10,000 Micronesians. Intentionally or not, these expenditures have the effect of a fiscal policy, for the
resulting increase in personal income pumps up consumer
demand, thus stimulating private investment and employment. The consequent expansion of the private sector
does have the beneficial effect of redistributing income
to individuals who have been unable to obtain a government job. But most businesses are in the service industries, particularly the retail trade, and most profit is
made by converting the wages of government employees
into imported commodities. The resulting economic
structure may be described metaphorically as "topheavy": the service sector is enormous and expanding,
the productive sector relatively small and declining.
From the foregoing description, it is obvious that
the economy of the territory is a dependent economy, by
almost any common definition of the term. However,
readers familiar with the dependency literature already
have realized that Micronesia is not dependent in the
same sense in which "dependence" is used by most "dependency theorists." The various reasons for this difference, many of which are related to the demographic and
geographic characteristics of the islands, are addressed
in the concluding chapter. For the moment, it is sufficient to note that (1) American goals in the area are
above all strategic and military, that is, political;
(2) the policy chosen to attain these goals involved an
American subsidization of the islands; and (3) the
implementation of this policy has far-reaching consequences for the patterns of choices made by Micronesian
workers, consumers, and businesses and for the resulting
structure of the territorial economy. The following
chapters analyze how the exogenous forces just described
for the whole territory interact with environmental,
economic, and sociocultural conditions on one island to
generate these patterns of choice and to create this
structure. I begin by showing that the island's contemporary sociocultural conditions themselves are a

creation of contact with the nineteenth century world economy and the beliefs and practices of Christianity.

3
Cultural Transformation

This chapter describes the aboriginal political economy of Kosrae and shows how it was transformed in the nineteenth century as a result of contact with the representatives of European and American societies. This information serves as more than mere historical background for the "meat" of the description and analysis to follow. As will become apparent, the present-day cultural features of Kosrae, although long- and well-established, are an historical product of contact with the worldwide economic system and with the ideology of the Christian religion. The island thus exemplifies the paradigm of the history of other Third World peoples enunciated by Wolf (1982:76): "most of the societies studied by anthropologists are an outgrowth of the expansion of Europe and not the pristine precipitates of past evolutionary stages." Before recounting this history, it is useful to describe the important environmental features of the island.

NATURAL SETTING

Kosrae is the easternmost of the Caroline islands. Like the ethnographically well-described members of the Caroline archipelago, such as Belau (formerly Palau), Yap, Truk, and Ponape, Kosrae is a volcanic island. A precipitous, forested series of mountains make up most of its interior. The steepness is interrupted significantly only by a valley formed by the Innem River draining towards the east and the Okat River towards the northwest. This same valley divides Kosrae geologically into two parts: the northern third of the island is dominated by a single mountain, whereas the southern two-thirds contains many jagged peaks, the highest of which is just over 2,000 feet in elevation. Because of the heavy rainfall, a multitude of small rivers and streams have cut into the hillsides, eroding rock and

soil onto a relatively flat coastal plain that surrounds
most of the periphery.

Unlike other high islands of the Caroline archipelago with large barrier reefs, Kosrae has a small
fringing reef of only a few square miles in area, most
of which is located along the northwestern and
northeastern coasts in the present villages of Tafunsak
and Lelu. The reef is broken significantly in only
three areas, in the east, northwest, and south. The
three resulting natural harbors provided a replenishing
and resting point for whaleboats in the mid-nineteenth
century. By the time of my fieldwork, only the easternmost harbor in the present village of Lelu was in use
for government and large private vessels.

The shoreline of the island is in some areas dominated by mangroves and in others covered with stretches
of lovely, sandy beaches. In two areas, along the
southwestern and northeastern coast of the island, the
mangroves form channels of natural waterways that were
important routes of canoe transportation in aboriginal
Kosrae. In former times, and to a lesser extent today,
mangrove forests were exploited for their hard wood used
in house construction and for the large crabs that
abound in this habitat. Elsewhere, along the northwestern, northern, and eastern shore of the island,
beaches stretch for miles. Economically the most important uses of their sandy, salty soil are for coconut
palms and pandanus trees.

Kosrae is actually an archipelago, for several tiny
islets are found within its fringing reef. Only the two
inhabited islands have any significance for this study.
(Map 3.1) The first is the large island on which the
majority of the population always has lived. This
island is about 42 square miles in area, including
several square miles of mangrove swamp. Henceforth, I
refer to it as the "mainland" or "large island." The
second important island, called Lelu, has an ancient and
modern economic and political significance out of proportion to its small size (about one-fifth square mile).
Aboriginally, this island was the home of the nobility
and their commoner retainers. Today, it still is the
official capital and most populous settlement of Kosrae.
The easternmost portion of tiny Lelu is dominated by a
mountain of 354 feet, and is largely planted with
breadfruit, bananas, and coconuts. In contrast, the
western half is completely flat, densely settled, and
almost totally surrounded by a stone sea wall. All or
most of it apparently was built up by prehistoric human
labor, the workers first constructing a stone wall,
then filling in the new space with large blocks of
coral, and finally overlaying finer stones, coral, rub-
ble, and sand (Sarfert 1919-20:23; Cordy 1981). The
powerful chiefs of old Kosrae lived in a district in

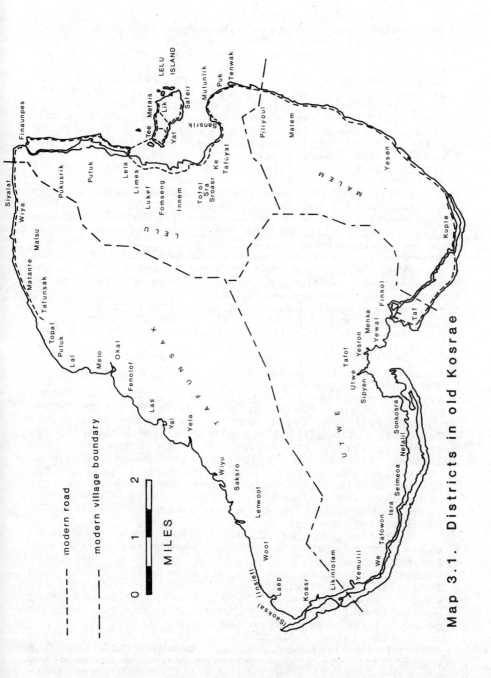

Map 3.1. Districts in old Kosrae

the western half of Lelu, in compounds surrounded by enormous walls constructed from huge basalt crystals. Although these megaliths are now little more than ruins, at one time they were a wonder of the Pacific, reaching heights of up to 25 feet. (Cordy [1981, 1982], an archeologist who has excavated this area, describes the grandeur of ancient Lelu "the stone city of Kosrae," in detail.) Similar and more famous walls exist at Nan Madol, on Ponape, over 300 miles to the northwest. On both islands, the reasons for their construction are unknown, but their placement around the dwellings of chiefs and their families suggests that defense was one function.

Aboriginally, transportation between Lelu and the mainland was by foot at low tide or by canoe otherwise. The shortest distance between the two islands is less than one-half mile, so the water and reef between them is an insignificant natural barrier. In old Kosrae, movement of goods and people between the two islands occurred daily, for the commoner population of the mainland was required to bring tribute in the form of food to the residences of the chiefs on Lelu. Today movement occurs by motor vehicle or foot on a causeway connecting the two islands, built after World War II.

The climate is pleasantly tropical. Daytime temperatures are usually in the 80s and may drop into the 70s at night. Rainfall averages around 200 inches annually over the whole island. The high elevations of the interior produce a minor variation between the western and eastern sides of the island, with the western portion receiving slightly more precipitation (OPNAV 1944; U.S. Department of State 1978: Statistical Table 54). There is only a slight seasonal variation in rainfall. April, the wettest month, receives about 23 inches; October, the driest, receives about 14 inches. Obviously, drought is rarely if ever a problem for Kosraen cultivators. Nonetheless, there are frequently periods of over a week with no rainfall, which result in periodic shortages of water suitable for drinking, bathing, and washing.

Typhoons that periodically cause enormous destruction farther west are rare in the Eastern Carolines. Severe storms did occur in 1891 and 1905, destroying houses and crops, but no typhoons have since been recorded. Currently, the main effect of strong rain and wind on the inhabitants is to prevent them from fishing on the ocean, as Kosraens justifiably are reluctant to go beyond the reef in high seas.

In the interior of the mainland, the soil is a product of the decomposition of volcanic rock that has eroded from the steep mountainsides. Aside from the shrub-covered ridges of the peaks of the highest mountains and the areas that are under cultivation, the

mainland now is covered by secondary tropical rain
forest.   If the analyses of tropical ecologists and
pedologists are correct, the dense vegetative cover is
an indication not of high soil fertility, but of high
rates of photosynthesis combined with the rapid decay of
fallen plant matter due to the high heat and rainfall
(Richards 1952; Nye and Greenland 1960).   Today as in
the past, the swampy lowlands are cultivated largely in
root crops, whereas the drier hillsides are planted in
breadfruit, bananas, and other tree crops.

HISTORICAL SOURCES

Most ethnographic studies of change include questioning elderly informants about how "the culture"
worked, or how "the society" was structured, in aboriginal times.   Unfortunately, my fieldwork on Kosrae began
about 50 years too late for this method to be used.
Depopulation and missionization in the mid-nineteenth
century combined to undermine the most centralized and
stratified sociopolitical system in all Micronesia
(Alkire 1977).   Today, few Kosraens regret this loss.
The period when paganism existed is now called the "dark
time," referring to cultural conditions before the missionary Benjamin Snow brought the light of Christianity
to the island.   Yet Kosraens do have a culture that
is uniquely their own.   They speak of facsin Kosrae,
"Kosraen custom," referring to the church-related moral
standards, values and social activities that dominate
much of their cultural lives.   But because these customs
are in no way aboriginal, and because no modern informant was born before the aboriginal political economy
largely had disappeared, any description of the precontact conditions of the island must rely mainly on historical documents, particularly on accounts of early
explorers and missionaries and on later reconstructions
by previous ethnographers.
The first definite sighting of Kosrae by a Westerner
was by Crozer in 1804, who gave the island the name of
Strong's island after the governor of Massachusetts.
Actual contact did not occur until 1824, when a French
scientific exploration team landed with the ship La
Coquille in June and remained on the island for 10 days.
Three men from this vessel wrote accounts of their
observations: the captain Duperrey (1828), the botanist
Lesson (1839), and Dumont D'Urville (1834).   Three years
later, a Russian explorer visited Kosrae in the course
of a scientific expedition, remaining on the island for
three weeks.   The captain of the ship, Lütke (1971, original 1835) published a detailed account of the island;
like the French, he was confused about the class structure and political organization.   A Prussian naturalist

from the same expedition, Kittlitz (1858), described the
indigenous flora and fauna and gives some information on
the cultural conditions of the Kosraen people.   All the
above sources have been translated recently by Ritter
and Ritter (1982), and together they provide an unusual
wealth of information (if interpreted carefully) on
aboriginal life in Kosrae.

Although hundreds of whaleships stopped in Kosrae
between 1830 and the 1860s, few left any account of the
inhabitants.   The next major source is the American
missionary Benjamin Snow. His letters, published by the
American Board of Commissioners for Foreign Missions
(ABCFM), are an important source of information about
events between his arrival in 1852 and his abandonment
of the mission in 1862, as well as scattered periods in
later years during his periodic return visits.

German sources include the trader Hernsheim (1883:
40-58), the naturalist and ethnologist Finsch (1893),
and the ethnographer Sarfert (1919-20). By far the most
complete account is found in Sarfert, who was in Kosrae
for three months in 1908-1909 purely for ethnographic
purposes.   His work encompasses two volumes, and most
reconstructions of the aboriginal culture that have
since been attempted rely largely on his account.

Since Sarfert, several ethnographers have worked on
Kosrae. Lewis' (1949; n.d.) study occurred after World
War II, in 1947, as part of the Coordinated Investigation of Micronesian Anthropology. Using data from the
early French and Russian explorers, from Snow's letters,
and from the German sources, he attempted to reconstruct
the aboriginal sociocultural conditions of the island,
and also presents a moderately complete account of
culture change before 1947. Wilson's (1969) work, written from an ethnoscientific viewpoint, consisted of
three short stays on the island in the early 1960s.
Schaefer (1976) was on the island in 1972-3 to investi-
gate the church and its role in the social life of Lelu
villagers. Ritter (1978, 1980a,b, 1981a,b) investigated
demographic patterns in the modern villages of Utwe and
Malem; his work from 1974-5 overlapped with my own.

THE POLITICAL ECONOMY OF OLD KOSRAE

Population and Settlement

The earliest estimates of the precontact population of Kosrae were made by the 1824 French expedition.
Lesson (1839:493) reported about 1,200 people distributed largely along the coasts and in the interior
valley of the mainland. Dumont D'Urville (1839:463)
estimated the number of inhabitants at between 2,000-
3,000.   From his visit three years later, Lütke

(1971:343-5) wrote that there were about 800 adults on
the mainland and Lelu combined. Later, the mission
estimated that the population prior to 1850 was 5,000
(Sarfert 1919-20:48), but the basis for this figure is
unstated. It seems clear that the island could have
supported this number, given the much higher densities
of other Micronesian high islands (Schneider 1968:383).
After an exhaustive analysis of the available evidence,
Ritter (1981a) concludes that the precontact population
was something over 3,000, but that this relatively low
figure probably was the result of mortality caused by a
late eighteenth century typhoon. This estimate of
3,000-5,000 is significant: after drastic depopulation
between about 1840 and 1880, Kosrae did not regain its
precontact population size until the mid-twentieth century. As a result, at the time of my research in Lelu
in 1975-6, almost all families had sufficient land
available for subsistence, at least in this village.

Available evidence suggests that the mainland was
settled exclusively by commoners, whereas the residents
of tiny Lelu included members of both social classes.
On the mainland, most of the population lived along the
coast, although clusters of houses also were established
in the interior Okat-Innem Valleys (Lesson 1839:493).
These house clusters were too small to warrant the term
"village." Thus, Lütke (1971), with the aid of a
Kosraen, identified 44 settlements on the mainland,
averaging only 14 adults in size; the largest settlement, on the northwest coast, had only 35 adults. This
dispersed settlement pattern still prevails in rural
areas of neighboring Ponape, but by the early twentieth
century most of the Kosraen population lived in one of
four nucleated villages.

For political reasons, these settlements were aggregated administratively into about 57 districts (Sarfert
1919-20:34), the boundaries of which were natural features such as rivers. (Map 3.1) Each district extended
from the coast to the interior mountains, thus including
areas with assorted ecological characteristics. Many
also included a section of reef, named for the district
of which it was a part. Control over one or more of
these districts was allocated to each of the nobility
with high titles; in turn, the titled man in control of
a district appointed an overseer from among the commoner
population of the district to carry out his orders.
With the disappearance of the prerogatives of nobility
in the nineteenth century, the districts today have lost
their former political significance, and their names are
used mainly as a means of identifying locations of
peoples' land and houses.

On Lelu, the nobility, their families, and their
commoner retainers lived within the walled enclosures
best called courtyards (Sarfert 1919-20:240). The chiefs

had many special structures used for their servants and
cooks, attendants of children, and menstruating and
pregnant women. In addition to their greater number,
the houses of the nobility were larger and more finely
constructed than those of the mainland commoners. The
courtyards of the various chiefs were separated by
trails and water-filled canals, along which tribute was
carried from the large island. The early French speak
of this area of tiny Lelu as if it represented a small
walled city, which is perhaps not an overstatement.
(Cordy 1981)
    Already in the contrast between the settlements and
living conditions of the commoners and nobility, a sharp
social distinction is apparent. This differentiation
also was realized politically, socially, economically,
and even linguistically, as I now shall document.

Clan and Class

    The population was divided into four matrilineal
clans (Sarfert 1919-20:329), which were broadly ranked
in prestige. The highest ranking clan was the Ton,
"freshwater eel," clan. Evidence from other parts of
the Pacific leads to the presumption that each clan was
comprised of several genealogical lines, or subclans,
some considered noble and others commoner on the ideolo-
gical basis of genealogical seniority (Sahlins 1958).
Because modern Kosraens are unable to give much information about the clans, most details on their place in
the social life of aboriginal Kosrae will remain
obscure. Their main significance might have been political, for it is agreed that the king of the whole
island was normally hereditary within the senior subclan
of the freshwater eel clan, called the Ton Yewal.
    The entire population of Kosrae also was divided
into two named social classes, membership in which was
ascribed largely by birth. Despite the fact that the
clans were ranked relative to one another, the three
highest clans counted commoners as well as nobility
among their membership, so that class rank crosscut clan
membership. Social interaction between the classes was
governed by a rigid etiquette similar to that of neighboring Ponape and in Polynesia. There was, for example,
a special form of respect language that commoners used
in addressing a noble, and numerous other linguistic
and kinesic patterns that demonstrated deference to the
nobility (Sarfert 1919-20:351-2). Many details of
interclass relations are unknown, but it is clear that
the nobility was in a highly favored social, political,
and economic position.
    Sarfert (1919-20:335-7) addressed himself specifi-
cally to the issue of the degree of heritability of

class membership. Long after the political system had
begun to decline, Kosraens told him that noble rank was
strictly hereditary within certain families of the three
highest-ranking clans. Sarfert probably was correct in
believing that these statements did not perfectly
reflect social reality, but the bulk of the evidence
indicates that although absolute ascription did not
exist, noble status was very difficult for a commoner to
achieve. It was not, however, so difficult for a noble
to lose. By virtue of their genealogical position,
individual nobles were eligible to compete for one of
the chiefly titles. If over the course of several
generations, no member of a noble line was successful in
acquiring a title, the noble status of the whole line
tended to be forgotten (Sarfert 1919-20:337-8). In the
long run, the status of noble, with its attendant rights
and privileges, had to be validated periodically by
successful competition for a title.

The Titles

It is difficult to overestimate the political and
economic importance of the acquisition of a title in
old Kosrae. Even modern Kosraens, who seem embarrassed
by other aspects of their pagan past, are proud of
having ancestors who were lem wal, "titled nobles," or
"chiefs." Sarfert (1919-20:340-1) lists 18 ranked
titles, at least nine of which carried control over
land, labor, and other resources. The highest title was
Tokosra, who may be considered "principal chief" or
"king." Most evidence indicates that the kingship normally was hereditary within the Ton Yewal subclan. The
missionary Benjamin Snow wrote in the 1850s that there
was much "logrolling" (quoted in Safert 1919-20:342-3)
in the succession, leading to the conclusion that genealogical ascription determined the eligible candidates,
but not necessarily which specific man would succeed to
the kingship. The holder of the second ranked title,
Kanka, was considered to be next in line for the kingship (although not always so in fact), so presumably he
too was normally of the royal subclan.
If the office of Tokosra remained within the Ton
Yewal, there was much more flexibility in succession to
other titles. From among the genealogical lines eligible to compete for titles, a new king appointed members to the various chiefly offices. He also had the
right to promote or demote incumbents and to strip them
of titles altogether. The noble members of a specific
clan did not have an automatic right to compete for certain titles, for the titles were not offices accruing to
specific clans. Rather, a noble of any clan was eligible to compete for any of the titles, with the possible

exception of the second highest ranking title, Kanka.
Thus, even after acquiring a title, an ambitious noble
could hope to improve his position further by moving up
in the chiefly hierarchy.

When a king died, the other title holders met to
select his successor. Nothing is known of the formal
rules of the selection procedure (whether a simple
majority or nominal unanimity was necessary, or whether
some chiefs had a greater voice than others, for example). Once selected, the new Tokosra received the
right to allocate all the land on the island, and the
commoners who lived on it, among the titled nobility.
This was done on the basis of districts, some chiefs
receiving control over many districts, some only a few,
and others, apparently, none. This allocation was at
the whim of the king: just as each clan had no permanent rights to specific titles, so the titles had no
permanent rights to a specified number of districts.
Each king could allocate control over the districts
among the titled nobility in any way he wished.

Chiefs had many jural rights over the natural and
human resources of the island. Each chief had the right
to receive tribute in agricultural goods and fish from
the commoners in the districts assigned to him, a right
that freed title holders from agricultural labor. Commoners also were obligated to provide services for their
chief. They cultivated special gardens maintained by
the chief of their districts for his own use, participated in fishing expeditions for use in the many feasts
that the title-holders sponsored, constructed the fine
houses and canoes used by the nobility, and often became
servants or specialized craftsmen in the service of
their chief. The tribute and labor rendered by commoners were seen as a chief's due, and ordinarily he
provided no formal reciprocation for them. Many of
these activities were organized by district overseers,
who were commoners appointed to their position by the
chief of their district. (Sarfert 1919-20:364-5)

Nominally, the king was the ultimate "owner" of all
land on the island. For administrative convenience, he
allocated political and economic control over specific
districts among the title holders. The king probably
was able to strip control over a district from a chief,
although the implementation of this "right" led to a
successful revolt in 1837. For their part, chiefs, once
acquiring a district from the king, appointed a commoner
overseer to see that tribute was rendered to themselves
regularly. Chiefs also had the rights to receive all
coconuts and kava roots cultivated in their districts,
for consumption of these was confined to the nobility.

The position of the Tokosra relative to the other
titles can be stated with a fair degree of precision.
All reports agree that he was the object of great

veneration, for the same formal symbols of deference
that the commoners were obliged to render to the nobility likewise were given by the nobles to the Tokosra.
A sea captain called him "the sole governor of the
island" (Hammet 1854:63); Snow dubbed him an "absolute
monarch" (Sarfert 1919-20:347); a visiting missionary
wrote "I never saw such deference paid to any mere man"
(E.W. Clark, ABCFM, Letter of November 4, 1852). On
the other hand, Sarfert (1919-20:347) was less convinced
of his absolute authority, calling him "primus inter
pares." The issue can only be resolved by considering
the different rights attached to the offices of king and
chiefs.

The king was not really, as Sarfert believed, "first
among equals," for he had privileges denied to the
holders of other titles. The most important of these
were the rights to appoint, promote, demote, or strip
nobility of their titles and to allocate control over
districts to the chief of his choice. He was thus in a
powerful structural position, having the privilege of
determining who among the nobility acquired the highest
ranking offices. In addition, he had more servants than
the other chiefs and probably more material possessions.
All other chiefs owned him a portion of the tribute paid
by the commoners in their districts. Sarfert (1919-20:
367) wrote that the chiefs would take one-half of the
tribute they received every day to the king's house, and
the latter would choose the best portions for his own
family and distribute the remainder among his servants.
As might be expected given his secular authority, the
king was viewed as ritually powerful and as endowed with
the character of a god (Sarfert 1919-20:355).

Nonetheless, the great obeisance paid by the chiefs
and their formal obligations to the Tokosra give an
exaggerated view of his actual power. Despite whatever
ideologies surrounded his status, in fact his influence
was countervailed by that of the titled nobility. There
are several indications of this. Two rebellions are
known to have occurred; in one, the Tokosra quarreled
with the high chief Selihk, and the subordinants of the
latter in the district of Tofol rose up and defeated the
king, replacing him with their own choice. In addition,
the king attempted by various means to ensure that the
chiefs remained loyal to him. One means of doing this
was for a king to give titles to his own kinsmen, as
Awane Lepalik I (King George) did (Sarfert 1919-20:349,
Genealogical Chart 3). His right to demote title
holders also was used to ensure support: King George
demoted the brother of his predecessor from Kanka, the
second-ranking title, to Sesuhfo, a low title. Finally,
kings did not allocate control over two contiguous
districts to the same chief, to make it difficult for
a single chief to gain support from large numbers of

commoners. Thus, the king's power in fact was circum-
scribed by that of the chiefs, and obedience to his
wishes was not always automatic and might have had to be
supported by the periodic use of force.

The final problem of this section is the status of
the district overseers, whom Lütke (1971:345) called the
"chiefs of the second class." The chief of the district, who appointed them, could replace an overseer
whose job performance was inadequate, or if the complaints of the people about him became too severe. The
overseers had more responsibilities but also more rights
than other commoners. Thus, an overseer was supported
in food by the people of his district, had servants from
among them, received some special obeisance from the
people as the representative of the chief, and had the
right to redistribute the shell money objects recipro-
cated by the chief to the commoners for extra services.
(Sarfert 1919-20:360-1, 364-5) Lewis (1949:21) reported
that the position was the object of competition among
commoners, implying that there was some material or at
least social advantage given to its incumbent. The
privileges attached to the position of overseer, then,
made it a valued position for commoners. Indeed it was
perhaps their primary avenue of social mobility, if it
is true that aborigially they could hardly hope to
become titled.

The Organization of Political Competition

The above description has summarized the "structural" aspects of aboriginal Kosraen social, political,
and economic relationships, that is, jural rights and
obligations of nobles and commoners, behavioral norms,
and the like. Equally important for the later cultural
transformation of the island is the "organizational"
side of social activity (Firth 1954). How, within this
structural framework, were labor and material resources
mobilized to achieve the goals of individuals and
groups? It is apparent that the jural rules of the
structure left a great deal of room for political maneuver and strategizing, and therefore promoted rivalry and
competition among the titled nobility. This competition
had great importance in influencing the trajectory of
change after contact.

As elsewhere in ranked or stratified societies, the
fact that formal positions of power and privilege were
limited in number led to competition between those candidates eligible to obtain these positions. The competition took several forms. There is evidence that the
use of force occurred on at least two occasions. After
1800 but prior to contact with the West, the people
of Matante district revolted and were aided by the

commoners of the southern and western districts.
According to Lewis (n.d.:24, footnote 2), the rebellion
grew out of quarrels over relative status between two
genealogical lines of the Penma clan. A second revolt,
already mentioned, occurred in 1837, shortly after contact. A king attempted to seize the large district of
Tofol from the chief Selihk, his sister's son. Selihk
and his six brothers felt powerful enough to oppose the
already unpopular king, and with the aid of many of
the commoners and probably some of the other chiefs,
defeated and deposed the king. Selihk died of his
wounds, but his brother became the new king, Awane
Lepalihk I, later known as King George.

The use of force is effective, if the attempt is
successful, but it is also a high-risk strategy. In
old Kosrae, undoubtedly most competition between chiefs
occurred through economic distributions. Specifically,
chiefs competed among themselves by means of tribute
payments to the king, by a rivalrous reciprocal exchange
similar to the potlatch, and by feasting. When commoners rendered tribute to their respective chiefs, the
latter were obliged to give about one-half of the produce to the king. But in addition to this "required"
payment, chiefs also would bring the king gifts of food
"of their own free will" (Sarfert 1919-29:367), an
action that can only be interpreted as an attempt to
gain the king's favor. "Getting on the king's good
side" thus led the chiefs to order the district overseers to have extra goods produced by the commoners, and
therefore stimulated productive activity in the districts.

Chiefs also competed through rivalrous gift-giving
resembling the potlatch of the Indians of the northwest
coast of North America. The practice might begin with a
simple basket of food given to a rival, but it could
snowball until objects such as mats, clothing, shell
money, and even canoes and land were included. Relatives
and other supporters would aid whenever the presentations outgrew the resources of the primary participants
(Sarfert 1919-20:138). In such distributions, chiefs
called on the commoners of their districts to produce
and contribute goods under the supervision of the
district overseers.

A main form of competition among chiefs were the
many feasts that chiefs sponsored and organized.
Sarfert (1919-20:138) mentions 13 festivals celebrated
regularly, including religious events, weddings, and
communal labor activities like the building of houses,
canoes, and walls, field clearing, and fishing expeditions. This list does not include "potlatch" contests,
nor at least three feasts that occurred at or just
before a death (1919-20:315-6), nor a huge festival at
the coronation ceremony of a new king (1919-20:252-3).

This list may be conservative, because of the deculturation that had occurred by Sarfert's visit.

At least two of these feasts were religious in
character, or in any event ritual occasions were the
cultural rationale for holding them. The epang festival
was the ritual of renewal of the taboo places on Lelu
dedicated to the god Sikaus. On occasion, perhaps every
three to six years, a titled noble would sponsor this
festival, which was named after this chief. The sponsoring chief told the king of his desire to hold the
epang, and the king commanded all the districts to make
preparations, that is, to begin the cultivation of new
fields and to make objects of decoration, canoes, and
probably mats. The competitive nature of this festival
is not in doubt: "The reason for all these preparations was that the epang was also an economic competition, ahkofai ["potlatch"], between the titled chiefs."
(Sarfert 1919-20:406) The chiefs were divided into two
groups. One group aided the titled noble who sponsored the event, the other the king. The implication,
although unstated by Sarfert, is that the epang was in
fact a competition between a particular title-holder and
the king, with the various chiefs taking either side.
It might well have served as a means by which the degree·
of political support of a titled noble could have been
gauged. A second large religious festival was in honor
of the breadfruit goddess Sinlakuh and was held each
year at harvest time. Snow (ABCFM, Letter of June
27, 1863) described this event as a kind of Kosraen
Christmas. Sarfert's informants told him that at the
time of this festival Kosrae was "one entire pile of
food" (1919-20:138).

These feasts certainly were one, and probably the
main, context for competition among the nobility over
titles. The missionary Snow refers many times in his
letters to the mission's problems with feasting and with
violations of the sabbath caused by preparations for
feasting. He battled frequently with the chiefs over
their refusal to give up the "heathenish practice." In
one of his letters the purpose of the feasts is revealed
clearly. A convert asked Snow if Christians should give
up attending feasts. Although knowing the opposition
that would be forthcoming from the chiefs by the policy,
the missionary decided to start new converts on the
right path from the outset, but wrote: "Still I shall
be greatly surprised if strong opposition and even per-
secution should not arise when the king and chiefs shall
see what an important source of gain and distinction is
interfered with by such an arrangement." (ABCFM, Letter
of March 25, 1858) Sarfert (1919-20:365) also believed
that the feasts were a major means of gaining political
rank: "The nobles also had competitions for honor and
prestige which caused all of Kosrae except themselves to

engage in intensive economic activity." Lewis (n.d.:13) concurs: "In general, production and consumption were stimulated by a desire for prestige through contribu- tions to feasts." That feasts and other kinds of dis- tributions are associated with political rivalries is a well-established fact of Pacific ethnography, although it requires independent documentation for Kosrae.

Political competitions over title acquisitions and promotions thus led the nobility to sponsor periodic distributions. One economic effect of their political rivalries was to stimulate the commoners in the dis- tricts assigned to them into productive activities above their own subsistence requirements. Another was the development of an exchange structure that economic anthropologists of the substantivist persuasion call "redistributive": goods produced by commoners under the supervision of district overseers were expropriated by the titled nobility and used to fund their political competitions. A portion of these expropriated products must have been redistributed to commoners in the form of feasts, public works projects, religious services, and chiefly hospitality. But the titled nobility also intercepted many of these products and used them to increase the consumption of themselves and their kin.

Far from the orderly paradise that the earliest French explorers believed it to be, old Kosrae was rid- dled by internal political rivalries and occasional violent conflicts. Kosraen chiefs held formal poli- tical offices (titles) that existed independently of their incumbents to which members of the nobility were recruited. Because recruitment to these offices was by no means automatic, the titled nobility may be viewed as political entrepreneurs who organized labor and channeled the flow of the products of this labor to their own material and political advantage. In the early years of contact with the West, these political rivalries persisted, provisioned by new kinds of goods obtained from visiting seamen. This persistence did not continue, however, for by the end of the nineteenth cen- tury the aboriginal sociopolitical system had all but disappeared. The next section documents the processes that resulted in this cultural transformation.

TRANSFORMATION

Early Contact, 1824-1852

Members of the French scientific vessel that first contacted Kosrae in 1824, and of the Russian exploration team that visited in 1827, left detailed written records of the earliest encounters of the island with the West. In spite of one incident involving theft and of the

Europeans' dislike for the autocratic powers of the titled nobility, relations generally were amiable. Because of their importance for later events, I shall concentrate on the trade relations that were established. The French and Russians supplied metal nails and various hand tools, cloth goods, trinkets, and two sows; the latter were objects of wonderment to the Kosraens, who had no pigs in aboriginal times. In return, the Europeans received water, woven textiles, and local foods like breadfruit, sugar cane, bananas, and drinking coconuts, the latter very expensively. The explorers were pleased with how easily this trade was established, and wrote that there was no lack of food for daily consumption while visiting the island. But they were disappointed that Kosrae was unable to furnish provisions that could be stored for use at sea. (Lesson 1832:473-4; Lütke 1971:304-5, 322-3, 398-9)

The distribution of the Western goods following their acquisition by the Kosraens also is relevant for later events. All the accounts agreed that most of the objects traded in were immediately or ultimately given to the chiefs and/or king:

> . . . it seems that the chiefs have an absolute right on the properties of men of common origin, which are born in the respective districts. We saw chiefs immediately appropriate axes or nails from natives who had exchanged for them objects which belonged to themselves. They turned towards us in showing us this action, and seemed not at all affected, so natural did it seem to them. But this passive obeisance is equally imposed on the chiefs in regard to the king, and we saw that all the presents which they received were immediately delivered to him. (Lesson 1839:490).

Similar statements were made by Lütke (1971:345) and Duperrey (quoted in Sarfert 1919-20:362). Besides revealing the remarkable degree of power of the title-holders over the commoners, these statements indicate that the chiefs were largely in control of the trade with Europeans, even from the earliest contacts, a pattern that continued until the 1850s. This chiefly control over the acquisition of Western goods had important impacts on political and cultural changes of later years.

Kosraens seem to have desired these Western goods intensely, but the goods they were able to offer in return did not have great value to European navigators. Thus, Lütke (1971:398) expressed disappointment that the island could not provide many products that could be used at sea, although there was no shortage of food available to the crews of foreign vessels while visiting

the island. He noted that the main usefulness of Kosrae
to future navigators would be "respite." What Lütke
meant by this term is unclear, but the nature of the
"respite" provided to later whaling crews is perfectly
apparent. The primary utility that Kosrae offered to
the whaleships of the 1840s through the 1860s was a service, namely, sex. In these decades, whalers acquired
"respite" in large quantities: the American trader,
Kirkland, who settled on Kosrae in 1850, told the missionary Snow that about 12 ships per year were visiting
the island. In the next decade, the number increased:
in one day in 1856, Snow counted 14 ships in Lelu harbor
at the same time. (ABCFM, Snow's letters of September 1,
1852 and October 1, 1856)

Beginning in the 1840s, the exchange of Kosraen
women's sexual favors for Western goods was promoted
vigorously by the chiefs and king, and all indications
are that they gained a substantial profit in Western
goods from the practice. In 1853, Snow wrote of his
attempt to stop the chiefs: "some few of the dirty
fellows seem to think that in this way one hope of their
gains is taken away." (ABCFM, Snow's letter of January
8, 1853) During the 1850s Snow pressured the king into
prohibiting the "vile practice," but always the chiefs
continued the activity behind the missionary's back.
At one meeting, the chief Sesa declared (probably correctly): "all right, no more gals, so 'long white man."
(ABCFM, Snow's letter of October ?, 1853) Snow's letters
thus show that the chiefs were most active in promoting
the traffic in women, even while their desire to please
the missionary led many of them to deny it.

Certainly by the 1840s and probably beginning in the
1830s, the population of the island began a precipitous
decline in numbers that was not reversed until the
1880s. One 1851 visitor wrote of a settlement in which
Kosraens "were simply being eaten up alive with the most
loathsome of diseases" (Haley 1948:166). Hammet (1854:
64), in December, 1852, saw some "disgusting objects"
suffering from what he believed to be syphilis. Lewis
(1949) thought this disease was yaws, but his medical
evidence has been analyzed by Ritter (1978), who concluded that influenza and sterility induced by gonorrhea
also contributed. Whatever its cause, depopulation was
drastic. In 1852, Hammet estimated the population at
1,200 and the trader Kirkland told Snow there were only
between 1,400 and 1,700 surviving Kosraens. At least
half the precontact population had died from introduced
diseases by the 1850s, and the number was to drop to
about 300 by 1880.

This drastic depopulation had both political and
cultural effects. Politically, it resulted in a change
in the principle of accession to the kingship. After
the death of Awane Sru I around 1835, his son, who was

of the Penma clan, became the new king, Awane Sru II.
According to Sarfert (1919-20:344), this was because
there was no masculine heir in the kingly subclan.
Because he somehow managed to accede to the kinship
against the will of the other chiefs, and was unpopular
with the people, Awane Sru II was expelled by the afore-
mentioned revolt of 1837 led by the seven sons of his
sisters. His successor, Awane Lepalik I (King George),
also was a Penma, as were most of the remaining kings
until the elimination of the office. (Sarfert 1919-20:
379-387)

Missionization, 1852-1899

When Benjamin Snow arrived to teach and preach the
gospel on Kosrae in 1852, he thus found the indigenous
inhabitants greatly reduced in numbers and the nobility
controlling the exchange of trade goods for women's
sexual favors with the crews of whaleships. Despite
these changes, available evidence suggests that the
aboriginal political system, with its rivalries among
the nobility, was thriving. True, the principle of succession to the office of Tokosra had changed, but demographic fluctuations occurred in aboriginal times as
well (Ritter 1978). King George did not appear to suffer much loss of respect or power because he was of the
Penma clan. The political activities and class relationships of old Kosrae were virtually intact; formal
etiquette and respect language (suhnak) still regulated
chief-commoner interactions; religious ceremonies and
feasts were still the context of political rivalries
between the chiefs; the four clans were still in existence; and the king still appointed the nobility to
titles, while the titled men still chose the king from
among the eligible candidates. Changes undoubtedly had
occurred, but the overall impression is one of continu-
ity, owing largely to the fact that the nobility were
successful in using imported Western goods to achieve
success in traditional political rivalries, that is, new
resources provisioned the old competitions. Yet, by the
end of this period, the traditional etiquette of social
interaction, the aboriginal religious ceremonies, most
of the privileges of nobility and kingship, and the
style and context of political competition, had all virtually disappeared. The proximate causes of this transformation were depopulation and missionization, which in
combination produced new forms of social and political
relationships and new cultural beliefs and values, all
of which are seen by modern Kosraens as their own unique
"customs" that define their cultural identity. As
demonstrated in this section, the key elements of modern

Kosraen social relations, cultural practices, and ideologies were developing by the turn of the century.

King George had been warned by the whaleboat captains that if he allowed missionaries to settle, the profitable exchange in women would be curtailed, and so he was somewhat apprehensive when Snow, his wife, and two Hawaiian helpers arrived in 1852. The monarch also expressed concern about the missionaries' potential interference with his political authority, but allowed them to remain when Snow assured him that the party was on the island for religious and educational purposes only, and would in no way interfere with his traditional powers.

Given the nature of the indigenous political and economic exchange system, together with the transactions in women that were occurring with the whalers, it is evident that Snow's "religious purposes" could not possibly have been fulfilled without "political interference." Thus, at the benediction of Snow's very first service, the chiefs and commoners present were asked to stand in the presence of the king, an act customarily forbidden to them under the suhnak etiquette (ABCFM, Snow's letter of January 18, 1853). Despite this and probably other "interferences" that are undocumented, King George supported the missionary effort. The monarch's material and moral support led Snow initially to be optimistic about the prospects for the quick Christianization of the island. But the king himself was weak morally, sometimes standing at services in an intoxicated state to deliver a lecture on the virtues of temperance. He did not seriously attempt to stop the chiefs from sending women to the ships, nor did he make any effort to curtail chiefly rivalry through feasting, a habit that Snow never was able to suppress.

Despite their initial enthusiasm, throughout the 1850s the missionaries had very little success, due largely to the longstanding opposition of the titled nobility. When King George died in 1854, his successors proved to be indifferent or outwardly hostile to Snow, largely because of the missionary's efforts to curtail the traffic in women that was the major source of trade goods, which in turn fueled political competition. Church attendance was irregular, due to the efforts of the priests of the pagan goddess Sinlakuh on the mainland and the attitude of the chiefs. Snow's efforts to stop the trade in women were unsuccessful. He blamed the captains and crews of whaleships for bringing the worst vices of civilization to the islanders, and many of his letters back to New England were little more than tirades against the worst offenders. Pagan practices like dancing, "heathenish songs," feasting, chiefly polygyny, royal incest, and kava drinking persisted. In brief, throughout the 1850s Kosraens, especially the nobility, remained largely unwilling to renounce their customs and to give up the means of their material profit in return for the dubious benefits of Christianity. For example, in 1858, Snow called a meeting of those who wished to be counted on God's side and stated that no one should attend who had anything to do with sending women to ships. Total attendance: one Samoan, eight children, and two adults. (ABCFM, Snow's letter of March 25, 1858). These two adults were the first converts, received into membership in April, 1858, after six years of almost fruitless proselytizing.

Meanwhile, Kosraen numbers continued their decline. Snow made several careful censuses in the 1850s. The first, in 1855, showed the population to be 1,106; by 1858, it had dropped to 748; by 1874, only 397 Kosraens were alive; by 1880 it had reached its low point of around 300 (Ritter 1978:55), after which it began a steady increase that continues into the present. The political effect of this depopulation already has been noted: the near extinction of the noble line from which kings normally were recruited. A probable effect of the terror that must have been created by such widespread death and sickness is the production of psychological stress. Snow's letters of the late 1850s clearly document the sickness that not only was depopulating the island but also disfiguring the survivors. In 1860, for example, Snow was told by visitors that the people had a "sickly, filthy, dying look" (ABCFM, Snow's letter of July 17, 1860). People's relatives must have literally been dying all around them, for reasons not clearly understood, and it would be surprising if these conditions were without psychological effects.

Another source of stress was the nature of the intensive contact that had been occurring for over two decades with groups of individuals who must have been among the least enlightened of the agents of Western civilization. An appreciation of the "intensity" of the contact is given by the figure of 75 ships, mostly whalers, that had called at the island between Snow's arrival in the fall of 1853 and the spring of 1856, an average of 21 vessels per year (Lewis n.d.:31). This intensity was unmatched until the 1930s. An indication of the "nature" of the contact already has been given: a sex-starved whaleship crew on the loose would not be expected to be a mild-mannered or well-intentioned group of gentlemen, so relations with whalers was surely quite bawdy and often exploitative, as many of Snow's letters document.

Finally, it is accepted widely that exposure to unfamiliar ideas and behaviors can lead to a breakdown of the cognitive assumptions of a culture (Wallace 1956, 1966) and, especially when combined with a condition of "relative deprivation" (Aberle 1962), result in a

synthesis of the old and the new that occurs at a revo-
lutionary tempo. New cultural beliefs and practices can
evolve in a very short period if these conditions are
present.

These contact-induced demographic, psychological,
social, and cultural conditions led to a situation of
stress, if not anomie, in which the prerequisites for
some kind of religious movement appear to have been
present. At least, the events of the 1860s become
intelligible under this hypothesis.

Between 1861 and 1863, Snow's letters document the
first "encouraging progress," in spite of continued
opposition from many of the nobles. Attendance and
attentiveness at church increased, until by 1862 over
100 were in regular attendance; more baptisms were
reported; and some of the converts even were preaching
on the mainland. But at the same time, there was also a
revival of the "heathen" religious festivals surpassing
that of any previous time since the establishment of the
mission. By 1863, the commoner priests of Sinlakuh, the
breadfruit deity, were reviving the yearly processions
and festivals held on Lelu. It appears that a kind of
nativistic movement (Linton 1943) also was occurring,
rivalling the mission's recent successes. (ABCFM,
Snow's letters of October 17, 1861; July 15, 1862; and
June 27, 1863; Lewis n.d.:34). There were two competing
religious ideologies and practices, the one Christian,
the other pagan, perhaps with most of the population
adopting a "wait and see" attitude.

If so, they were not long in "seeing." Due to the
rapidly declining population and the relative unfruit-
fulness of Snow's efforts, in 1862 the American Board
ordered the missionaries to leave Kosrae. Their new
station was at Ebon, in the Marshalls. Snow left the
mission in charge of an Hawaiian helper and a small band
of converts. However, he made yearly visits back to the
island, and continued to report on the progress of the
mission. Unhampered by Snow's presence, the pagan king
was engaged in persecuting the 27 recently baptized
Christians. When the latter petitioned the Tokosra to
cease the revived pagan dancing and singing, he treated
them contemptuously and seized a piece of the land the
church had been cultivating. One week later, while
supervising the replanting of the land for his own use,
he quite suddenly dropped dead. If it is true that most
of the population was committed to neither of the competing religions, this event must have shown which side
was right, or, in Kosraen eyes, at least which deity was
stronger.

Subsequently, conversion proceeded rapidly, in spite
of continued opposition by the new king and at least two
of the chiefs. Between June, 1863, and January, 1864,
there were 50 new converts, including two chiefs. By

1867, there were 188 members in good standing, besides
those who had died after joining (17 in 1867 alone) and
those who had been excommunicated for failure to conform
to the rigid moral standards set by Snow in regard to
fornication, smoking, drinking, and feasting. As documented in Chapter 8, the first three transgressions continue to dominate Christian ethics on the island. But,
despite his other (albeit belated) impressive successes,
Snow never was able to eliminate the feasts, complaining
in a letter in 1867 that the "church had fallen into
some of the habits of the island in regard to feasting
at their funerals" (ABCFM, Snow's letter of October 14,
1867). Today, feasting at funerals as well as at other
religious and social occasions is integrated into the
church's ideology and practices, with significant
effects on the modern economy.

King George's fear, expressed in 1852, that the mission would interfere with political affairs, had proven
to be justified. Indeed, once the mission had the alle-
giance of most of the commoner population, and of some
of the titled nobility, the political system itself
began to decline. The nobility increasingly lost status
and number after 1863. By 1868, Snow reported that there
were only seven chiefs under the king, controlling the
only seven districts left inhabited after the drastic
depopulation. The same year, an event occurred that
reveals the decline in the political influence of the
titled chiefs:

> Arrangements were made and the people were allowed
> to choose 7 representatives from the 7 districts of
> the island, to sit once a month with the king and
> his 7 chiefs, to deliberate concerning the civil
> affairs of the island and to enact laws and regula-
> tions for the welfare and prosperity of the island.
> It would not be wise to predict very much upon this
> movement, as the king is not overliberal and is
> exceedingly jealous of all encroachments upon his
> power and upon any course that may diminish, however
> slightly, the good prospects of the royal treasury.
> (ABCFM, Snow's letter of January 21, 1869)

The other side to the loss of chiefly power and
privilege after the large-scale conversion is, of
course, an increase in the relative prestige and political power of the commoners. It is apparent that the
formerly disenfranchised and disadvantaged commoners
were gaining something more than eternal life through
their conversion. I do not wish to argue here that the
commoners realized that the church was a new avenue of
social mobility, nor to speculate that their conversion was rooted in political and perhaps material self-
interest. Nonetheless, subsequent events reveal that

one major result of the adoption of Christianity was an improvement in the social standing of commoners, the rise of a more egalitarian ethic and social structure that still persists, and the greater participation of commoners in the political process.

These social trends are evidenced by events of 1871, 1874, 1879, and 1884. In 1871, a church committee expelled the wife of the king and her sister from the church, "from evidences of guilt that might not have been sufficient in a more enlightened church." (ABCFM, Snow's letter of October 7, 1871) It is probable that the committee, which must have been composed mainly of commoners, needed little evidence, but was testing its power by excommunicating two noble women, a step that would have been unthinkable only ten years before. By 1874, the church members, including by this time many of the nobility, felt themselves powerful enough to depose the Tokosra, Awane Salik II. With the chief Kanka presiding, and with the visiting Snow amazed at the forcefulness of the manner of the commoners, the congregation met at the church, voted the king out of office, and elected by popular vote a new Tokosra. (Sarfert 1919-20:384-6) This represented the first time that commoners had a direct vote in the selection of a king, and hereafter their voice was an important one, as Finsch (1893) noted in his 1880 visit.

Unlike his predecessor, the new king was a faithful Christian. Interestingly, he too was deposed in 1879, for working too energetically in the Christian effort. The American mission board had decided earlier to move the Marshall Islands Training School from Ebon to Kosrae, largely for reasons of the bad health of the missionaries on the Marshallese atoll (Bliss 1906). They petitioned the king for land and in 1879 Awane Sru IV sold them the district of Woot, dispossessing in the process the family of the overseer and giving them no compensation. Commoners apparently had come to regard the land on which they lived and worked as their own: the king's action was such an affront to the overseer's family, and perhaps such a threat to the newly won rights and independence of the commoners, that he also was thrown out of office (Lewis 1949:47-8).

Another blow to the old distinction between noble and commoner came at a church service in January, 1884, when King Awane Sru VI abolished the suhnak, the system of social etiquette and respect language that heretofore had governed relations between the classes and between statuses within the family. Symbolically, this abolition eliminated the customary formal distinctions beween noble and commoner. Again, the church was behind it, having made the request of the king. Today, most remnants of this "high" language and behavior have disappeared; pronominal forms of the respect language persist in public speaking contexts (e.g., the informal _eltal_ vs. formal _ellos_, "they"), but this is its only current manifestation.

Between the late 1860s and early 1880s, the aboriginal stratification system thus was weakened, but not totally destroyed. In 1880, the German ethnographer Otto Finsch wrote that the commoners still treated the king with a "degree of submissiveness that I have met nowhere else" (1888:455). The king still exacted tribute in labor, food, and by now, copra (Lewis n.d.:38-9). Individual nobles still were appointed to titles, although only five title-holders were left to meet with the king in council (Finsch 1893:455). Nonetheless, it is clear that the power and privileges attached to the titles had declined significantly. For example, when a king died in 1888, depopulation had been so drastic that only one suitable hereditary candidate existed, the chief Sesa. The office that had been fought over 25 years earlier was refused by him, and the son of the man who had succeeded in 1863 was made king, due to the lack of a willing hereditary candidate. He lived only a few months; when he died, Sesa again refused the office. It was necessary to send to Honolulu for a grandson of King George's sister, who had left the island in 1863. In 1890, he returned to Kosrae to become the Tokosra Awane Sa, and reigned until 1910. By this date, there were only three chiefs besides the king. (Sarfert 1919-20: 386-8). This further decrease in the number of titles cannot be attributed to depopulation, for by this time the population had begun to increase, in 1905 to 516 (Lewis 1949:58). Rather, it is the decline in the nobility's power, privilege and function that accounts for the loss in numbers of titles.

As indicated previously, contact with foreigners, especially whaleship crews, was quite intensive from the 1840s through the 1860s. By the 1870s the great whaling era had passed in the Pacific and for the first time in 30 or 40 years, Kosrae was relatively isolated from outside influences. It was probably during the last decades of the nineteenth and early decades of the twentieth century that the Kosraen church evolved the complicated formal structure and rigorous rules for membership described in Chapter 8. It therefore is unfortunate that so little is known of the "Kosraenization" of the Christian church during this period.

A major part of my analysis in future chapters concerns how contemporary social relations and cultural practices on Kosrae interact with recent exogenous inputs to the island. In chapters 8, 9, and 10, I show that a substantial fraction of the cash income in the village of Lelu is channeled into the improvement of church buildings and into ceremonies and feasts connected to the church and to life crisis events. The

present chapter has demonstrated that many social features and cultural practices of modern Kosrae themselves were created by the interaction between the
aboriginal political economy and the depopulation and
missionization that occurred in the nineteenth century.
Modern sociocultural conditions on the island then are
not "aboriginal," although Kosraens have come to think
of them as their own unique "customs."

4
Colonial Masters

Kosrae has experienced the rule of four colonial powers: Spain, Germany, Japan, and the United States. Each has had its own interests, and its own effects on the island's population. This chapter reviews the colonial history of the island. In line with the objectives of this work, I confine the discussion to the effects of various colonial masters on the development of modern Kosraen cultural practices and norms and on the economy.

GERMAN ADMINISTRATION, 1899-1914

Germany was not the first colonial power to gain control over Kosrae and the other islands of Micronesia. Spain claimed the area in 1885, but it did little on Kosrae other than declare Spanish sovereignty over it. In 1899, Germany acquired the Mariana and Caroline islands from Spain, adding these islands to its protectorate in the Marshalls, and thus acquiring internationally recognized rights to all the islands that now comprise the Trust Territory. Due to its small population (only 516 in 1905) and economic unimportance, Kosrae was the only high island in the Carolines without a government station. Direct contact with outsiders was limited, for a government ship carrying cargo, mail, and occasional orders from the German governor on Ponape arrived only once every three months (Sarfert 1919-20:8). Kosrae became, and so remained until the 1930s, an official backwater.

At the time of Sarfert's visit in 1910, the Tokosra had appointed men to only three of the titles. What little remained of the perquisites of noble status did not extend to significant rights over land in use by the descendants of commoners. Even the king had lost most of his prerogatives: he owned only the district of Innem, and this was acquired through ordinary inheritance from his father. Although his food was provided by younger male relatives, he was unable to exercise any

53

claim to tribute, and had little income (Lewis 1949:52).
Sarfert referred to the king as a "figurehead," noting
that the persistence of the office was due to the influence of the German government, with whom he served as
middleman.   Many people wished to eliminate the kingship
altogether.   (Sarfert 1919-20:388-9).   But when this
king died in 1910, the German government ordered another
election so that someone might be held accountable.   A
son of an old king was at this time the pastor of the
Lelu Church; in spite of some disagreements, he became
the next, and last, Tokosra. The kingship hung on until
his death in 1957, but the office probably would have
been eliminated much earlier but for German interference
and his longevity.
     Certainly by the German administration, and probably
even earlier, the real secular power was the church, for
by this time Christianity was the established religion.
In fact, as early as 1872, a member of the Hawaiian
Mission had written: "The population indeed, is small,
only about three hundred, but they are the most civi-
lized and refined of all I have seen in Micronesia.
The gospel is firmly planted here" (quoted in Sarfert
1919-20:391).   In 1905, the Kosraen Church became the
first in Micronesia to receive its independence from the
American Board of Commissioners for Foreign Missions.
By 1910, it had promulgated laws against some of those
"heathen" practices that Snow had considered most abom-
inable, such as kava drinking, extramarital sexual relations, and pagan dancing and singing, and against the
new sins introduced by seamen, alcohol and tobacco.
Punishment for violation of these moral standards was
excommunication, a sanction that was, and by many people
still is, taken very seriously.   Kava drinking is today
a dead issue, but prohibitions against promiscuity,
alcohol, and tobacco still dominate Christian morality,
as shown in chapter 8.   Snow never was able to root out
another aboriginal cultural practice, feasting, and
today the major social and religious holidays and life
crisis ceremonies include large feasts, which are discussed in chapters 8 through 10.
     Aside from their intervention that allowed the
office of Tokosra to persist in spite of the fact that
its rights, powers, and functions were virtually gone,
the Germans had little discernible influence on the
church-centered culture that was evolving.   Their main
interest in Micronesia, as indeed in all of Oceania, was
economic.   The production of copra for export through
German traders began in the 1870s, but it was not until
between 1890 and 1900 that the copra trade became the
primary means of earning cash income. After the Germans
established official control in 1899, the government
ordered Micronesians to increase their plantings of
coconuts to increase the volume of trade and profits for

the German trading companies. On Kosrae, Sarfert (1919-20:101) wrote that the people were so eager to make copra for export that they harvested the nuts prematurely. Few other economic opportunities were available, for the island now was visited by only a few ships each year. Copra's overriding importance as an agricultural export continues even until the present, although today only a minority of Kosraens earn significant amounts of cash income from its production.

JAPANESE ADMINISTRATION, 1914-1945

Three important events occurred during the Japanese administration of Kosrae in the interwar years: (1) the exploitation of the island's natural resources that began in the 1930s; (2) a Japanese land survey carried out in 1932 that resulted in the appropriation of most of the interior of the mainland by the Japanese government; and (3) the development of a new kind of social group that subsequently became an integral part of the formal structure of the Kosraen church.

When the Japanese navy took possession of Micronesia at the outbreak of World War I, they placed Kosrae under the branch government of neighboring Ponape. At first, a single Japanese police sergeant was stationed on the island for purposes of administration and law enforcement. By the 1930s, however, the island became an important center of Japanese military and commercial activity in the Carolines. As discussed in chapter 2, the Japanese throughout Micronesia put a great effort into development because of their own economic and military requirements, not because they wished to develop the area for the benefit of the inhabitants. Nonetheless, there were certain "spread effects," such as improvements in infrastructure and market reliability, that allowed Kosraens to prosper in the decade of the 1930s (Lewis 1949:56).

During Japanese times, the coconut palms that the Germans had "encouraged" the islanders to plant came into full production, and by 1936 Kosraens were producing about 500-600 short tons of copra (calculated from figures given in Bascom 1965:96). Between 1934 and 1940, the total value of exports increased about six-fold, from 33,000 yen to 204,500 yen (or, roughly, from $8,000 to $50,000). Until 1937, copra constituted most of the value of exports to Japan, but by 1940 rope, cordage, and thread made from the husks of coconuts and hibiscus fibers were equally important. (OPNAV P22-5, 1944:150; Oliver 1971:34) The products were purchased by the Nanyo Boeki Kaisha (South Seas Trading Company), which was active throughout Micronesia. This company, still remembered as NanBo by older Kosraens, had

established trading stations in the villages of Lelu,
Malem and Tafunsak by 1938 (OPNAV P22-5, 1944:139-40).
In addition to establishing a large and reliable export
market for the island's products, NanBo operated shipping lines based on Ponape and sold processed foods,
clothing, textiles, metal products, and other goods
imported from Japan at its retail outlets. The value of
these imported goods increased from 33,000 yen in 1934
to 233,000 yen in 1940 (OPNAV P22-5, 1944:151; Oliver
1971:35). Many of these imports were consumed by
Japanese and other foreign residents, the number of
which grew substantially, but older modern informants
stated that their income and consumption levels grew in
the 1930s. These high levels were not to be duplicated
in the American trusteeship until the 1960s.

As elsewhere in Micronesia, the Japanese provided
the infrastructure required for increasing production
and marketing. Their road system on Kosrae was extensive; they constructed refrigeration and warehousing
facilities on the south side of Lelu harbor, in which
products were stored waiting for export; a long dock was
built in Lelu harbor from which supplies were loaded and
unloaded; a small dam was constructed on the Tafoyat
River for supplying water to workers and, after the war
began, to Japanese troops. Most significantly, even
before the war was imminent, the Japanese improved
transportation to and from the island. In 1932, 28
steamers called at Kosrae, a figure comparing favorably
with the 35 that stopped at Ponape during the same year.
In 1934, there were 33 arrivals and departures, again
favorably comparing with Ponape's 40. (OPNAV P22-5,
1944:117). This was a great improvement over the estimated five or six vessels per year prior to about 1920
and throughout the 1950s under American administration.

The most impressive economic accomplishment of the
Japanese on Kosrae was their ambitious program of agricultural development. In 1938, the Nanyo Kohatsu Kaisha
(South Seas Development Company) attempted to expand
their impressive program of sugar cane development in
the Marianas to Kosrae. The experiment failed, as did
a similar one for cotton (Lewis 1949:57), for unknown
reasons. Undaunted, the Japanese imported laborers
from Ocean Island, Korea, and Okinawa to undertake the
raising of foodstuffs for export to the Marshalls, where
increasing numbers of troops were gathering for the war.
Modern informants recalled that the Japanese used
Kosraens to clear and lay out rows, whereas the imported
laborers did the actual planting and tending of the
crops. Potatoes, cucumbers, watermelons, and, especially tapioca (cassava), were planted. Aerial photographs made by the U.S. Navy in 1944 reveal the extent
of these plantings. The largest areas of cultivation

were at Tafoyat and Pilyioul, but the land also was
cleared extensively at Tofol, Ke, Innem, and Fomseng,
all in the present municipality of Lelu. From maps made
by the Navy from these photographs, I estimate the areas
completely cleared of forest and intensively planted
with these crops at between 600 and 700 acres. Today
these areas are planted with subsistence gardens or
covered in secondary forest.

As mentioned, foreigners were imported to supply labor for these projects. Some appreciation of
their numbers is given by the naval historian Dorothy
Richards. At the end of World War II, the American Navy
was faced with the necessity of repatriating 976 people
from other Pacific islands and 4,523 Japanese, Koreans,
and Okinawans. The 1,542 resident Kosraens at the war's
end thus were swamped numerically from about 1940 until
the surrender of the island to the Americans in 1945.
(Richards 1957, volume II:48-9)

According to modern informants, during the war the
Japanese forced most Kosraens to engage in hard labor.
When bombing by the Americans began, people were forced
to flee their villages and take refuge in the mountains
of the mainland. Kosraens feared that the Japanese
were considering murdering the indigenous population in
order to conserve the food supply, for the American
blockade near the war's end was so effective in pre-
venting the entrance of ships that the island's land and
sea resources had to support over 7,000 people. For
several months after the war, Kosraens lived mainly off
C-rations acquired from the American troops, indicating
that the gardens probably were stripped of food during
the period of the blockade. Kosraens perceived the
American occupying force as the emancipators of the
island from the Japanese; the date of their arrival,
September 8, 1945, (which I will later call "Liberation
Day") is still a major holiday.

A second happening during Japanese times is important because in 1975 it was the focus of disputes
between the U.S. administration and Kosraen land owners.
This is the land "survey" carried out in 1932. All evidence suggests that by this date the land was under private ownership, even the steep interior of the island.
Land still was quite abundant relative to the Kosraen
population, which still did not approach its precontact
numbers, but the interests of the Japanese in developing
the island for export, military use, and possibly colonization led them to attempt to acquire rights to land.
They legislated a policy under which all land covered at
high tide (that is, all areas of mangrove) was made
legally "public land." In 1932, the Japanese government
carried out a survey with the ostensible purpose of
clarifying ownership and issuing titles to land held by

Kosraens; actually, it resulted in the alienation of
most of the interior of the island to the Japanese
government. Lewis (1949:56) reported that Kosraens were
left with little more than the acreage actually under
cultivation. When the U.S. administration began, the
American government apparently assumed that the land was
acquired through legal processes, but people today claim
that they or their ancestors were afraid not to agree to
the terms of the survey, and did so essentially under
conditions of force. As a result, in 1974, 6,142 hectares of the island were "public domain," while only
4,459 hectares were under the private ownership of
Kosraens (U.S. Department of State 1978:14 of statistical appendix). The complaints of Kosraens who claim to
be the true owners of this public land against the
administration were still under adjudication at the time
of my 1975-6 field research. Kosraens had disputed
every marker placed by the Japanese survey team in 1932
that would limit their ownership, most claiming that the
land belongs to them all the way up the summits of the
mountains.

The final event of interest during Japanese times
is the innovation of a new category of social organization that has, over the past three decades, become associated with the church and that dominates much of the
extrafamilial social life of the island. The Japanese
instituted this organization, called kumi ("group"), in
several other areas of Micronesia (School of Naval
Administration 1948:155). According to modern informants, the groups began when the Japanese were searching
for an organizational means to accomplish tasks related
to public works, like construction and maintenance of
public buildings, roads, sea walls, docks, and play-
grounds. An elderly man said that the groups arose when
the Japanese officials asked the king and some other
influential Kosraens about the best way to get the people to work well. It was agreed that dividing the population into groups and inducing a spirit of competition
between them would result in maximum output, and at the
same time make the work "happy." There were four such
groups, called itsi, ni, sang, and yung (the Japanese
ordinal numerals for "first" through "fourth"). Before
the institution of the kumi, I was told, people were
very lazy about public works projects, and only threats
and force induced them to attend and work hard. But
after a rivalrous ethos was added, most of the people
participated eagerly. In addition to giving people an
incentive to work hard, the groups were the organizational basis for the division of labor in public works.
From these beginnings, the kumi have developed today
into one of the most important of all Kosraen organizations, as documented in Chapters 8 and 10.

AMERICAN TRUSTEESHIP

As shown in chapter 2, the policy of the United
States administration towards all of Micronesia has
undergone two phases. Kosrae has shared this territory-
wide experience. For almost two decades of its administration, the United States did little to promote
development by providing opportunities, reliable markets, infrastructure, and services. The island's economy during this period may be characterized fairly as
subsistence-oriented. Beginning in the mid-1960s, and
continuing until the present, enormous economic changes
have been introduced through the agency of the Kosraen
branch of the Trust Territory government. The remainder
of this chapter establishes the context for the analysis
of the rest of the book by describing these changes and
their general effects on the whole island. Future chapters will concentrate on Lelu village, where I worked in
1975-6.

The Early Phase, 1947-1963

After the creation of the strategic trusteeship
in 1947, the Americans divided Micronesia into six
administrative districts. Kosrae was allocated the
subordinate status of a subdistrict, under Ponape. As
such, it had no resident American administrator, but
an Island Council was established as a liaison between
the District Administrator on Ponape and the local
population. This council consisted of an island Chief
Magistrate and Secretary-Treasurer, both elected by the
population at large, together with Magistrates and
Secretaries for each of the four villages. In 1975-6,
this council was still in existence, although many of
its powers had been alienated to the burgeoning bureaucracy of the local branch of the Trust Territory administration (Peoples n.d.).

Because of its relatively small population of 1,700
in 1947 (Lewis 1949), and its political subordination to
Ponape, Kosrae received few services after the war.
Wartime bombing by the Americans destroyed most of the
public works and physical infrastructure constructed by
the Japanese, and no effort was made by the new administration to rebuild them. Most of what the bombs did
not destroy was allowed slowly to deteriorate through
disuse and lack of maintenance: the Tafoyat dock was
eroded by the reef, the inland dam filled up with silt,
and most of the roads were reclaimed by the forest.
Long periods, often several months in outlying areas
like Kosrae (Oliver 1971:78), elapsed without shipping.
In short, the administering authority failed to rebuild,

much less improve, the physical infrastructure of the Japanese, and did not provide the support services, notably regular shipping, necessary for the island's population to recover its prewar living standards. This pattern held throughout Micronesia (Oliver 1971 and chapter 2), but was especially true for those islands that were not District Centers.

Kosraens reacted to these conditions by returning to subsistence agriculture, earning only a small cash income from the production of copra, which comprised 95% of the total value of exports. During Lewis' study in 1947, some bananas were exported, presumably to the Marshalls for use by American military personnel on Kwajelein atoll. Interestingly, Lewis reported that there were 19 restaurants in operation in 1947, and that 67 men had acquired licenses for all sorts of other businesses. Other men wished to acquire licenses for additional restaurants and bakeries, but were discouraged by the Island Council, "due to the excessive number already engaged, many unprofitably, in such ventures" (Lewis 1949:91). Lewis believed that the explanation for the large numbers of people who wished to engage in trading activities despite their unprofitability was "the customary aspiration of each [Kosraen] to be doing what his neighbors are doing." (Lewis 1949:91) Another part of the explanation may be the lack of alternative sources of income. With so few opportunities available, people naturally crowded into those that offered some chance of success. But because so many adopted the same strategy, the numbers became excessive for the small level of demand, so most were unprofitable or short-lived.

The economy of the island remained stagnant into the 1960s, and the level of cash income certainly declined from Japanese days, according to modern informants. Wilson, who made three short field trips to the island in the early 1960s, reported that copra, remittances from Kosraens employed in Ponape or the Marshalls, and teacher salaries were the most important sources of monetary income. The budget for the whole island in the early 1960s was only about $250,000 per year, and much of this went towards salaries of American personnel and for supplies and equipment. (Wilson 1969:32-3) Although Wilson's statement that income earned through copra production averaged only about $15 per person per year in the early 1960s is probably an underestimation, it is most unlikely that many Kosraens earned more than about $100 in cash annually until the growth of the budget after 1963. This income was expended on small quantities of imported rice, flour, sugar, tinned meats and fish, and other foodstuffs, and on household necessities like kerosene lanterns and stoves, clothing, and toilet articles.

Government Wages and Dependence, 1964-1976

American policy throughout the Trust Territory
since 1963 has been to transfer increasing amounts
of money from U.S. taxpayers to Micronesia through
Congressional appropriations and other forms of federal
assistance (see chapter 2). Some of this money is spent
on the salaries of American personnel in the islands,
but most of it is distributed to Micronesians. At
the island level, this distribution takes the form
of improvements in physical capital and infrastructure,
increases in the quantities of public services available, and, most importantly for purposes of this book,
increases in cash income earned through government
employment.

Kosrae has participated in these benefits. I am
unable to document the annual increases in the budget
allocated to Kosrae in successive years between 1964 and
1976, because these statistics were kept in Ponape until
1977. However, I have good information on employment
with the Kosraen branch of the government for 1975. In
that year, the Trust Territory (T.T.) administration
employed 291 of the resident 4,200 Kosraens on a year-
round, full-time basis, and paid them $898,542 in wages.
This figure does not include the wages of employees of
the Post Office, Municipal Government, Ponape District
Legislature, Congress of Micronesia, and judiciary, or
of part-time carpenters and road and sea wall laborers,
all of whose wages were also paid by one or another
governmental institution funded by the United States.
Nor does it include any employment by local private
businesses or by the Philippine-owned Micronesian Construction Company, which was on contract with the T.T.
government in 1975 to construct a new administrative,
health, and educational complex. Income earned solely
through working in the various departments of the local
branch of the T.T. administration, then, averaged about
$213 per capita in 1975, or almost $3,100 per employee
for the year. As shown in Table 4.1, over one-fifth of
all Kosraens of suitable age had government jobs.

There is, of course, great variation in yearly wage
income of government employees, based on formal training
and education, work experience, and job classification.
The highest paid Kosraen employee received over $11,000
per annum, the lowest just under $1,500 in 1975. This
wage differential is creating significant inequalities
in living standards that are magnified by the fact that
a great many households have no members on the payroll
of any government agency nor any private sector
employer.

In addition to its differential effects on households and family units, employment with the government
is differentially distributed across the four villages

TABLE 4.1
Distribution of government jobs and wages by village, 1975

Village	(A) Total Population	(B) Population, Both Sexes, Aged 20-60	(C) Members With Jobs	(D) (C) as % of (B)	(E) Total Remuneration	(F) Remuneration Per Capita
Lelu	1500b	450b	107	24%	$342,928	$229
Malem	939c	287c	77	27%	$254,510	$283
Tafunsaka	1100b	350b	71	20%	$200,993	$180
Utwe	679c	225c	36	16%	$100,111	$133
	4218	1312	291	22%	$898,542	$213

aTafunsak village figures include approximately 150 Kosraens who live in Welung, a settlement on the westernmost coast of the island that is politically a part of Tafunsak village but residentially separate.

bEstimates based on the census carried out in September, 1973 (U.S. Department of State 1977).

cThese figures are taken from Ritter's (1978:150, 470, 472) demographic data.

in Kosrae (see Table 4.1). Malem villagers have the
highest percentage of government employees and the
highest wages per capita and per worker. Lelu village,
where I conducted research in 1975-6, also has a large
proportion of its population of potential workers
employed with the T.T. administration (column D). Of
the four villages, Utwe, which is still relatively
isolated on the south coast of the island, has been the
least affected by the government payroll.

The 291 Kosraen employees of the local branch of
the Trust Territory government worked in the various
departments of a complex administrative bureaucracy.
The Education Department was the largest employer in
1975, with 89 Kosraens working mostly as teachers,
either in the four village elementary schools or at the
island's high school located in Tafunsak village. Other
large departments included Public Works, Public Health,
and Public Safety (Figure 4.1). Many of these jobs,
such as administrator, teacher, and nurse, require a
formal college education, which many Kosraens have
attained at the Universities of Guam or Hawaii, or at
one of several colleges in the mainland United States.
Others, such as electrician or mechanic, require formal
technical training, which some have acquired at the
Micronesian Occupation Center in Palau.

As the above data indicate, the employees of the
administration are engaged in the provision of public
services and goods to the island's population. This
increased volume of governmental services alone has
raised living standards significantly. Elementary and
secondary education are provided out of the T.T. budget,
and even those who go elsewhere for a college degree
usually receive some form of financial assistance.
Medical care is also free, although a nominal fee is
charged for drugs. Police, agricultural extension,
community, and administrative services are also provided free of fee or tax. In fact, at the time of my
research, the only taxes were a Head Tax and a Public
Works tax levied by the Island Council for repair of
village roads and sea walls and salaries; these totalled
$3 monthly per adult male. In 1975, transportation to
and from the island was also improved. The government
field trip ship came only about once per month, but
three foreign companies operated vessels that called on
the island irregularly. Altogether, about 25 vessels
visit Kosrae per year. This has increased travel opportunities, and Kosraens regularly visit their kin who are
employed by Global Associates in Kwajelein, or by the
T.T. government in Ponape or Saipan.

The supply of public goods also has increased. By
1975, roads (although unpaved) connected four of the
five major settlements. The administration financed the
materials for a water system in Malem, Utwe, and

64

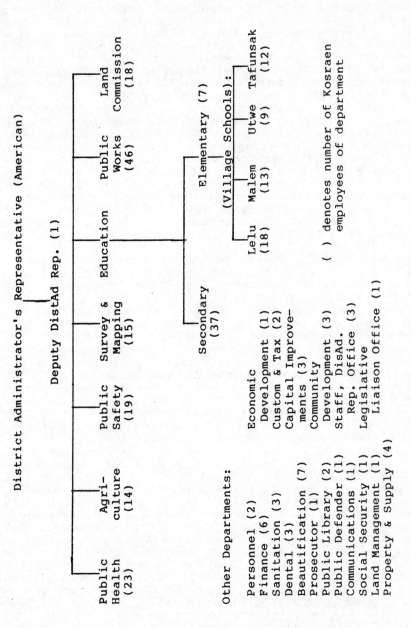

Figure 4.1 Structure of Administrative Bureaucracy

Tafunsak villages before I arrived; just after I left, a water system for Lelu also was completed. Only Lelu village had electricity, but plans existed to extend power lines to the other villages as well. A new dock was completed in Lelu harbor after my departure. An impressive new hospital, high school, and administrative complex was completed in the late 1970s on public land in the mainland portion of Lelu, which is now the governmental center of the island. In 1975, the island had no airstrip, but the administration proposed the construction of a $16 million airport on the reef at Okat Harbor in Tafunsak village. A smaller, interim airstrip was constructed in 1977 on the reef in Lelu. The government also planned to encircle the island with a new road and to construct a major thoroughfare through the interior valley running from Innem to Okat. Engineers from the Navy have constructed farm roads in parts of the island. Although Kosraens find employment in this new construction they have not paid, nor will they pay (at least directly), for any of these improvements in infrastructure and public goods.

At the time of my fieldwork, Kosrae was still a sub-district under Ponape. Kosraens' dislike of this subordinate status intensified in the late 1960s and early 1970s, when Kosraen leaders began to believe that the district government on Ponape was not giving their island its fair share of Trust Territory benefits. The leaders applied for, and received, permission to separate from Ponape district, and in 1977 Kosrae became the newest and smallest district in Micronesia.

Cash income, government services, and the supply of public goods thus have increased in Kosrae, as throughout Micronesia, since the mid-1960s. What have been the effects of this change on the local economy? How have these exogenous inputs combined with local cultural practices and economic conditions to influence the pattern of change that has occurred? These questions are addressed in the following chapters. I begin by describing one critical set of endogenous conditions, namely, the agricultural economy of Lelu village.

5
Agricultural Production

The preceding chapter demonstrates that the economy of Kosrae has become increasingly monetized since the mid-1960s. An increasing proportion of the economically active population is engaged in labor for a monetary wage, and an increasing proportion of the total goods and services consumed are purchased with money rather than produced with unpaid family labor. Despite this trend, production of indigenous foods for subsistence uses continues among family units, even among those households that have wage-earning members. Households with one or more members who have found employment for wages have curtailed subsistence production, but not eliminated it, nor even reduced it as much as they would if the island's agricultural economy did not have certain characteristics described in this chapter. In general, wage-earning households are engaged in two interlocking "spheres" of materially productive activities: (1) production of indigenous foods, largely but not exclusively for the use-value of family members, and (2) production of public goods and services, for which they receive a wage that they exchange for imported foodstuffs and durables. This chapter describes the organization and performance of the subsistence sector of the economy of Lelu village in 1975-6. It focusses on the characteristics that allow the coexistence of wage labor with subsistence production and thus prevents the complete proletarianization of the labor force. Discussion of the cash sector of the economy is reserved for chapter 6. I begin with an overview of Lelu.

THE VILLAGE

Today, as in old Kosrae, Lelu is the administrative capital and most populous village on the island. In 1975, the headquarters of the local branch of the Trust Territory government was located on Lelu island. In the late 1970s, the administration constructed a new high

school, hospital, and government complex on public land
in Tofol, on the mainland portion of the village. (Map
5.1) The Lelu harbor is the official port-of-call for
both government and private vessels, so practically all
human traffic and cargo to and from the island must pass
through the village. Because the island's credit union,
the main branch of the consumer cooperative, and the
largest stores are located on Lelu island, the village
also is the main center of commercial activity. Despite
its status as the administrative, transportation, and
commercial hub of Kosrae, Lelu still retained more of
the character of a village than a town at the time of my
research.

To choose a precise numerical figure for the population of Lelu would be somewhat arbitrary, because individuals come and go on the government's field trip ships
and on private vessels each time a ship visits the
island. For 1975, the population was around 1,500, of
which only about one-half were adults (Peoples 1977;
Ritter 1978 thoroughly discusses Kosraen migration).
About 85% of the resident villagers live on the small
island, which is now connected to the mainland by a
causeway built after World War II by Kosraens. The flat
western half of Lelu island (called Tee) is densely
populated with residences, cookhouses, and businesses,
whereas on the easternmost portion (called Safeir)
settlement is confined mainly to the southern coast.
Except for its extreme eastern tip, Lelu island is completely surrounded by a sea wall, generally kept in good
repair.

It is important to note that, although in 1975 most
villagers lived on the small island, the bulk of the
cultivable land is located on the mainland portion of
the village. Most Lelu families inherited only a house
site on the tiny island, and most or all of their coconut plantations and subsistence gardens are located on
the mainland. Some families, mainly those that live on
the Safeir section, do have subsistence gardens established on the mountain that dominates the eastern half
of the small island. However, for most families that
live on Lelu island, the care and harvest of gardens
requires a trip to the mainland by canoe or motor
vehicle, which consumes about one-half to one hour,
depending on the mode of transportation and the precise
location of the mainland plot. Fortunately for these
families, Kosraen gardens do not require much labor to
maintain or harvest, so daily trips are unnecessary.

In early 1976, when I left the village, there were
25 families who regarded themselves as more or less permanently settled on the mainland portion of Lelu. Most
families who lived on the mainland moved there only in
the last few years, since the administration completed a
new road that runs from the causeway south around the

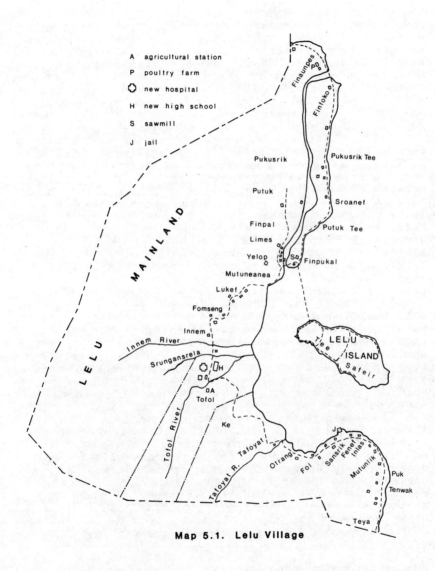

A   agricultural station
P   poultry farm
⬡   new hospital
H   new high school
S   sawmill
J   jail

Map 5.1. Lelu Village

perimeter of the island to Utwe village. These families
give several reasons for their relocation, among which
are the high density of Lelu island, the failure to
inherit an acceptable house site on the small island,
the closer proximity to their mainland gardens, and the
completion of the road that greatly facilitates transportation to the services and jobs on Lelu island.
Besides these families who live on the mainland virtually full time, about 20 other families have constructed houses that they visit for periods of several
days while working in their gardens or making copra for
a prolonged period, or, they often say, "just because we
want to." As a result, many of the mainland houses of
Map 5.1 are unoccupied much of the time.

Due to Kosraen residence practices, determining
the number of households in Lelu village, and indeed
defining the term "household," is difficult. First,
young married couples frequently rotate their residence
between the dwellings of both the wife's and husband's
parents before eventually constructing and settling down
into a house of their own. It may be several years
before such couples establish an independent household,
and, until they do, their household membership is ten-
tative and may change almost monthly. Second, it is
fairly common for a group of brothers to live in a
single compound, either jointly inherited from their
deceased father, or together with their father and
mother. When this occurs, each brother (or son) usually builds a separate house for his own nuclear family
within the compound. Because these living arrangements
often involve on-again, off-again economic cooperation
and occasional partial sharing of subsistence tasks and
cash income, whether to consider each dwelling a separate household or a segment of a single enormous household is problematic. Third, the term "residence" is
ambiguous in the Kosraen context, for young unmarried
men and women often live part of the time with their
natural parents, and part of the time with other relatives. As a result of such practices, a neat definition
of "household" is impossible, and an investigator cannot
unambiguously enumerate the number of households in the
village. In general, I use "household" to refer to
related individuals, usually a single nuclear family,
living in a single dwelling and pooling cash incomes and
other products of their labor. By this definition,
there were about 150 households in the village in 1975.

ECOLOGICAL ZONES AND LAND USE

Five terrestrial ecological zones may be distinguished in Lelu, based on characteristics of vegetation, slope, and use (Map 5.2). Kosraens have terms for

each type and also can make finer distinctions than those adopted here.

Mangrove forests occur along the shoreline wherever rivers or streams have washed sufficient quantities of silt from the mountainsides. This zone provides three major resources for Lelu people: hard, heavy mangrove wood for construction of residences and cookhouses, leaves of the nipa palm for roof thatch, and crabs for food. Due to the availability of imported substitutes, the importance of all these products is declining. No area of mangrove forest is under private ownership today. The Japanese established a law that all land below the mean high water mark, which included all mangrove area, was public land. This law was retained by the United States, and its precepts are followed by Kosraens, who may cut wood and nipa palm or fish for crabs in any mangrove area they choose.

Strand vegetation growing on coralline sand overlaid with humus occurs along the coast wherever mangroves are absent. The entire western half of tiny Lelu island, apparently built up by human labor prior to the coming of Europeans (Cordy 1981), also is strand. Most of the population of the village lives on land of this type. Except for house sites, this zone generally is planted with coconuts, breadfruit, bananas, pandanus, citrus, and occasionally sugar cane. Coconuts are by far the dominant crop, and almost the exclusive one on the mainland areas of strand. But on Lelu island, where most of the villagers live, for reasons of convenience of access, breadfruit and bananas commonly are interplanted with coconut palms.

From aerial photos and maps made by the Division of Land and Surveys, I estimate the area of strand at about 200 acres. This is only about 4% of the total area of Lelu village. Kosraens recognize that this sandy, salty soil is the best land for coconuts, but its small area is not sufficient to meet the demand for land for the copra trade. Therefore, cultivation of the coconut has been extended to land in other ecological zones.

The two largest areas of wet lowlands are the valleys formed by the Tafoyat River and by the complex of the Innem, Tofol, and smaller surrounding rivers. Kosraens correctly consider this land most suitable for the cultivation of taro, although breadfruit, bananas, and coconuts often are planted here as well. Whereas most of the wet lowland area around Tafoyat is under cultivation, this is not the case in the much larger area between Tofol and Fomseng. Here the land slopes gently towards the interior and is waterlogged constantly, conditions that make this whole area ideal for taro cultivation. Yet as one travels away from the road along the course of one of the rivers, cultivations usually cease several hundred feet inland and secondary

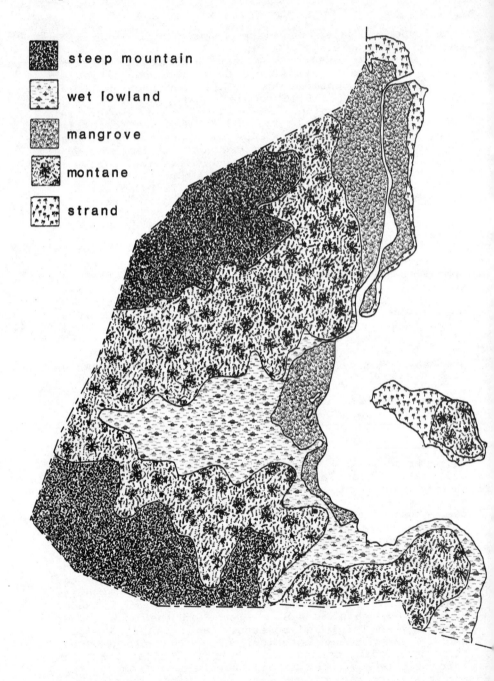

Map 5.2. Ecological Zones, Lelu Village

Legend:
- steep mountain
- wet lowland
- mangrove
- montane
- strand

forest begins. Some of this area certainly was cultivated and settled in aboriginal times (Lesson 1839).
Thus, much potential taro land was unused in 1975-6.

The montane ecological zone is the largest type in
area and the most complex in natural vegetation. This
relatively dry and often very steep land is best suited
for the cultivation of breadfruit, plantains, and bananas, but due to the small area of strand in Lelu, coconuts usually are interplanted with these three main
crops in montane areas. Sugar cane and yams also frequently appear in this zone. As with the wet lowlands,
much montane land is not currently under cultivation.
In fact, only the montane of eastern Lelu island is
planted fully. On the mainland, most of the steep, dry
land on the south side of Lelu Harbor, from Teya to
Tafoyat, is cultivated, but even here there are areas in
which secondary forest is overtaking abandoned banana
"groves." In the other montane areas, large portions of
the zone are not utilized for gardens. Plantings of
breadfruit, bananas, and coconuts could be extended over
their 1975 acreages.

The fifth and economically least important zone in
Lelu is the steep mountains of Finkol and Matante. This
land is so steep and the soil so thin that only scrub
vegetation and grasses grow here. I believe it to be
uncultivable. It is, at any rate, almost all public
land, lost to private ownership by the Japanese "survey"
carried out in 1932.

Of the five land types identified, the strand, wet
lowlands, and montane areas are suitable for cultivation, but only the strand zone was planted at anything
close to its capacity during my fieldwork. It is impossible to estimate the area of wet lowlands and montane
actually under cultivation, for the aerial photographs
made in 1975 are incomplete. I am convinced, however,
based on my own 1975 ground surveys, that not more than
one-third of the land suitable for taro actually is cultivated, and not more than two-thirds of the montane
land is planted in breadfruit, plantain, banana, and
coconut. Secondary forest covers the remaining land of
these two types.

CULTIVATION METHODS AND LABOR REQUIREMENTS

Before beginning research, I had expected Kosraens
to pratice shifting cultivation, also known as slash-
and-burn, in which plots are cultivated for one or more
years and fallowed for a decade or more to restore soil
nutrients and structure. No reference to such a system
on the island occurs in any published source, and informants were puzzled by my questions about how long the
land had to be "rested" after a crop was removed. Their

bewilderment stems from the fact that the fallow period, in the sense of a systematic abandonment of a plot after a harvest, seems to be unknown. They declared that taro, for example, could be planted indefinitely on the same plot, and indeed I observed that the root tip and stalk of hard taro usually were replaced into the same hole from which it had been dug a few minutes before. Once, I observed the early stages of tropical forest succession overtaking some banana and breadfruit trees and, thinking the plot had been abandoned to fallow, asked about it. But the reply was "el alsracngwesr in imohm," "he's too lazy to slash the undergrowth." All informants agreed that bananas and plantains could be grown indefinitely on the same space so long as the land was slashed of weeds regularly. People said that the fruit would shrink as weeds grew up around the stalk, but they maintained that once the area was cleared of undergrowth, the fruit would regain its former size. I finally concluded that allowing the land to revert to forest to restore its fertility is indeed not practiced. This is not difficult to explain for tree crops, for their roots extend far down into the soil. I can offer no such explanation for the two major shallow-rooted varieties of taro. Thus, the wet lowland and montane land in Lelu now in secondary forest have not been abandoned to fallow; they simply have been abandoned.

The changes in agricultural technology that have occurred since the time of contact have not influenced profoundly the techniques used. Some labor-saving implements have been introduced. Steel machetes replaced the shell knife over a century ago (Finsch 1893); the spade usually is used in planting new crops; and steel axes and chain saws have replaced the shell adz for use in clearing new land. Some traditional wooden tools have changed not at all. The digging stick is used in harvesting "hard" taro (Cyrtosperma, also called giant swamp taro). A short twig tied onto a long pole helps in twisting breadfruit from high limbs. A stout carrying pole is employed for toting bunches of heavy fruit from garden sites. A sharpened stick wedged into the ground still is used for husking coconuts. Land-intensive methods such as irrigation, fertilization, and thorough weeding are not used except occasionally in tiny gardens planted with Western vegetables. Sprayers for the application of pest- or fungus-control agents are available from the Agricultural Station, but seldom were used in 1975. Although unsophisticated, the tools and methods used in subsistence cultivation are adequate and remarkably labor-efficient, as discussed below.

As was true also in aboriginal times, adult men and adolescent boys are responsible for almost all garden work, including land preparation, planting, slashing of undergrowth, and harvesting. Except for fishing, women's role in the provision of food is mostly limited to its preparation after harvest. There are, however, two occasions in which women or girls participate in garden chores: in the rare and usually temporary circumstance in which no males of suitable age are available to a household, and when an important man in the kumi helps his group to raise money by paying women to slash weeds from his land (see chapter 8).

That portion of everyday subsistence obtained by producing indigenous foods in one's own gardens requires very little expenditure of labor. This condition arises from the fact that the crops of overwhelming importance in the daily diet are bananas, plantains, and breadfruit, all of which are long-lived and require little labor to plant, maintain, and harvest.

Although breadfruit trees produce fruit only seasonally, they are abundant when available. Sarfert (1919-20:95) believed that there were two periods of ripening, June through August and December through February. My own data indicate a lengthening of these periods. The variety that matures first in the fall was in full production by the end of October, 1975, and other varieties matured successively through March. The summer harvest also began somewhat earlier than Sarfert believed, in May, with the last harvests occurring in August. The "peak" harvest periods in 1975 and 1976 were between November through January and June through July, and breadfruit was certainly the major staple of most households during these months.

Sarfert (1919-20:93-4) identified 18 varieties, and Wilson (1969:85) 16, but at the time of my field work only six were of major economic importance, although others were cultivated. The ripening of these is not completely successive, but there is a definite order with overlapping periods. Ikunlal is always the first to ripen, followed by muhsunwe and srafon, puhtaktek, fok kwekwe, and finally foksruhsrak. During about eight months of the year, one or the other of these varieties is very plentiful, and a few breadfruit are available for nine or ten months.

Breadfruit is a true cultigen, not part of a natural biotic community, so it must be cleared of undergrowth periodically. This is done, at most, only about three or four times per year, requiring a maintenance labor investment of just a couple of hours per tree per year.

The time required to harvest a breadfruit tree primarily depends upon its location. If a household has trees planted near its dwelling, an entire day's supply can be harvested in less than an hour. More commonly, the family lives on Lelu island and only has trees planted on the steep montane land of the mainland.

Harvesting then requires a trip by canoe, motor vehicle, or foot to the stand of trees. The tree usually
is climbed, the fruit twisted free with a long pole,
gathered, and tied onto a carrying pole, after which it
is carried on the shoulder down the steep slope. Each
trip, undertaken during the harvest season one to three
times weekly by most households, consumes less than
one man-day, and bananas often are harvested on the same
trip.

Bananas and plantains are discussed together,
because they are cultivated in the same manner. Both
usually are prepared by frying or boiling. Like breadfruit, they are best planted on the dry montane soil
of the steep hillsides, but also are interplanted with
taro in the wet lowlands zone and with coconuts in the
limited strand areas. Once planted, suckers form off
the main stalk, forming a "stool," or clump of banana
stalks. Only one stalk per stool produces at any time.
When the fruit is harvested, the producing stalk is cut
down about two or three feet from the ground level, and
another stalk from the same stool will grow new fruit.

Like breadfruit, bananas and plantains then are
perennials. Once planted, informants stated that a
stool will produce fruit indefinitely, as long as the
land is slashed of undergrowth every two or three
months. An elderly informant, for instance, stated that
his father planted the stools he currently was harvesting.

Like breadfruit, the time required to harvest plantains and bananas varies primarily with the location of
the stools. Some are grown around house sites on Lelu
island, making harvesting time negligible. But most are
planted on the montane areas of the mainland. Harvest
of these distant plants requires a trip to the mainland,
locating the mature fruit, cutting the stalk and tying
the fruit onto a carrying pole, and transporting the
crop on one's shoulder down the mountainside. The males
of some households go to the mainland to harvest bananas
only once a week, others as often as three times weekly,
each trip requiring a man-day or less. Unlike breadfruit, which usually rots by three days after it has
been harvested, cut bananas are hung in the cookhouse
for a week or more, and bunches are cut off as required
for cooking.

In addition to breadfruit, plantains, and bananas,
two genera of taro are important in the diet of some
Lelu households. "Soft" taro (Colocasia sp.) can be
used for feasts, for which it is made into a poi-like
dish called fahfah by men skilled in the preparation of
this highly valued ceremonial food. In 1975 in Lelu, it
was not consumed on an everyday basis by any household
of which I am aware. A special situation existed at the
time of my field work that made it impossible to acquire

data on the labor hours ordinarily devoted to this root
crop. Soft taro was struck by a disease (diagnosed as
Phytophtora colocasia by the Agriculture Department) in
August, 1971, which rendered the tubers inedible. In
the next year, it spread to most of the island from its
original beginnings in the Innem-Tofol area. Attempts
to control the fungus by the Agriculture Department
failed. Bordeaux was provided to the farmers, but the
frequent rains washed the agent off the plants, making
two or three applications per week necessary for effective control. In these days when imported rice is an
inexpensive and readily available substitute for soft
taro, most people were unwilling to make the necessary
monetary investment in the fungicide. Only in 1974 did
the disease begin to abate, but its continued presence
in 1975 made many Lelu people hesitant to resume extensive plantings of soft taro. Many had ceased planting
altogether, and most planted only a minimum quantity for
their anticipated ceremonial needs.

The disease did not affect the other important kind
of taro, giant swamp taro (Cyrtosperma sp.). This
genus, also called "hard" taro, is not as highly prized
a foodstuff as is Colocasia. Due to the disease that
afflicted the latter, Cyrtosperma was consumed more
often than soft taro in 1975; for some households, it
ranked fourth behind plantains, bananas, and breadfruit
as a staple. Soft taro requires about a year to mature,
giant swamp taro about 18 months. Frequent replanting
is unncessary for both kinds: when the root is removed
from the stalk at harvest, the crown of the plant is
simply replaced in the ground, usually in the same spot
from which it was removed. As already mentioned, informants stated that this could be repeated indefinitely,
so long as the plot was periodically slashed of weeds
and undergrowth.

The foregoing description of the cultivation
requirements of the major staple crops partly explains
why so little labor is devoted to their production.
Although, as shown in a later section, Lelu villagers in
1975 did not even approach subsistence self-sufficiency,
it is remarkable that males spent only about 8% of their
daytime hours in subsistence agriculture. Further,
fishing, the other major productive activity intended to
supply the household with daily food, consumed only 6%
of the total hours available to men, and only 5% of
women's labor time. (see Appendix A) A later chapter
documents the significant interhousehold variations in
the amount of labor time devoted to subsistence activities. At this point, I only wish to note that, in the
aggregate, Lelu householders allocate only a small proportion of their time to subsistence pursuits, and that
one reason for this is that the important cultigens do
not require much labor.

LAND TENURE

A significant quantity of cultivable land in Lelu is under the control of the T.T. government. As discussed in chapter 4, over half the acreage on the whole island was ceded to the Japanese government as a result of the 1932 survey. Officially, this is classified as "public land," but Kosraens call it "government land," that is, land the government will use for its own purposes. At the time of my fieldwork, the exact boundaries of the public lands were being determined through survey and adjudication. I believe that, with the exception of a large area of fine montane land at Tofol, most public land on the Lelu mainland was of the type I have called the steep mountains, and hence is uncultivable. The Division of Land and Surveys and the Land Commission also were surveying and issuing titles to privately owned land. In 1975, this enormous project was not nearly complete and was a major source of dispute and discussion by Kosreans. The following discussion applies only to lands under private ownership.

Under Kosraen custom, land may be sold, traded, or given away, and Kosraens often say that it is "up to the owner" about how he wishes to dispose of his land. Although there is no customary or legal restriction against selling land to other Kosraens, there is a normative one. Individuals who sell significant quantities of land are considered somewhat stupid, or, equally bad, not to be thinking of the future of their heirs. I know of only one Lelu man who has acquired a great deal of land by purchase. Also the owner of a large retail store, he acquired about 22 acres by purchase or trade from various individuals, some of whom erased their debts to his store by means of the transaction. Most of the land he purchased now is planted in bananas, which he used in making of banana turnovers for resale in his store. He also employed three men in 1975 part-time to clear and manage his plantations, the only Lelu man who did this to my knowledge. Land-swapping also sometimes occurs, usually when two men lack land of a certain type and trade to their mutual advantage, or as a means of consolidating holdings that otherwise would be inconveniently scattered.

However, most land is acquired through inheritance. My time on the island was too limited to allow a detailed investigation of inheritance practices on a case-by-case basis. There is a great deal of flexibility in both the norms and practices of land inheritance. Whenever the question is asked "to whom does a man give land when he dies?," the most common answer is "it's up to him." In practice, almost all men give some land to each of their sons. Some will pass land to daughters as well, especially if their husbands have insufficient land, if they are unmarried, or if they have illegitimate sons. It is considered desirable for all male heirs to receive land suitable for cultivation of all the major food crops, and for a house site, but circumstances often make this impossible.

If an older man has married sons, he allows them to use his land for purposes of household subsistence and copra-making. Even if the sons establish separate residences, as frequently happens nowadays, they help support their parents with frequent food gifts. As he grows older, a man ordinarily writes down on a piece of paper the manner in which he wishes the land to be divided among his heirs after he dies. This will (or "paper," as Kosraens call it) becomes a binding document, especially if witnesses were present. From then until the man dies, title to the land is divided, with the various heirs receiving use-rights and the father retaining residual rights (these terms are from Wilson 1969). This allows the heirs to "plan" (Kosraens use this word): they now can plant coconuts, breadfruit, and bananas, which produce for decades, free of concern that the father will leave the plot to another heir. (I also was told that sometimes sons will stake a preliminary "claim" to parcels by planting crops on them). On the death of the father, full rights of ownership are transferred to the heirs. If circumstances do not allow a written will to be left, a man should communicate to several witnesses which parcels he wishes to be left to which heirs. Failing either of these mechanisms, the eldest son or a brother of the deceased divides the land among the descendants, ideally in an impartial manner.

The absence of a fixed principle, such as primogeniture, governing the inheritance of land has the positive effect of ensuring flexibility in the transmission of land through the generations, but it also promotes land disputes. If a man dies suddenly and has left no written will or oral statement, disagreements among potential heirs are likely to follow. Even when an oral statement is left in the presence of witnesses, it frequently happens that future arguments occur over what the deceased really said or meant. Uncertainty of tenure is then common, as it has perhaps been for decades. But the disputes were particularly acrimonious at the time of my fieldwork, because of the work of the Land Commission. Realizing that permanent legal title will be granted as a result of the land Commission's adjudication, claimants pressed their alleged rights vigorously. At the time of my visit, all of tiny Lelu island had been surveyed and legal title given, but most of the mainland parcels were unregistered.

The cultural preference for leaving some land of all available types to all male offspring tends to result in a fairly equitable distribution of land holdings among a

man's sons. Recalling that the Kosraen population
dropped to around 300 in 1880, one obvious source of
variability in quantities of land held by individuals is
the history of differential fertility since the late
nineteenth century among various family lines. This
variability is dampened somewhat, however, by the common
practice of adoption. Couples with no children of their
own ordinarily will adopt infants from close relatives
or, less often, from friends. This practice has the
fortunate (although unintended) system-wide effect of
redistributing land held by childless couples. Thus,
Ritter (1981b:54) discovered a strong tendency for male
adoptees to maintain close relationships with their
adopted parents if the latter have no natural sons, in
anticipation of receiving land from the adopting couple.
Because Wilson (1976) and Ritter (1981b) have discussed
Kosraen adoption fully, I shall not further consider it
here, except to note that it probably tends to even out
land holdings.

Two factors thus tend to even out the distribution
of land between households: the preference for leaving land of various types to all sons, and adoption.
Despite these, there is of course variability in the
amounts of land held by individuals, or, in the case of
divided title between an elderly man and his adult sons,
collections of individuals. Unfortunately, I have no
quantitative data on this variability for mainland parcels, where most gardens are located, because the Land
Commission had not completed its work on the mainland in
1976. I can state, however, that I know of no Lelu
household that lacks a supply of land adequate for its
everyday subsistence needs. Most households whose gardens I visited have land that is not presently cultivated at all. This condition affects the way that
households with one or more employed male members have
reacted to wage labor, as discussed later in this chapter. The condition will not, however, exist for much
longer: already some men complained of a shortage of
land of certain types, and several men told me of their
concern that they did not have enough land to pass some
along to all their sons. For 1975, however, I feel con-
fident with the following generalization: the great
majority of Lelu households own or have access to sufficient land to allow them to be self-sufficient in indigenous cultivated foodstuffs.

The pattern of ownership is striking, and somewhat
inconvenient to the households affected, in one regard:
many men have holdings that are scattered on the mainland portion of Lelu. For example, one man has land in
the wet lowlands zone planted in taro at both Innem and
Tafoyat, and has land planted in plantains, bananas,
breadfruit, and coconuts in the montane zones of Otrang
and Inlas. Rather than owning large, continuous tracts

of land, many men have three or more smaller, spatially
fragmented holdings. As a result, they or other male
members of their households often must visit more than
one location in harvesting trips to the mainland. This
common fragmentation of parcels is explicable by the
demographic history of the island. As the population
declined between about 1840 and 1880, the number of
occupied districts also fell (Finsch 1893:451). When
the population began to increase in the 1880s, the power
of the nobility had been so eroded by missionization
that they no longer could enforce their land claims.
De facto ownership passed into the lands of commoners
and their descendants. But the population was so
reduced in number that, around the turn of the century,
adult men possessed enormous amounts of land:

> when talking about people and land the natives refer
> to one man as being the owner of an entire district.
> For example, the districts of Laap and Koasr belong
> to my translator Kephas; Malem, Taf and Finkol
> belonged to one man; and the District of Utwe to two
> brothers; I presume this would also be the case for
> other districts. (Sarfert 1919-20:389)

Wilson's (1969:278-94) data on land ownership on the
mainland portion of Lelu also indicates that whole districts, and in many cases more than one district, were
held by a single individual about three generations ago.
Once all the land was owned by the relatively few surviving families, succeeding generations acquired most
of their land by inheritance. The practice of passing
along land suitable for cultivation of the major crops
to all male (and sometimes female) offspring led inex-
orably to fragmentation of parcels and to scattering of
holdings. This present pattern might be even more pro-
nounced were it not for the practices of adoption, free
sale, and exchange of land that are allowed under
Kosraen custom.

ORGANIZATION

As mentioned previously, in Kosrae all work relating
to the cultivation of indigenous foodstuffs for subsistence uses is allocated to males. By early adolescence,
and sometimes even younger, boys are assigned garden
tasks, and ordinarily they continue to work on the land
throughout adulthood or until physically unable to do
so (although the grown sons of an elderly couple are
expected to provide much of their parent's food). Women
and girls only rarely engage in subsistence gardening,
although they do fish for the household and handle
most of the cutting and drying of copra for the export

market. In old Kosrae, when food normally was prepared by baking in the earth oven, men did the cooking; nowadays, with the availability of cooking utensils and kerosene stoves, women usually prepare the everyday meals, although men frequently do make the earth oven when food is cooked by this method.

With respect to the acquisition of locally produced food for everyday consumption, the household ordinarily is the social unit that cooperates in production and that shares the products of labor. Each household has access to land that is either owned by its head, or to which it has use-rights by virtue of a kinship relation, usually to the father or sibling(s) of the head. Most of the agricultural technology also is owned by the household. Chain saws for clearing new land is the major exception; when used, these are rented from the Agricultural Station. Households do vary significantly in their ownership of some kinds of fishing equipment (see Appendix H). The two most expensive kinds of nets, surround nets and throw nets, are owned by a minority of households, for example. But, as also for the canoe, such equipment is so easily borrowed from related households that for each family unit to purchase its own would be wasteful. Thus, two of the factors of production, land and tools, are owned by households, or use-rights to them are almost automatic.

Access to the third factor of production, labor, also is controlled by the household. This is more complex, for there are several exceptions to this generalization. (1) When new land is cleared for cultivation, voluntary work groups often are recruited from among a man's relatives and friends. (2) Some men do occasionally employ groups of people to "bush" (clear weeds by slashing with a machete) their gardens. For example, a man may hire a group of boys who wish to earn money for a school party or for a joint church contribution; or someone may employ the women of a kumi (Chapter 8) to help them acquire cash for their group's contribution to year-end ceremonies. These arrangements are always short-term, usually for a day or half-day, and are intended as much to help the groups with their activities as to accomplish the task. (3) Kosraen kinship is sufficiently extended that a household with a serious shortage of labor of one sex frequently calls on their relatives to lend a laborer. The individuals who help in this way usually are adolescent boys and girls. Sometimes they may temporarily change households, both residing with and contributing their labor to a nonparental relative. This practice is sufficiently common that Kosraens have a term for it: mwet kuhlacnsap ("person who helps," i.e., one who leaves his or her natal household to contribute their labor to another). (4) It is quite common for elderly couples to live by

themselves in a dwelling separate from their grown
children. The sons of the couple, who usually live
nearby if not in adjacent dwellings, regularly supply
their parents with both storebought and indigenous
foods. (5) Small-scale food exchanges between neighboring and related households are common. For example,
when a boy returns home from a family's garden with
breadfruit, one or two fruit may be given to a neighbor
or relative. Such exchanges generally are balanced,
each household receiving roughly what they give, and are
a material symbol of good relations between the families; except for elderly couples, so far as I know these
exchanges are not a significant source of food for any
household. Despite such complications, the labor used
in producing indigenous foods for subsistence purposes
is by and large domestic labor, that is, the labor of
the household members themselves.

Thus, in Lelu in 1975, access to the means of subsistence production was governed by principles of domes-
ticity and kinship. It should be emphasized that I am
here referring to the provision of indigenous foodstuffs
for the everyday subsistence of households. Almost all
households also purchase some portion of their food at a
local store and all households are engaged periodically
in production of food for ceremonial feasts, which are
organized by higher-level social groupings, such as
church and kumi.

CONCLUSION

This chapter so far has established the following
conclusions. First, more land of both the wet lowlands
and montane type are available to Lelu people than is
actually under cultivation. Second, the most important
subsistence crops (breadfruit, banana, plantain, and
taro) require little labor to plant, maintain, and harvest. As a result, Lelu men and boys, who do virtually
all the agricultural tasks, in the aggregate expended
only about 8% of their time in subsistence agriculture.
Third, despite some variability in acreage owned, all
households currently have access to land. I believe,
but cannot document, that most or all have enough land
to be self-sufficient in native foods. Fourth, with
some caveats, most households produce most of their
indigenous foods using their own land, technological,
and labor resources.

Together, these conditions of the village's agricultural economy mean that even those Lelu people who
have found employment for wages have not yet been
transformed into a fully proletarianized labor force.
By this statement, I mean that all households continue
to be engaged, to a greater or lesser extent, in

autosubsistence activities. Wage labor has not resulted
in the loss of access to the means of (subsistence) production by workers or their households. Those households containing job holders are engaged both in subsistence cultivation and fishing, and in employment for
a monetary wage. Households with jobs of course spend
less effort in subsistence production than do those
with no employed members (Appendix A) largely because of
the relative scarcity of male time in job households
(chapter 7). But because even job households have
access to land, and because Kosraen cultigens require so
little labor, job-holding men themselves do garden work
on Saturdays or, less often, after work. Moreover, adolescent boys take up part of the subsistence labor slack
created by their father's wage work. Thus, all households continue to produce and consume indigenous foods,
and the conditions of the village's agricultural economy
allow this to occur.

    Despite this fact, it should not be thought that
these conditions have spared the inhabitants from a high
degree of dependence on imported foods. My data on production and consumption are sufficient to allow a rough
estimate to be made of the level of subsistence self-
sufficiency of Lelu village in 1975. This estimate, and
the assumptions behind it, is presented in Appendix D.
Using quantities of calories as the measure of the proportion of food for everyday consumption produced
locally, Lelu people produced between one-half and two-
thirds of the food they consumed in 1975. A minimum of
one-third of their food supply was imported. Because,
as shown in this chapter, more land is available to Lelu
people than they actually cultivate, the reason for
these imports is not an absolute shortage of land.

6
The Dependent Cash Economy

As Chapter 4 has shown, the cash sector of the Lelu economy has blossomed since the mid-1960s, due almost entirely to the expansion of wage labor opportunities with the local branch of the Trust Territory government. In the rate of growth of wage labor and monetary income, and in its pattern of response to this growth, Lelu in some respects is a miniature replica of the dependent economy of all of Micronesia. As the present chapter shall document, most of the new income is expended on imported commodities, such as building materials for new houses, motor vehicles, and a variety of imported foodstuffs. Stimulated by the increased availability of cash in the village, businesses develop that circulate cash even to individuals who have not obtained a government job. As also in Micronesia generally, these businesses concentrate in retail, entertainment, transportation, and other service industries. After describing the growth in cash incomes, in imports, and in the private sector, I develop a sectoral model of the village economy that depicts its structure and reveals the flow of cash between its sectors.

INCOME

From data summarized in Appendix E, I estimate the minimum total cash income of Lelu people in 1975 at about $650,000. Regular employment with the local branch of the administration accounted for $343,000. If employment with other governmental agencies, such as the Post Office or the Ponape District Legislature, is included, $400,000, or over 60% of the village's cash income, was earned through jobs funded directly by the United States. With about 150 households in the village, an average household earned about $4,300 cash. There is, of course, great variation around this mean. Some households had more than one source of cash income, either because they had more than one member on the

government payroll, or because they had employed members
and also owned a store or other business. Some of these
earned over $10,000 in cash during 1975. Other house-
holds had no employed members and owned no business,
but relied almost entirely on income earned from copra
sales; their cash income was only a few hundred dollars.

These figures underestimate the total income of the
village, because they omit the value of the cultivated
produce, fish, and other foods that every household also
produces for its own use. Data given in Appendixes B
and C allow a more complete accounting of the value of
goods and services produced in 1975. Assigning the
prices of agricultural, fish, and pork foodstuffs at
market outlets in 1975 to the approximate total production of these foods, I estimate the cash value of the
subsistence sector of the economy at $250,000. Like the
figure for cash income, this estimate also should be
considered a minimal one. Lelu villagers then had a
total of at least $900,000 real income in 1975, and more
likely something over $1,000,000. The real per capita
income is then at least $600, the real mean income per
household at least $6,000.

These figures may sound impressive to those who have
worked in other underdeveloped areas, but they still
appear low by the standards of industrialized countries.
Indeed, even the most well-to-do Kosraens do not enjoy
the high standards of material consumption of an average
North American. However, the level of living of Lelu
households are higher than these statistics indicate on
the surface because they do not have many of the expenses of households in the industrialized nations. At the
time of my fieldwork, no income tax was paid, although
an income tax bill has since been passed by the Congress
of Micronesia. In Lelu, electricity was available,
costing an average of only about $4 per household per
month. The services of physicians and other health
agents were free, although a nominal fee was charged for
medicines acquired from the local hospital. Rent is
practically unknown, even in the rare instance in which
a family occupies the house or land of another. A fine
new house could be constructed from materials costing
between $2,000 and $3,000. Almost anyone who has lived
in underdeveloped villages in Asia, Latin America, or
Africa would, I am sure, agree that Lelu people are
living quite well by the standards existing in most
rural areas in those continents.

IMPORTS

Available data suggest that the consumption of
imports has increased roughly in direct proportion to
the increase in wages paid to government employees since

the mid-1960s. These data were acquired from the annual accounts compiled by the Kosrae Island Cooperative Association (K.I.C.A.), a consumer cooperative, from 1966-1975. The co-op began operations in May, 1965. Until 1973, there was only one store on Kosrae, on Lelu island. A branch in Utwe village opened in August, 1973, followed by branches in Tafunsak in April, 1974, and in Malem in March, 1975. Table 6.1 shows the magnitude of the increase in total merchandise sales by the K.I.C.A. from 1966-1975. All these sales were of imported goods, for the co-op does not sell any locally produced goods, so the table also reveals the approximate magnitude of the increase in imports for the same period. However, it does not show the total absolute level of imports, because several other retail outlets also order and sell merchandise independently of the consumer cooperative.

As shown in Table 6.1, the 1975 value of retail sales at the consumer's cooperative was over eleven times the value in 1966. The lower rate of increase at the Lelu outlet since 1973 compared to sales over the whole island is only apparent, because prior to the opening of branch stores in other villages in 1973, 1974, and 1975, people of these other villages came to Lelu to shop at the K.I.C.A. In 1975, $377,102 of the cooperative's total merchandise sales on the whole island were of foodstuffs and cigarettes; $199,166 of the sales at the Lelu outlet only were sales of the same two categories. Thus, it appears that about one-half of the total value of merchandise purchased at the four branches of the K.I.C.A. represent purchases of imported foods and cigarettes.

Categories and Patterns of Expenditure

The major categories of imported goods sold on the island are materials for new housing, motor vehicles, foods, and household goods. Most families purchase household goods and (especially) foods, on an everyday basis, typically by sending a youngster to some local store to pick up one or two items as they are needed. Houses and motor vehicles represent special purchases because most households must save a portion of their earnings over a period of many months to buy these goods. Since April, 1967, this saving has been facilitated by the Kosrae Island Credit Union (K.I.C.U.). A government job holder usually asks the K.I.C.U. to deposit a sizeable fraction, often 50%, of his bi-weekly paycheck in his account with the Credit Union. Over a period of months, he thus builds up shares. Under the rules of the K.I.C.U., he can borrow at any one time an amount equal to twice the value of his shares, at the

TABLE 6.1
Kosrae Island Cooperative Association total merchandise
sales, 1966-75, for whole island and Lelu village

Year	Kosrae Island $ Amount Sold	Lelu Village $ Amount Sold
1966	$ 63,136	$ 63,136
1967	$129,072	$129,072
1968	$189,915	$189,915
1969	$234,615	$234,615
1970	$293,131	$293,131
1971	$211,083	$211,083
1972	$252,102	$252,102
1973	$354,782	$312,954
1974	$523,753	$396,434
1975	$729,675	$402,759

Source: Records of the Kosrae Island Cooperative
Association

interest rate of 1% monthly. Most saving by this method
is not made for purposes of having a "nest egg" or
having a supply of funds available for emergencies. It
is, in fact, what might be called "target saving": most
people save now in order to borrow later for purchases
of some expensive good. Thus, the head of the K.I.C.U.
estimated that about 80% of all loans were made for consumption of items like building materials (60%) or motor
vehicles (20%). This pattern of saving followed by subsequent borrowing is discussed further below. The following pages and Appendixes F through H summarize expenditure patterns on the major categories of imports.
    Village Housing. The economic history of Kosrae
since World War II is revealed strikingly by the extant
housing. A housing survey conducted in Lelu (Appendix
F) revealed that private dwellings may be divided into
three categories, based on their physical characteristics and age. (1) In 1975 there were about a half-dozen
very old, large dwellings built of cement; most also had
a second story constructed with imported or local mangrove wood. These were built after the war by men who
were able to earn, by copra-making, fishing, or off-
island wage labor, the $500 or so necessary to purchase
cement for floors and walls, and galvanized metal for
the roof. According to their owners, four of these
were built in 1949, 1951, 1952 and "between 1945 and
1950." The others also were built before about 1955.
(2) On Lelu island, there were about a dozen of the

second major type of dwelling. This type is defined by
the fact that only materials available on the island
itself were used in their construction: mangrove wood
for the floors, walls, and support structure, and the
woven thatch of the nipa palm for the roof. Almost all
these were built during the early or mid-1960s. By
1975, most of these "traditional" style dwellings were
badly dilapidated and in need of repair or replacement.
(3) By far the most numerous is the "modern" style
house. It is built entirely of imported materials:
corrugated and galvanized iron for the roof; flat sheet
metal, cement block, or (most commonly) plywood for the
walls; screens or louvers for the windows; and concrete
for the floor. Virtually all these modern houses (I
have specific data on 27) were built in the late 1960s
through 1975. The oldest private dwellings, then, were
built around 1950; the few surviving traditional-style
houses were constructed mostly in the 1960s; and most of
the modern houses date from the late 1960s and early
1970s.

The recent economic history of the island explains
why housing styles break down surprisingly neatly into
these categories. After the war, a few of the wealthier
men were able to earn enough money to build a large,
long-lasting structure. But most people had to be content with the traditional style built out of local mangrove wood and nipa palm. This latter type will last
only about 10-15 years. When they had to be replaced in
the 1960s and early 1970s, many people were working for
the government and so most were replaced with the modern
style. Thus, the few traditional dwellings represent,
in a sense, "survivals" from the economic condition of
the village in the 1950s and early 1960s, and one by one
they are being replaced by the much-preferred modern
type.

In 1975, there were at least six modern style houses
constructed that replaced traditional ones; there were
at least another 14 built as new households, many for
young married couples. To build a new house for oneself
or, as is common, for one's parents, a job holder nearly
always begins a few months ahead by depositing a portion
of his paycheck with the Credit Union. When the shares
have accumulated, he then can borrow an amount up to
twice their value to purchase the imported materials
required to start the construction. Usually the house
is built in two, three, or sometimes four stages, often
months apart, for most men alternately deposit and later
borrow money. After the first two stages, the house
usually can be occupied, although it may have no window
glass or screen, nor an interior wall or ceiling. Most
houses take about two years to complete, with a year or
less before the family moves in. In almost all cases,
voluntary work parties are recruited to acquire labor

for mixing and pouring cement and carpentry. The relatives and friends of the owner who help with the construction receive food and cool drinks while working
plus, ordinarily, a basket of food to take home to their
families. However, a few men are beginning to hire for
cash one of the four or five men in the village who are
recognized as especially skilled in carpentry.

In 1975, a small, modern style house with a concrete
floor, corrugated iron roof, and sheet metal walls could
be constructed for as little as $500. A larger struc-
ture, complete with louvers and plywood walls, cost
between $2,000 and $2,500. Based on interviews with
numerous people who had recently constructed new dwellings, I have a high degree of confidence that the average total cost of a house in 1975 was between $2,500 and
$2,800, including the dollar cost of food to reciprocate
the labor services of kin and friends. Using this figure, the monies spent on new housing in Lelu may be
estimated (although the estimate is complicated by the
practice of purchasing building materials in stages).
There were at least 20 new houses constructed in 1975,
and deposits made at the Credit Union for others. At
the minimum, total expenditure on new housing was about
$60,000.

Almost none of this sum was spent on locally produced commodities. Iron, cement, and louver materials
obviously could not be produced on the island economically, but even the wood for frames and walls was almost
entirely imported, either as plywood, beams, or studs.
Many Kosraens believe that imported woods are superior
in appearance and durability to local mangrove wood.
Another contributing factor was the absence of an
operating sawmill in Lelu in 1975. Philip Ritter
(personal communication) reports that modern-style
houses in Utwe village are usually built with local
mangrove wood for frames and rafters. Utwe had two saw-
mills in operation in 1975. Lelu people probably would
have used more local timber if the village's lone sawmill had been working.

Motor Vehicles. In 1975, there were between 45
and 50 trucks and automobiles and 40 to 50 motorcycles
under private ownership. The Kosrae Island Cooperative
Association and two private retail stores sold trucks
and cars by special order, and one of these stores frequently had motorcycles in regular stock. Many vehicle
owners, however, purchased their vehicles off-island,
where competition was more intense and prices generally
lower, even after transportation costs were included.
Most vehicles, whether auto, truck, or motorcycle, were
made in Japan.

A vehicle survey carried out by an assistant and
myself shows that 16 trucks or cars were purchased in
1975, with a total market value of $45,000. Seven

individuals purchased motorcycles in the same year,
worth about $3,200. Thus, villagers spent a total of
around $50,000 on motor vehicles, somewhat less than the
expenditure on new dwellings. Motor vehicles quite
often are borrowed by close relatives; partly for this
reason, expenditure patterns differ from those of
houses. The latter usually are purchased out of a man's
own savings, or the savings of, at most, a group of
brothers jointly financing a house for their father. But
the expense of purchasing a truck quite often is shared.
Usually one man is considered the primary owner of the
vehicle, but his sons, brothers, and often cousins give
some money to "help" him with the expense. In return,
these men also have use of the vehicle when they need
it, although they will ask permission. The "help" is
usually less than $100, and the owner himself does bear
the brunt of the expense.

Foods. As discussed in the previous chapter, in
1975 I believe that all Lelu households grew a portion
of their food on land that they owned or to which they
had access through kinship ties. Few, if any, households relied totally on imported foods. However, many
households, particularly those with jobs, made almost
daily visits to the consumer's cooperative or to a private retail store to purchase rice, tinned fish and
meats, sugar, flour, or other imported foods. Bread, a
popular food, was purchased at one of the village's
bakeries or retail stores. Although it was baked in the
village, I consider it and other baked foods to be
imports, because all the materials used in their preparation were imported. Practically the only locally
produced foods bought for everyday consumption were fish
(caught by a member of the fishing cooperative or by a
casual fisherman) and a few Western vegetables (most of
which were grown by Utwe villagers). From data summarized in Appendix G, I estimate that about $220,000
was spent on food during 1975 by the whole village for
everyday consumption. At least 90%, and more likely
95%, of all foods purchased were imported; Lelu people
then spent over $200,000 on imported foods for everyday
consumption.

It should be noted here that these figures do not
include the significant expenditures made by villagers
on foods consumed in ceremonial contexts, such as
funerals, marriages, church holidays, and other feasts.
These events, and expenditures on them, are discussed
in chapters 8 through 10. I justify partitioning the
demand for food into "everyday consumption" and "ceremonial consumption" in those chapters.

Household goods. This category may be divided into
"perishables" and "durables" used jointly by the members of a household. The former includes goods such as
bleach, laundry and bath soap, kerosene, toothpaste, and

other items that are used up relatively quickly. In a four week period in 1975, a sample of 10 households spent $258 on such goods. Assuming an average household spent around $25 monthly on household perishables, the whole village's purchases were valued at around $45,000 for the year. Durable household goods include stoves, tools, cooking utensils, electric appliances, lamps, radios, and so forth. As Appendix H shows, most households had a considerable stock of these goods. I have no reliable data on the dollar value of durables. At a minimum, perhaps $70,000 was spent on perishables and durables together in 1975, and the figure more likely is higher.

Expenditure on houses, vehicles, foods, and household goods accounted for approximately $400,000 (60%) of the total village income of $650,000 in 1975. In chapter 10, I estimate that Lelu people spent an additional $100,000 on foods, clothing, and other goods purchased for use in ceremonial contexts. The remaining $150,000 is a residual category for my data. Casual observations suggest that it was spent mainly on entertainment at local theaters and billiard halls, alcohol, cigarettes, travel, college education off-island, clothing, savings, gasoline and other motor vehicle expenses, and personal items.

COPRA

Into the 1960s, Kosraens earned the bulk of their personal income from the production and sale of copra, the dried meat of the coconut. All copra produced on the island is sold at the Kosrae Island Cooperative Association, which is the local purchasing agent for the Micronesian-wide buyer, the United Micronesian Development Association. The Copra Stabilization Board, which operates throughout the Trust Territory, helps to protect producers from the notorious fluctuations in the world market prices of the product. As I understand its operation, when world copra prices are higher than average, the Board sets the prices to be paid to Micronesian producers somewhat lower than market rates so that, in effect, producers pay into a fund. When world prices fall to below-average levels, the Board uses the accumulated fund to subsidize the prices paid to producers. Despite this sensible arrangement, the variations in prices received by producers are enormous: when I arrived in Kosrae in March, 1975, producers were receiving a record $20.50 per 100 pound bag; by the next fall, the price had dropped to $6.50 per bag.

Copra production is still the main income-earning, agriculturally productive activity organized using household labor and privately owned land. A man will,

often with the aid of his teen-aged sons or other relatives or friends, gather and remove the husks from the
fallen nuts at his plantation. The nuts are taken to a
drier, either a simple platform with a removable rain-
proof roof, often called a sun drier, or a more elaborate smoke drier. The actual removal of the meat from
the inside of the shell is almost exclusively women's
work, and ordinarily they handle the drying operations
as well. Not every household owns a drier. In 1975,
there were, to my knowledge, only four copra driers in
Lelu, of which three were smoke driers. One man commonly rented his drier for a fee, but most others allow
relatives and friends to use their driers at no formal
charge, although there is usually reciprocity of some
kind.

It makes intuitive sense that the production of
copra should have fallen proportionately to the increase
in income resulting from government wages. However,
this appears not to have occurred. I cannot document
this conclusion with confidence, for the records that I
obtained from two sources on copra exports between 1967
and 1975 do not agree. My own observations and the
reliable statistics kept by the K.I.C.A. on production
by specific individuals in 1974 suggest the following
response. Most households have indeed decreased their
copra production, but others have partly made up the
difference in the aggregate figures by increasing their
production. K.I.C.A. records show that in 1974, Lelu
producers earned $50,670, for a mean copra income per
capita of $34. Table 6.2 shows that most men made less
than $500 worth of copra in 1974, and most of these made
less than $200 worth. A few men made over $1,000, and
one outstanding producer who has an exceptionally large
plantation earned over $4,500 from his copra labor.

Even employed men occasionally make copra, if only
to keep the nuts that have fallen from their palms from
being wasted. Typically, employed men do not themselves
participate in the gathering or husking of the nuts, but
have their sons or younger male relatives do the work.
By means of this strategy, the employed man's own scarce
time is conserved, while the household earns additional
cash income from the labor of its unemployed young or
adolescent men. The Time Budget data of Appendix A give
a quantitative idea of how the presence of a government
job affects the amount of labor devoted to copra production. If households are the unit of observation, the
male labor force of those households in which one or
more male members had jobs spent 4% of their time in
copra production, whereas males in jobless households
allocated 7% of their time to producing copra. On the
other hand, if individual adult men are the observation
units, those men without jobs spent 17% of their time in
copra work; those men in the sample with jobs engaged in

TABLE 6.2
Frequency table, dollar value of copra produced by number of producers, Lelu village, 1974

Amount Sold	Number of Producers
under $500	91
$ 501-1,000	23
$1,001-1,500	5
$1,501-2,000	2
$2,001-2,500	1
$4,501-5,000	1

Source: Records of Kosrae Island Cooperative Association

no copra production at all. Thus, although employed men tend to make very little copra themselves, their unemployed male kin frequently do so in their stead.

Of the 23 men who made between $501 and $1,000 worth of copra in 1974, 16 were unemployed in 1975; of the five who made between $1,001 and $1,500, three were unemployed; none of the four who made over $1,500 worth were employed. The pattern is by now evident: most households, even those with government employees, continue to earn a few hundred dollars per year through the sale of copra. A few, largely those without government employment, have intensified their production, and probably now are producing more than previously (unfortunately, available records do not allow this conclusion to be stated with confidence). Two factors account for this pattern. First, government employees are improving their living standards, and those without jobs or businesses are eager to keep up as much as they can through copra production. Second, thanks to the large number of retail stores that exist by selling imported goods to government employees and their families, a much wider range of goods and services now are available for purchase on the island, and this gives unemployed men an incentive to increase their copra production.

BUSINESS

In 1975, Lelu people earned about $400,000 from employment in public services with the Trust Territory administration or with some other American-funded agency. An additional $60,000 was earned through the sale of copra to the export market. Only about $40,000 to $50,000 was earned through producing other local resources for sale to fellow villagers, including mainly lagoon and ocean fish, but also a multitude of small-scale individual-to-individual sales of pigs, handicrafts, canoes, mats, coconut oil, and other items. The remainder of the cash income, or $150,000, came from service industries in the private sector, either in the form of profits of retail stores, theaters, bakeries, billiard halls, and other businesses, or in the form of wages earned through private sector employment. (see Appendix E and section on INCOME) From these figures, it might appear that Lelu people were dependent on the Trust Territory administration for about 60% of their total cash income.

Actually, however, this would be a serious under-estimation. Although 40% of the total cash income of the village was earned through private sector activities, income from nongovernmental sources would be much less than it is without the dollars earned from employment with some governmental agency. That is, in addition to the direct dependence of government job holders on U.S. appropriations, many of those working in the private sector are dependent indirectly on American taxpayers. Their opportunities exist mainly because government employees use their wage income to purchase the goods and services that they supply.

A simple listing of the businesses active in Lelu in 1975 reveals this fact. The majority were retail stores, 15 in number, which sold imported goods exclusively. By the end of 1975, there were four bakeries in operation, two beginning during that year. In addition, the women of several households regularly baked bread, doughnuts, turnovers, and sweet cakes that they sold wholesale to one of the large local stores. Like the bakeries, they bought the flour, sugar, yeast, and other baking materials from a local store at retail prices, transforming them with their own labor into the finished product. Entertainment services were another significant source of income: the village had two billiard halls and three theaters, one of which opened in 1975. The owner of the island's largest retail store, with two branches on Lelu island, also owned a hotel; in 1975 it was occupied by an American involved in the government's land survey. The same man also contracted with one of the foreign shipping companies to provide a passenger terminal, ran a taxi service, and employed several girls to bake bread for retail sale at one of his store branches. The Kosrae Island Fuel Transportation Company, started in 1972, sold parts for autos, scooters, and outboards, made repairs on motor vehicles, and sold gasoline. The Kosrae Terminal and Stevedoring Company had a contract with the government to provide steve-doring services whenever a ship came into port, employing many men for short periods. One of the theater owners improved an old building next to his movie house and, when I left in February, 1976, was planning to start a restaurant. In 1975, another store owner was constructing a fine new building with cement blocks, which he was planning to turn into a theater or restaurant. In late 1975, a man was successful in obtaining a loan from the Economic Development Load Fund to purchase vending machines for candy, cigarettes, and soft drinks, just because, he said, "there are none on Kosrae." A group of men decided that it would be profitable to start their own construction company to bid for government capital improvement projects and had applied for a large loan to purchase heavy equipment.

Two features of this list are significant. First, most businesses were engaged in the service industries, notably import and retail, baking, recreation, and transportation. The private sector of the village is dominated by services; only two businesses, considered below, were engaged in profit-making activities that produced some good using local resources. Second, it is apparent that most of these businesses depend for their existence on the cash income that other villagers earn from government employment, and that many would fail altogether should government jobs or wages be reduced significantly. Their profit-making potential is based largely on their capacity to transform the wages of government job holders into imported goods and into entertainment. I shall return to both of these points in the conclusion to this chapter.

As the preceding discussion shows, the retail trade is a significant component of the expansion of the private sector generated by government wages. In Lelu in 1975, 15 stores were in operation. They fall into three classes, based on the size of their inventories and annual sales. The three largest stores had an inventory of over $10,000 (in one case, certainly well over $20,000). These were general merchandise stores, selling a variety of imported foods and soft drinks, cloth and clothing, tools, household utensils, cleaning products, and so forth. All these stores order most of their merchandise from off-island, largely from wholesalers in the United States, Japan, and Australia. Four other stores, which I consider medium-sized based on their inventory of several thousand dollars, also sell general merchandise. The owners of two of these told me that they order some of their merchandise from off-island, but purchase much of it, at normal retail prices, from the Kosrae Island Cooperative Association or from one of the three large stores. The eight small stores in Lelu, and an unknown number in other villages, depend entirely on the K.I.C.A. and, to a lesser extent, on one of the large stores, for their merchandise. Their inventory is quite small, usually less than $500, and is limited largely to foods and drinks and household products, that is, to consumer perishables that most families purchase in small quantities almost every day. Five of the eight small stores have not devoted a special structure to their retail business; rather, a section of their family dwelling has been set aside for their merchandise, or a small appendage has been added onto their house. In 1975, all the small stores used family labor exclusively. One of the medium-sized stores employed a clerk, whereas the counters of the others usually were tended by the wife or a child of the owner. Even two of the large stores were tended by family members. The owner of the third, however, which also is the largest retail outlet on the island, employed two men as clerks, and also hired several local girls part-time as bakers.

Thus, only the largest stores, and the consumer cooperative, order most of their merchandise wholesale from off-island. The small stores, and to a lesser extent the medium-sized ones, purchase their inventory at retail prices, usually from the consumer cooperative. This practice leads to great variations in prices to consumers. For example, a 15-ounce can of mackerel that sold for 45¢ at the co-op and at one of the large stores cost as much as 75¢ at the small stores; a 50-pound bag of rice sold for $15.50 at the co-op, but cost $18.00 at one of the small stores.

How is it that these tiny retail outlets stay in business, since competition with the co-op or one of the larger stores should presumably force them to lower their prices or go bankrupt? In fact many of them do close up periodically or permanently. I cannot quantify this conclusion, but informants stated that small stores, run by families and employing no wage labor, periodically are opened and exist for a few months, then fail. Interestingly, the reason often given for the failure is that the family literally "ate" its inventory, for practically all the goods kept by these stores are imported foodstuffs, especially canned meats and fish and rice. Some Kosraens say that a lot of money can be made from stores; this certainly is true of the large ones, as is indicated by their expansion through investment in the past few years, but I doubt that more than three or four of the smaller stores are significant money-making enterprises.

But some of the smaller stores and all of the four medium-sized ones have been in business for years. How have they survived? Partly they have done so with the help of the patronage of their kin. But I also was told that many in the past had gone bankrupt due to the overextension of credit to their relatives, who never got around to paying their debts. The Kosrae Island Cooperative Association, I was told, nearly was forced out of the business in its early years due to default by debtors, and so no longer will extend credit.

Despite the hazards of allowing customers, especially relatives, to buy now and pay later, I believe that the small and at least some of the medium-sized stores owe their existence partly to their willingness to give credit. To understand why extending credit is a viable business tactic in Kosrae, whereas in other parts of the world it so often is cited as the major reason for failure, it must be recalled that government employment yields a steady and reliable cash income. Credit ordinarily is extended, and erased periodically, according to the following pattern. A household with a job typically has credit with one or two village stores. The family makes purchases on credit, often sending a child to buy single items. The family's debt usually builds up between pay days (every two weeks); when the job holders receive their wages they pay off their debts for the last two weeks. I observed this practice among several households with jobs in the consumption/production survey made in November and December, 1975. Its wide generality also is revealed anecdotally by the reply I received from a young woman when I asked if her (jobless) household had credit with any stores: "do we get paid every two weeks, so that we can wipe out our debt?," she laughed. The pattern of consumer purchasing behavior also is relevant: Kosraens have no concept of "weekly shopping," but buy goods, especially food, as they are needed, often making several trips to some local store in a single day. Finally, the ability of these stores to survive owes much to convenience: one can make purchases at almost any time of the day or night, even rousting the owner out of sleep to do so.

Even though their prices on most items are higher than those at the consumer's cooperative or at one of the large stores, small and medium sized stores persist because they offer a certain convenience and are willing to extend credit. It is apparent that extension of credit is a practice that involves less risk today than formerly. With regular pay periods for government employees, storekeepers are more assured than in the past that customers will pay off their debts regularly every two weeks.

Lest I give too one-sided a view of commercial activities in Lelu village, notice must be taken of two organizations that do transform local resources into consumer goods, making profit in the process. The first organization is the Kosrae Fishing Cooperative Association (K.F.C.A.). This co-op began in October, 1973, for the purpose of organizing the market sale of fresh fish. To gain membership, shares are purchased by fisherman for $10 yearly. Individual members, who also

may reside in other villages, bring their fish to the
co-op's market outlet in Lelu, receiving 40¢ per pound
for tuna and 35¢ per pound for all other kinds of fish.
Retail prices are 5¢ higher for each kind of fish. In
1975, records kept by the head of the co-op indicate
that 10 Lelu men sold fish wholesale to the market, for
a total fishermen's return of $12,000. One of these men
in the six month period from July to December sold 5,016
pounds of fish to the market for a return to himself of
about $2,000. Most Lelu members sold far less--the man
who sold the second highest quantity sold only 1,517
pounds in this six month period, earning him about $600.
In addition to the sale of fish using the cooperative as
an intermediary, some fishermen also sell their catches
directly to consumers. Although villagers do purchase
fish for the everyday consumption of their households,
demand for fresh fish is especially high preceding various ceremonial feasts. The records of the co-op indicate that in 1974, the K.F.C.A. paid its members from
all over the island only $3,341 (wholesale) for the fish
they supplied to the market. If accurate, then the
money earned from fishing increased dramatically in
1975, when Lelu fishermen alone earned around $12,000
from sales to the K.F.C.A. If the problem of supplying
spare parts for the outboard motors of the island's
fishermen is solved, fish sales can rise even higher,
for many villagers complained to me that there was an
insufficient supply of fish at the K.F.C.A. outlet.

The second business that converts the wage income of
government employees into private profit by increasing
production is a poultry farm. The owner also owns one
of the three large retail stores and the most profitable
billiard hall in the village and has a government job.
Formerly, there were as many as four poultry farms, producing from July, 1972, to June, 1973, 3,983 dozen eggs
worth $5,036 to the owners (from the records of the
Agricultural Station). But by September, 1975, all
these farms had closed, the Lelu man's operation being
the last to do so. His egg-laying facility was located
on the northernmost tip of the mainland, at Finaunpes.
The poultry house had an iron roof with bamboo walls,
interspaced to allow plenty of air circulation; inside
were individual cages with chutes into which the eggs
fell. From a mean 1973 price of $1.25 per dozen, the
price of eggs had risen in mid-1975 to $2.50 per dozen
(perhaps because of lack of competition, although the
owner said it was due to rising feed costs). Although
not mechanized, clearly the enterprise was profitable,
according to the owner himself; equally clearly, falling
sales had nothing to do with its closure, for eggs are
highly prized as a food. Why then did the owner sell
off all his chickens at his store and stop producing
eggs in September, 1975?

According to the owner, there were two reasons. The first was feed problems. Until 1974 this man, two men from Malem, and a Tafunsak man had poultry farms. Together these men ordered feed from Guam through the consumer's cooperative. But when the three men from other villages closed their farms (for reasons unknown to me), the price of feed rose (from $9 per bag in 1972-3 to $19 in 1975), because the previous low price was based partly on the relatively large quantities ordered. This was bad enough, but the owner's wife (who tended the counter of the store in which the eggs were sold) said that people understood about the rising feed prices and liked eggs so much that they bought them anyway. Unfortunately, with only one poultryman demanding feed, the co-op ceased paying attention to the single order and the supply of feed became irregular as well.

The second reason was the poor water supply at Finaunpes. The site acquired its water from the Tafunsak village pipe line (there was no water system in Lelu until after I left the field in February, 1976). Unfortunately, Finaunpes is at the very end of the Tafunsak water line, so most of the water was used up before it reached the henhouse. The chickens were getting too old anyway, the owner said, and the two problems of feed and water led him to choose not to reorder replacement hens. However, when I talked with him he was undaunted by this setback: he planned to wait for the water system to be installed in Lelu so he could relocate his farm on the small island near his home to take better care of the hens. To avoid the feed problem, he planned to bypass the consumer cooperative and do his own ordering.

Aside from individual copra production, these two businesses were the only activities of significant scale in Lelu in 1975 that produced some local commodity for sale to the market. Some of the other villages had members who planned to start piggeries and who had acquired loans from the Production Development Loan Fund, but the hog cholera epidemic (see chapter 9) squelched this opportunity, at least temporarily. The only sawmill under private ownership in Lelu was never in operation in 1975, for reasons unknown to me. Both the fishermen's cooperative and the poultry farm faced difficult obstacles in obtaining the supplies and services needed to carry on their operations, obstacles that were primarily logistical and organizational.

THE STRUCTURE OF DEPENDENCE

As a means of describing the relative importance of various activities in earning income, an economist might divide the village's cash economy into primary (extractive), secondary (industrial), and tertiary (service) sectors. Such a division would show that the economy is "topheavy," with most of the wage-earning labor force engaged in public or private service industries. The economist's description of this structure would note correctly that the dollars the United States has expended on the island have had effects similar to deficit spending, as if the administration had intended a fiscal policy. Because the Trust Territory bureaucracy has hired labor in public projects and services, employment levels have risen, the income of government workers has increased, and the resulting climb in demand has created new opportunities in the private sector of the economy. Of course, these impacts more likely are an unintended consequence of the means chosen to implement American political goals in Micronesia (chapter 2), rather than a conscious policy.

To show the relationship between the cash and subsistence sectors of the village's economy, an economic anthropologist might use the concept of "exchange spheres." Cash circulates in a sphere of "wage labor-cash-retail sale-imported goods and services," whereas subsistence goods circulate in a sphere of "household labor-subsistence goods-household sharing of products." Conversions between the spheres, for example, "traditional subsistence goods-cash-imported goods," would be revealed correctly as insignificant quantitatively. This description of the structure reveals an important fact about the growth of the cash sector of the economy, namely, that the American-funded public goods and services have not generated an increase in production in the primary (food producing) sector. With the exception of the few village fishermen, in general those who do not engage in wage labor do not produce goods to sell to those households that have obtained government jobs. As shown in the previous chapter, this is partly due to the fact that job-holding households have retained access to the means of subsistence production; that is, they still have the use of land, and the light labor requirements of the major subsistence crops allow subsistence production to continue in a household even after one or more of its male members have obtained employment.

Both the sectoral and the exchange sphere depiction of the structure of the Lelu economy reveal important facts about the relationship between various activities. However, in order to reveal other relationships, I have developed another kind of sectoral model that depicts the structure of the cash economy of the village in somewhat more detail (see Figure 6.1). The activities through which cash income is earned are divided into four sectors, shown as boxes in the figure, with the whole figure representing the village's cash economy. The dollar amounts entering each box indicate the approximate sums earned through expending labor in each

102

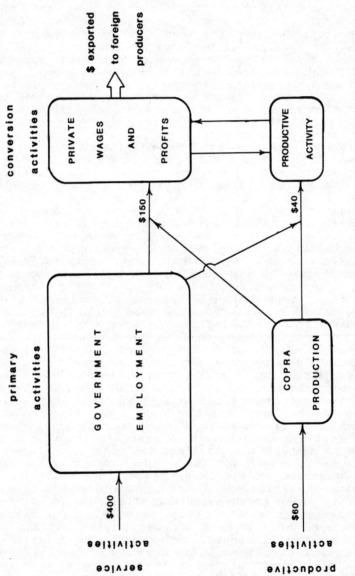

Figure 6.1. Sectoral Structure of Lelu Cash Economy, 1975

($ thousands)

kind of activity. The relative size of each box shows
the quantitative importance of each activity in earning
cash income. In the figure, Primary Activities represents labor that earns income directly from some external (off-island) source. In 1975, employment with some
governmental agency and copra production were the dominant primary activities. Conversion Activities refers
to those means of earning money (private sector wages
and profits) by converting the income of government
employees and copra producers into consumer goods and
services and imported goods. As shown in this chapter,
it is through conversion activities that the large
increases in income from government wage labor are
redistributed to those who do not work for the government, thus generating economic opportunities for most
villagers. Service Activities refers to those activities that earn cash income through employment in service
industries, defined as in our own economy. Productive
Activities denotes those activities that produce consumer goods for market sale, mainly fresh fish, pigs,
and handicrafts, using local natural resources of land
and sea. Production for household subsistence of
agricultural goods, fish, pigs, handicrafts, and so
forth are not included because the figure depicts only
those activities that earn cash income.

Figure 6.1 reveals several facts about the structure
of the Lelu economy. First, the large size of the two
"service" boxes relative to the two "productive" boxes
represents the domination of the cash sector by service
industries. Second, it is apparent that the cash economy is a system of the "throughput" sort. Income earned
through employment with a governmental agency or copra
production passes through the hands of only one or two
local middlemen before it is exported to the foreign
producers of the imported foods, building materials,
motor vehicles, household goods, clothing, and so forth
consumed by the village. Although most of the money is
spent locally at a store or other business, the fact
that most local enterprises are retail stores engaged in
the sale of imports means that government employment is
creating demand for goods produced in the United States,
Japan, Australia, and other foreign countries, however
small this demand might be. A third revelation of the
diagram is that the approximately $460,000 earned from
primary activities "multiplies" due to conversion activities into the estimated $650,000 total village income
in 1975. In part, this reflects the fact that unemployed villagers do sell some locally produced commodities to government wage earners, such as fish, pork,
handicrafts, and eggs. More importantly, it reveals
the indirect dependence of the private sector on the
demand generated by employment with the administration.
At present, businesses that "service" job-holding

households with imported consumer goods, baked foods, and entertainment dominate the sector labelled Private Wages and Profits. Should the United States administration reduce the wages paid to its Kosraen employees, these businesses certainly would experience reduced profits, unless income is increased from some other source. As shown in chapter 2, this relationship exists throughout Micronesia.

This structure does not follow as an inevitable result of the input of dollars by the American government. For example, the sizes of the two sectors of Conversion Activities relative to one another might be different if local-level ecological, economic, and sociocultural conditions were different. I now turn to a consideration of such local conditions and how they interact with wage labor.

7
Employment and Household Subsistence Choices

Chapter 5 concluded with the estimate that Lelu people depend on imported foods for one-third to one-half of their caloric intake. In chapter 6, I estimated that almost one-third of the total cash expenditure in the village was spent on imported foods consumed in the everyday diet. In this chapter, I move down one level of integration from the previous two in order to examine the effects of wage labor on the food choices of a few sample households. I confine the description and analysis to decisions made by household units about the production and consumption of foods, both imported and locally produced by members of the household, for everyday demand. A portion of the aggregate pattern of production, consumption, and investment described previously results from choices made by domestic units about how to allocate the resources available to them. To examine the factors influencing these choices therefore helps explain the patterns reported in the preceding two chapters. Such factors do not, however, totally account for such patterns, for almost all households participate in economic activities organized by higher-level groups, such as church and kumi, and by extended kinship networks, in the context of life crisis ceremonies. The effects of such "suprahousehold" organizations are considered in chapters 8, 9, and 10.

It will be useful to recall four important characteristics of the local agricultural economy that were established in chapter 5. (1) All households continue to have access to land on which to establish subsistence gardens. (2) Only men and boys work in agriculture, except under special circumstances. (3) Production for everyday household subsistence is organized using domestic labor, or, far less often, extrahousehold labor recruited through kinship ties. (4) The most important tree and root crops consumed on an everyday basis require little labor to plant, maintain, and harvest. Each of these is a condition of the village's agricultural economy that predated the growth of wage labor

105

opportunities. My aim in this chapter is to show how these endogenous conditions interact with employment to affect the subsistence choices of Lelu households. If any of these conditions were different, wage labor would have a different impact on households, and a different aggregate pattern of production, consumption, and investment would result.

HOUSEHOLD ECONOMIC ALLOCATIONS

Each household has access to resources that are used to fulfill the everyday subsistence wants of its members. These resources include labor (under 1975 conditions, the time and energy of its male members of suitable age), land (which it either owns or enjoys use-rights to by virtue of kinship ties), and money. To acquire the everyday food supply households allocate these resources; it will be assumed that their allocations are determined jointly by their preferences and by the relative availability of labor, land, and money. The following description shows how the allocations of sample households without any employed members ("jobless households") compare to the allocations of those with one or more employed members ("job households"). The aim is to give an idea of how government employment affects the economies of job households; this "comparative statics" method is the only way of achieving this aim, because data on household allocations before the days of government employment are lacking. Empirical data for this comparison are drawn from sample surveys conducted in Lelu in 1975; the relevant data themselves are summarized in Appendixes A, B, and G.

Labor

To determine the effects of wage labor on the allocation of labor time, by both sexes, I conducted a time budget survey among 17 Lelu households (Appendix A). Several results of employment are revealed. First, the only difference in time allocation by women and girls related clearly to wage labor is that the women of some jobless households bake bread to wholesale in one of the village's stores or to retail in the family's own bakery (Table A.2). This is another of the spread effects of the expansion of employment, already mentioned in the previous chapter. Second, employment has a profound effect on the time allocations of adult men (Table A.4). With regard to the provision of food for household uses, men without jobs spent 21% of their time in subsistence garden work and fishing, whereas men with jobs expended only 10% of their time in these same activities.

However, these figures do not necessarily accurately
portray the contrast in male participation in subsistence activities between job and jobless <u>households</u>.
As shown in chapter 5, many subsistence tasks are done
by adolescent males, and it is possible that job households have reacted to wage labor by intensifying the
subsistence labor of these boys, thus meliorating the
effect of employment. However, including their labor in
the comparison makes little or no difference in the
realm of subsistence: the male "labor pool" of jobless
households still spent about twice the amount of time in
gardening and fishing as their employed counterparts
(Table A.1). Third, over three-fourths of the potential
work time of employed adult men was consumed by their
jobs, and these men had only one-third the amount of
leisure of their unemployed counterparts (Table A.4).
This confirms the complaints of several employed informants about how "busy" they have become since obtaining
a job.

Land

Due to my limited time in the field, I have little
direct information about land use; I cannot, for example, quantify variations in acreages under cultivation
between job and jobless households. However, an indirect measure of land use is available. This takes the
form of interhousehold variability in labor hours
devoted to subsistence activity and in pounds of produce
harvested (Appendix B, Tables B.1 and B.2). Significant
variability is revealed between job and jobless households. In the nine job households, potential agricultural laborers (all males, weighted by age) worked a
mean of 17 hours per worker and harvested a mean of 201
pounds of produce per worker during the four-week period
of the production/consumption survey. In the six jobless households, the corresponding figures are 31 hours
per worker and 323 pounds of produce harvested per
worker. I am fairly certain, but cannot document, that
there are no consistent differences between job and jobless households in the amounts of land available to them
for subsistence cultivation. If so, it may be concluded
that job households cultivate a smaller percentage of
the land available to them than jobless households.

Money

The discussion of monetary allocations is confined
to expenditures on food. I conducted two surveys in
Lelu that yield quantitative data on monetary expenditures on foodstuffs (Appendix G). In the two-week

108

survey in October, 1975, those five households with jobs
spent a mean of $61 on foods; the four jobless house-
holds spent only $32 on food. In the month-long survey
of November and December, 1975, job households expended
a mean of $124 on food, while jobless households spent
only $56.   Despite the small size of the sample, it
appears that those households with employed male members
spent about twice as much money on food as unemployed
households.   As the data in Appendix G indicate, rice
and canned fish and meats are quantitatively the most
important imported foods consumed in the everyday diet
(they are not, however, the main imports consumed in
ceremonial contexts).

Putting the preceding data together, the following
pattern of differences in allocations between job and
jobless households emerges. Male members of the jobless
households spent about twice as much time in subsistence
gardening and fishing, jobless households probably utilized more of the land available to them, and jobless
households expended about one-half as much money on
storebought foods.   These data may be aggregated into
one conclusion: job households tend to allocate money to
purchase imported foods for daily consumption, rather
than allocating the labor time of their male members to
produce indigenous foods on their own land.   This conclusion is quite intuitive.   The data merely give a
quantitative indication of the magnitude of the predict-
able difference between the two sets of households.
Although the pattern of allocation of job households is
hardly surprising, what is it about employment that
accounts for the differences in subsistence choices
between job and jobless households?

Perhaps the most obvious reason why employed households tend to rely more on imported foods is a widespread preference for imports combined with their
greater cash incomes.   If this were the case, then it
follows that all families would prefer to consume
imported rice and tinned meats and fish in their everyday diet, but only those with one or more employed members have the income needed to satisfy their taste for
these imports.   It then would be the relative availability of one resource, namely, money, that alone accounts
for the observed difference in allocative pattern
between the two sets of households: by removing one
constraint on household resources (the lack of money),
wage labor allows job households to consume those foods
they "like."   Jobless households, unable to afford
imported foods, must satisfy their subsistence wants
with indigenous foods.

However, my data indicate no preference for those
imported foods that are consumed in the everday diet of
the vast majority of Lelu households (see Appendix I).
In the category of foods that I translate as "staples,"

locally produced yams, breadfruit, and Colocasia
("soft") taro all are preferred over rice. Thus, the
latter is not eaten two or even three times daily by
most employed families merely because they prefer its
taste to locally produced staples. In the "protein"
category, imported chickens, imported turkey tails
(sic), and locally hunted wild pigeons were the most
highly preferred foods. However, only a few well-to-do
households consumed these frequently on an everyday
basis, due to the high price of chickens and turkey
tails and the difficulty of hunting wild pigeons.
Almost all chickens and turkey tails were consumed in
ceremonial contexts. The same applies to a "preferred"
source of protein, imported beef; although consumed by a
few well-off households with freezers, for most its high
cost and irregular availability precluded its consumption on an everyday basis. Pork also is primarily a
ceremonial food. The relevant comparison in the protein
category is between the lower three categories of preference, for with the exception of beef and pork, all of
these foods were consumed in the everyday diet (but see
chapter 6 on egg production). Although consumed more
often than any other "protein," canned mackerel and sardines fell into the lowest category of preference.
Fresh fish, mangrove crabs, and lobster were preferred
over the most common imports that substitute for them.
With the notable exception of bananas and plantains,
both of which are regarded as monotonous and/or as "low
class" by most villagers, Lelu people prefer many of
their local foods to imported substitutes.

I do not wish to overplay this conclusion. Obviously, asking people to "rank" a group of common foods
probably is not a very reliable way to determine the
preferences that exist in their heads (although it
should be noted that my formal survey on this subject
confirmed my subjective impressions on food preferences,
and also that prior to going into the field I had
expected imported foods to be preferred over local
ones). The preference survey data does, however, indicate that Lelu job holders do not purchase imported
foods to feed their households simply because they and
their families "like" imported rice and canned meats and
fish better than local foods. There is more to their
subsistence choices than their higher incomes and their
preferences. What else contributes to the tendency of
job households to substitute imports for indigenous
foods?

THE ECONOMICS OF TIME ALLOCATION

I have just tried to show that differences in the
availability of monetary resources, when combined with

widespread preferences, do not account in any simple way
for the difference in allocative patterns between the
two sets of households. In this section, I argue that
differences in the availability of another resource,
men's labor time, is an important reason for the
observed patterns. Employment may meliorate the effects
of one constraint on job households (lack of money), but
at the same time it imposes an additional constraint
(relative shortage of men's labor). Once stated, this
argument also is intuitive: obviously, if employed men
devote a sizeable proportion of their time to wage work,
then their households have less total male labor available for gardening and fishing. However, the argument
is obvious only in the context of the empirically determined, local-level economic and environmental conditions
summarized in chapter 5; if these conditions were different, wage labor would not affect job households in
the same way or to the same degree. Before pursuing
this point, I shall defend the argument with empirical
data and with a microeconomic model.

The following data support the argument. First,
objectively the time they spend at work consumes most of
the labor time available to employed men; as Table A.4
shows, about three-fourths of their potential working
time is taken up by their jobs. Further, the administration schedules the working hours of its employees
as 8 to 5, Monday through Friday. This schedule greatly
interferes with garden work and indeed practically pre-
cludes its continuation at previous levels. In general,
the two hours or so of daylight that remain after work
can be used productively by only those fortunate job
holders who have garden land located near their house
sites. As described in chapter 5, most of the population lives on Lelu island, but the gardens of most
households are located on the mainland. As a result,
for most job holders the round trip travel time to their
gardens is one-half to one hour, leaving insufficient
time to locate and harvest mature tree and root crops.
When these considerations are combined with the cultural
prohibition against subsistence work on Sunday, a prohibition that is almost never violated, it is easily
realized that most employed men have only Saturday
available for gardening. In sum, the 40 hour week and
unfortunate scheduling of employment objectively consumes the labor time and conflicts with subsistence
activities of employed men.

Second, there are statements of employed men that
they have little time to engage in subsistence activities. One of the major costs of obtaining a government
job was widely considered to be a reduction in the
amount of time an employee could devote to agriculture.
Such subjective perceptions of informants are supported
by the time budget data of Table A.4, which shows that

indeed employed men had very little leisure. As mentioned previously, the labor of adolescent boys to which most employed households have access potentially can meliorate the effect of employment time on total hours devoted to subsistence. However, few job holders are willing to work these boys (most of whom themselves are in school and have homework) long enough to maintain as high a level of food production as unemployed households. There are exceptions to this pattern. One employee, for instance, was depositing most of his earnings in the Credit Union to construct a new dwelling for his family. He also had a teen-aged son who was not in high school, and who harvested his father's gardens three or four times weekly. This boy's labor, combined with that of his brothers who were in school, allowed this employed household to maintain an unusual level of self-sufficiency during the period of my survey.

A microeconomic model suggests why the increased scarcity of employed men's time reduces the labor hours that their households devote to subsistence activities. Table A.4 shows that job holders work much longer hours than jobless men, albeit at greater return. Theory predicts that each hour devoted to leisure is more valuable to employed than to unemployed men, because "free time" is in shorter supply for job holders. Therefore, each hour that an employed man detracts from leisure and devotes to subsistence pursuits has a relatively higher opportunity cost in foregone leisure. To work the extra long hours required to maintain previous levels of subsistence production, an employed man would be engaged in a high degree of "self-exploitation"; on average, they are unlikely to tolerate this for long periods. Similarly, the two categories of households differ in the relative mixes of cash and time they have available: for job households, not only is time more scarce, but cash is more plentiful. The value of the total time not spent working relative to the value of cash therefore is greater for job than for jobless households. Job households thus tend to substitute food imports bought with cash for local garden produce and fish "bought" with their labor time (of course, imported foods are also ultimately bought with labor time as well). This effect occurs also because the imported rice and tinned meats and fish that are consumed every day by most job households are far easier to prepare as well as to acquire than their locally produced counterparts. The household thus conserves the labor time of its female as well as male members by consuming imported foodstuffs. (Linder 1970 shows why there is a generalized increase in the scarcity of time as incomes rise, and why this translates into a greater emphasis on activities that conserve time in the home.)

It is worth noting that I do not claim that employment makes it _impossible_ for a job household to maintain
a high level of subsistence self-sufficiency; rather,
it alters the constraints on these households such that
their choices are more likely to be patterned in the
direction of reduced time spent in subsistence. Nor do
I claim that the relative scarcity of men's time is the
only causal factor; for example, job households may have
acquired more of a taste for imported foods, although my
data do not detect this and I would be surprised if it
is the case. My claims are two: first, the simple
availability of more cash alone to job households is
insufficient to account for their allocations; second,
the loss of men's time due to employment reduces a
household resource (male labor), which results in a
decline in autosubsistence activities. The possible
policy implications of these conclusions are pursued
elsewhere (Peoples 1986).

ENDOGENOUS FORCES AND WAGE LABOR

As the past three chapters have shown, wage labor
has profoundly influenced almost every aspect of the
economy of Lelu village. Its impact, however, has been
exerted in interaction with the preexisting conditions
of the island's agricultural economy. If these conditions varied, so would the effects of wage labor. In
the context of the present chapter, the economic allocations of Lelu households would be affected differently.
Three "what if" examples will illustrate this point.
(1) If indigenous cultigens required a great deal of
labor input, job households would be less able to maintain gardens for subsistence uses. Wage laborers then
would be more of a village proletariat than they were in
1975. (2) The same result would follow if government
employees did not continue to have access to land owned
by themselves or their fathers. Local land tenure conditions have ensured that all households retain access
to the means of subsistence production. (3) If women as
well as men worked in agriculture (as is often the case
on Micronesian atolls) households with employed male
members would be able to maintain a greater degree of
subsistence self-sufficiency than they did at the time
of my field work.

The influence of such endogenous conditions on the
pattern of response of villagers to wage labor opportunities is illustrated by a comparison between Lelu and
the Awa, a highland Papua New Guinea people studied by
Boyd (1981). Among the Awa, traditionally subsistence
production tasks were allocated to both men and women.
To men fell the work of pollarding large trees, the
building of fences to deter pigs, and the construction

of bamboo pipelines to irrigate taro gardens. The turning of soil in tilled grassland gardens was exclusively
women's work. The Awa maintain a variety of garden
types, each with specific labor requirements. For some
types, such as gardens cut in the forest and irrigated
plots, male labor input is high, while other types, such
as sweet potato and yam-taro gardens, require smaller
amounts of male labor.

In the early 1960s, Awa men began to contract for
wage labor work on the coast. They signed up for two
years initially, but many repeated the contract. This
pattern of circular migration resulted in a significant
shortage of men's labor in Ilakia village in the late
1960s: from 1968 to 1970, between 46% and 62% of the
adult male population were absent at any one time. The
agricultural tasks that they traditionally performed
were shouldered by the remiaining men, and represented a
substantial seasonal burden to them. In Lelu, the time
diverted from subsistence work in the household economy
by wage labor has not produced as heavy a load upon
unemployed men, for several reasons. First, because most
Lelu employed men are physically present in the village,
they are able to work in subsistence activities on
Saturdays and, for some men, after their jobs on week-
days. Second, cash incomes are far higher on Kosrae,
allowing a household with an employed member to purchase
much of its food. Third, it appears that the major Awa
root crops (yams, taro, and sweet potato) require more
labor than the modern Kosraen tree-crop staples. These
differences seem to result in a greater burden on Awa
men who remain in the village than on Lelu men who are
unemployed.

However, one endogenous condition has the opposite
effect: unlike Kosraens, traditionally Awa women were
engaged heavily in subsistence cultivation. Boyd's data
show that those Ilakia Awa households that are female-
headed (due to the absence of men on wage labor contracts) have altered their garden strategies. They
plant significantly more gardens of the types that
require little male labor. This preexisting division
of labor norm, lacking on Kosrae, allowed the Awa of
Ilakia village to maintain their level of production per
capita, even though a large percentage of the male labor
force was altogether absent from the village. Under
present division of labor conditions in Kosrae, a maintenance of past subsistence production levels by job
households would be highly burdensome to the male labor
force of such households.

This comparison highlights the importance of
local-level conditions as an influence on how villagers respond to opportunities presented from the outside. We see that, because of the preexisting division
of labor, Awa are likely to maintain a higher level of

self-sufficiency in foodstuffs than Kosraens. Stated formally, Kosraen household subsistence choices are constrained by the normative division of labor that does not allow as high a level of self-sufficiency as otherwise would be possible. Only with a knowledge, derived empirically, of endogenous conditions can the responses of Kosraen households to the exogenous input of wage labor be understood and, perhaps, predicted.

8
An Overview of Contemporary Kosraen Culture

So far, I have shown how the preexisting conditions of Kosrae's agricultural economy interact with employment for the local branch of the American administration to affect economic patterns in Lelu village. The remaining chapters describe and analyze the impact of contemporary Kosraen cultural conditions on the village's economy. I make no pretense of describing fully the beliefs and values of Kosraens, but concentrate on those cultural aspects that affect most profoundly the production, exchange, and consumption of material goods. As established in chapters 3 and 4, these cultural features themselves are the historical product of the interaction between the island's aboriginal political economy and nineteenth century depopulation and missionization. Four aspects of modern Kosraen culture have important economic consequences: the Christian church, the kumi, kinship relationships, and ceremonial practices. The first three are described in this chapter, whereas chapters 9 and 10 deal with ceremonial customs.

THE CHURCH

A discussion of the Christian church is the most appropriate topic with which to begin a description of contemporary Kosraen culture, for it is clearly more of a cultural "focus" than any other institution. The church is an essential part of Kosraen cultural identity, in the sense that adherence to its strict rules of membership and participation in its many activities and organizations are primary factors that distinguish Kosraens from other Micronesians. More importantly for present purposes, it has significant effects on the island's economy, because much of the time and monetary resources of loyal church members are committed to its religious and social activities and to the maintenance and improvement of its physical structures.

115

My strong impression is that, in spite of the political and economic changes that have occurred since the late nineteenth century, the church has been the main bastion of Kosraen cultural stability. For instance, the rigid moral standards that the missionary Snow established for membership still persist. Church members are forbidden to smoke, to drink alcoholic beverages, to fornicate or commit adultery, and to quarrel openly with their neighbors. If a member commits, or is publicly known to commit, any of these sins, he/she is said to have "fallen" from church membership. (The word "fallen" may not be accidental: it is the same word used by Snow in his letters of January 7, 1864 and October 26, 1868). To be readmitted into the church, one must attend a special meeting held on the first day of each month (mahlwem sasuh, "new month") and confess his or her sin in front of the members present. When Snow instituted this "confession complex," as it has been called by Schaefer (1976), he probably intended it to be a temporary measure to be abandoned whenever Kosraens became strong enough Christians to resist the temptation to regress into pagan or whaler-introduced sinful practices. However, during the church's relatively isolated evolution from about 1870 to 1920, the practice of public confession and formal forgiveness by the assembled church members became institutionalized and is seen by modern Kosraens as one of the most essential parts of their variant of Christianity.

The church is not a monolithic institution, but a quite complex structure with many suborganizations. In the broadest terms, there are two structural levels. First, each of the four villages has its own separate church buildings, officers, suborganizations, and finances; these are described below for Lelu village. Second, there are two overarching, island-wide organizations. One is called the "Church All." The officers of this body are the pastors, deacons, and deaconesses from all of the villages, along with a secretary, a treasurer, and a number of committeemen. These individuals meet periodically to discuss matters of policy affecting all the village churches, for example, what should be the church's official policy towards other faiths that wish to proselytize on the island? The other island-wide organization is the "Etawi All." It consists of a president, vice-president, secretary, treasurer, and various committeemen. The first four are elected annually by a vote of all Etawi members (see below) from all of the villages. The committeemen are appointed annually by the president-elect. Schaefer (1976:124-7) presents a brief discussion of the functions of these bodies, which are outside the scope of the present description.

Village Churches

My information about the village-level churches is
drawn entirely from the Lelu church, but is probably
generally correct for the other villages. Each village
church contains several suborganizations, each with its
own officers and, in some cases, committees. To sim-
plify the presentation of this complex structure, I
shall discuss the suborganizations in order of the relative difficulty of acquiring membership, beginning with
the easiest to join. The officers are discussed in a
later context.

Kumi. Like the other villages, the adult and young
adult population of Lelu is divided into four groups, or
kumi. The groups are named itsi, ni, sang, and yung,
the Japanese word for "first," "second," "third," and
"fourth," respectively (I use the Kosraen spelling common in 1975). Each kumi has its own separate officers
and finances. In 1975, the main responsibility of the
kumi was the organization of resources for feasts and
ceremonial events connected to the church. Any member
of the village may join one of the groups and participate in its joint activities, whether or not one is also
a church member. I know of no adult in Lelu who had not
joined one or another kumi, with the exception of one
extended family whose members belong to another
Christian denomination. Indeed, if an individual did
not belong to a kumi, he/she would be excluded from much
of the social and recreational life organized by the
village. I shall discuss further the activities of this
important organization in a later section of this
chapter.

Etawi (Christian Endeavor). This organization is
divided into three subgroups based on age: "Little
Etawi" for young children, "Youth Etawi" for persons of
teen-age through 30, and "Adult Etawi" for persons older
than 30. Meetings, which include hymn singing, Bible
study, prayer, and lessons, are held each Sunday afternoon for about one hour. Although anyone may attend
these meetings, formal membership is restricted to those
who either have not yet sinned, and thus "fallen," or
who have sinned and been reinstated. Each Etawi age-
group has its own separate finances. Its ostensible
functions are bible study and inculcation of Christian
beliefs and values.

Choir. Each village has its own choir, which often
presents special music at Sunday morning worship and
also sings at most funerals and on some other special
occasions. To join the choir, one need only attend the
practices held one or more nights per week and be a full
member of the Youth or Adult Etawi. In Lelu, there were
about 60 choir members in 1975.

Church. Members of both Youth and Adult Etawi who
lead exemplary lives may contact a member of the Church
Committee and ask to become a full-fledged member of the
Lelu Church. The committee votes on each specific
application and presents the petitioner in front of the
other full Church members for a vote on the "new month."
The successful applicant is baptized, after which he or
she has the right to partake of the quarterly Lord's
Supper. Only people who "are Church," as Kosraens say,
are eligible to hold one of the plethora of offices connected to the church's suborganizations. Joining the
Church then confers full membership rights, eligibility
for participation in all activities, and rights to compete for one of the church offices.

At any one time, not all villagers are active members of all these suborganizations, with the exception
of the kumi. This is because of the frequent "falls"
that occur when members commit one or more of the main
sins. Young children are automatically Christians, and
it takes an act of sin in their later life to "fall"
from membership. A great many, in fact almost all males
and most females, do commit a major sin at some point in
their lives, which results in their excommunication.
The custom of excommunication produces what is still a
fundamental social distinction in Kosrae, that between
mwet muhtuhn alu (people outside the church) and mwet
Christian (Christians, that is, full church members).
The majority of women and girls are outside the church
for only short periods, because the two "habitual sins"
of smoking and drinking are practically unknown for
females; illicit fornication and quarreling are responsible for most of the "falling" of women and girls.
Some men who are outside the church also are excommunicated only temporarily, until the next "new month"
when they can confess and be forgiven, but others are
hard-core sinners who have been outside the church for
years or even decades. Typically, these men express a
desire eventually to rejoin the church, but are unable
to stop their long-engrained habits of smoking and
drinking. Most men outside the church are young men
under the age of about 40, although there are a few
notable exceptions of men who continue to smoke and
drink into their 60s. A high percentage of men are outside during their 20s, but as they grow older there is
increasing pressure from the community and their families to repudiate their past practices and become full
church members.

Church Offices and "Work"

It would be easy to overemphasize the social significance of the distinction between Christians and those

outside the church. Certainly, it should not be taken to parallel that between noble and commoner in old Kosrae, because movements between the two categories are frequent and no formal respect is shown to ordinary church members by outsiders. To observe everyday social relations, a foreigner would not know, for example, that one party was a deacon while the other was outside the church. Non-Christians are not shunned or ostracized from community life, and through the kumi are allowed to participate in many church-sponsored activities like feasts and the annual Christmas marching and singing, to be discussed later.

Despite the fact that nonmembers are in no way social outcastes, the distinction between church and nonchurch villagers is an important one, for there are culturally valued and coveted statuses from which people outside the church are barred, namely, the holding of church offices. These offices are fully institutionalized social positions that give high esteem to their incumbents. Some of these positions are elective, by vote of the church members, and thus have an implicit competitive character. The formal ceremony at which new officers are installed for the upcoming year is one of the most important annual church events, involving a sizeable feast and speeches by both new and old officers. There are two such installation days each year. The one held in November installs officers, elected by the whole membership of Etawi on Kosrae, in the island-wide Etawi All organization. Thus, on Thanksgiving day in 1975, a service was held at the Lelu church, and attended by some members of other villages, to bestow office on the President, Vice-President, Secretary, and Treasurer of Etawi All. Another ceremony is held in December to install officers for the village-level Adult and Youth Etawi, who are elected by the members of the respective Etawi in each village. In Lelu, on December 14, 1975, nine village-level officers were installed at a joint meeting of the Lelu Youth and Adult Etawi. These officers were the President, Vice-President, Secretary, and Treasurer for both the youth and adults, together with an adult Sponsor for the Youth Etawi.

The above elected officials do not exhaust the social positions of the church's hierarchy. At the island level, there are the members of the Church All body mentioned in the previous subsection. At the village level, each church additionally has a pastor, several deacons and deaconesses, a secretary, a treasurer, and a choir leader. Each of the village's four kumi, which are loosely connected to the church, has a leader, a secretary, a treasurer and, for part of the year, two song leaders, all elective. Also at the village level, both Adult and Youth Etawi have four standing committees of twelve members each, the incumbents of which are

appointed annually by the President-elect of each
suborganization. These four committees are <u>Alu</u> ("worship"), <u>Kahsruh</u> ("helping"), <u>Tol</u> (also called the
Committee in Liyeacng Lohm, "maintenance of the building"), and <u>Fahsr</u> ("walking"). Each of these committees
has specialized functions, which are outside the scope
of the present discussion. There are also other minor
offices, but by now the point is evident: over the
decades, the Kosraen church has evolved a quite complex
hierarchical system of offices that give high social
standing to those who successfully acquire them. This
plethora of positions was, to me, the most impressive
aspect of the Kosraen church.

Because they are limited in supply and culturally
desirable, the higher church offices are the objects of
competition, although largely covert. The means by
which an individual succeeds in this competition is
"work" (<u>orekmuh</u>) in the church. By this concept,
Kosraens mean abstention from drinking, smoking, and
illicit fornication, maintenance of good social relations (<u>toasr</u>, or "anger," literally "heaviness," against
one's neighbors or relatives, also is considered a sin
that must be confessed), study of the Bible and other
religious materials, active and visible participation in
church events, frequent food and monetary contributions
to church feasts and special projects, and the like.
Kosraens seem to place more emphasis on "work" than on
the inward state of one's soul as a criterion for church
leadership and even for membership. Their Christianity
is an intensely public one, of which the custom of public confession of sin and public forgiveness by the congregation is only one manifestation.

Of particular interest for this study is the extent
to which leadership in the church depends on the level
of one's material prosperity. Two observations show
that the correlation between wealth and leadership is
far from perfect. First, some of the wealthiest (and
best educated) men in the village and on the whole
island are outside the church altogether, due to their
failure to meet cultural standards of Christian morality. Second, many of the most important church leaders
only have average wealth. Thus, in Lelu in 1975 none
of the holders of the following high offices were
especially well-to-do: Pastor; Adult Etawi President,
Secretary, and Treasurer; Choir leader; and Sunday
School principal. On the other hand, only one of the
holders of high office would I consider below average in
wealth, and the three active deacons and the new Vice-
President of Adult Etawi who was elected in 1975 were
well above average.

The reason for this lack of a consistent correlation is that, although material wealth helps in being
elected or appointed to a high church office, it alone

is neither necessary nor sufficient. Without a prolonged period of what Americans would call "clean living," no rich person can attain one of the high positions. Having money does increase one's chances,
because part of "work" is monetary contributions to aid
in feasts, work days, and special projects. It is not
necessary, however, because poorer men can make equal
contributions of money, albeit at greater personal
material sacrifice, and often can devote more time,
energy, and indigenous foods to the church.

However, holding a church position does yield
material benefits to those office-holders who are also
businessmen. This effect, which unfortunately I cannot
quantify, occurs because the church often purchases
imported building materials or food for the various
social events or special projects that it sponsors. A
1975 example of this is the Sharon Inn, a large con-
crete-walled building constructed by the Lelu church
during 1974 and 1975 and dedicated on September 6, 1975
with a huge, island-wide celebration and feast. The
imported concrete, glass, iron, wood, and rebars used in
the construction cost over $14,000, and almost $16,000
were spent on food for the people who contributed their
labor on 98 work days and on the Dedication Feast. The
church records that I obtained show that a significant
amount of this sum was spent at the large stores of two
church leaders. A minimum of $3,000 worth of the mate-
rials purchased for the building went to these storeowners, and another $5,000 to the local consumer coop-
erative. The almost $16,000 spent on imported food were
distributed among the cooperative, the same two storeowners, and other stores. The retail-import businesses
on Kosrae, especially those owned by church leaders,
thus receive a boost in their sales as a result of
church-sponsored activities.

Church Finances

The regular contributions made at various services
are not burdensome (Kosraens have no concept of tith-
ing) and clearly are inadequate to fund such a large
project as the Sharon Inn. As I understand church
finances, money is acquired regularly through passing of
the collection plate three times each month. Money is
collected at the afternoon meeting of the Adult, Youth,
and Little Etawi on the first Sunday of each month; this
is called Money in Mahlwem ("Monthly Money"). This fund
is used mainly to pay church bills such as electricity,
to give financial help to the sick and elderly, to
defray various transportation expenses, and to contribute to the food expenses of some church event. Another
collection is made at the afternoon Etawi meetings on

the third Sunday of each month; this is called <u>Money in Muhsah</u> ("Building Fund"). Typically, this fund accumulates until the church undertakes a construction project, when it becomes quickly exhausted. A third offering is taken at the morning Sunday School services on the second week of the month; I have no information about the disbursement of these monies. The final regular collection is taken four times per year at the quarterly Lord's Supper held in each village. All the money contributed on this occasion is donated to the island-wide Etawi All.

Only small amounts of money are given on these regular collections. I obtained church records for three of the above four collections for the Adult Etawi of Lelu village for 1973, 1974, and 1975 (Table 8.1). In 1975, the Youth Etawi, which maintains separate finances and accounts from its adult counterpart, received $489 for the Building Fund and $617 for the Monthly Money from its members. Although these amounts are small, they were only a fraction of the church's total income in 1975.

Voluntary contributions received through the periodic passing of the offering plate then are insufficient to finance such a large construction project as the Sharon Inn. By what other means does the church acquire such resources? Conversations with the church secretary and records kindly provided me by the same individual furnish the data needed to answer this question. Only a small part of the money came from the Building Fund. In 1974, Lelu people contributed $989 (about $80 per month) to the Building Fund (Table 8.1). But for all of 1974, $9,705 were contributed and applied to the purchase of materials used in the construction and of food to feed the workers. So only one-tenth of the total revenue raised in 1974 and spent on new construction was acquired out of the regular fund nominally set aside for this purpose. The other nine-tenths came from special donations, intended specifically to help finance the Sharon Inn. $3,976 were collected when the church asked all male Etawi members to give $30 for the project (some gave even more; one man gave $100). Another $4,183 were acquired from unsolicited donations given by individuals and various suborganizations of the church (e.g., the four <u>kumi</u> collected $511 from their members; Youth Etawi, Lelu choir, and other suborganizations received $2,262 in voluntary contributions). The remaining $557 of the $9,705 collected in 1974 were private gifts of building materials and money, the latter earned by men who worked for the administration on sea wall repair and donated their wages to the project.

I presented these data on how the church acquired money in 1974 (more was acquired in 1975, but this is discussed in chapter 10) for a special building project

TABLE 8.1
Regular collections of Adult Etawi, Lelu village

Source	1973	1974	1975
Monthly Money	$412	$506	$ 728
Building Fund	$673	$989	$1,006
Lord's Supper	$186	$300	N/A

in such detail to demonstrate that, in the words of one foreign resident, "the church always gets money when it needs it." As shown in Table 8.1, in general the regular contributions are not burdensome. But whenever, as happens every few years, extra resources are required for new facilities or for the improvement of existing ones, special contributions are requested. One man went so far as to call these levies a "tax." This is certainly an overstatement, since people could refuse to give, but nonetheless active participation in church affairs can be an expensive choice monetarily. Although some poorer members said that their obligations were an economic hardship, most still seemed happy to give as much as they can, saying that they are willing to sacrifice because the church is so important to them that they want the buildings and grounds to be as nice as possible. In addition, there is a spirit of inter-village rivalry: the church in Malem village had completed and dedicated a new building early in 1975 and Lelu people did not want to be outdone.

Conclusions

The foregoing information suggests that the Kosraen church has at least two important effects on the economy of the village. First, both the church and the kumi sponsor large-scale feasts, ceremonies, and building projects. Because of the cultural importance attached to participation in church-sponsored social activities, because Kosraens desire that church buildings and properties have an impressive appearance, and because the village-level churches compete to have fine physical structures, some of the income earned from wage labor is channeled into expenditures on church building projects and on church-sponsored ceremonial events. Part of the "work" of church officers is devoted to organizing the members, and indeed other villagers, to contribute to these public activities. The church thus channels a part of the income earned from government employment

124

into the public expenditure category that economists
call "social overhead capital." As a by-product of the
stimulation of consumption in this category, the church
increases the demand for building materials, and probably also for imported foodstuffs (see chapter 10), and
thus helps to energize the import-retail service industries.

I cannot document the second conclusion, but only
wish to mention its probable existence. As shown, part
of the cultural definition of Christian morality is
abstention from use of tobacco and of alcoholic beverages. The church long ago prohibited the sale of liquor
on the island, a prohibition still in effect at the time
of my research and maintained largely due to pressure
from church leaders. Like many such prohibitions, this
one is violated frequently, and liquor also is imported
(legally) from off-island. Nonetheless, it is likely
that moral standards of "clean living" enculturated by
the church has the effect of lowering the aggregate consumption of liquor and tobacco. Most Kosraens seriously
frown on smoking and drinking; even if a man himself
commits these sins, he is likely to administer a good
beating to any of his children who follow his bad example. Given the social problems resulting from alcohol-
ism and from high monetary expenditures on liquor in
other areas of Micronesia, this effect is probably significant and entirely laudable.

KUMI

In chapter 4, I mentioned that the Japanese introduced a novel organizational form, the kumi, to the
Kosraens during the 1930s. To increase labor
efficiency, they divided the population into four
groups, called kumi, and assigned various tasks in
public works projects to each of the groups. Although
their functions and activities have altered since
Japanese times, the kumi organization not only persists
but has become integrated into the church structure.
Along with the church, kumi-organized social events are
the focus of much of the public activity that occurs
outside the contexts of kinship, subsistence, and job.

At the time of Lewis' study in 1947-8, the kumi
were largely mutual help organizations. They provided
labor for the construction of houses, canoes, fences,
and so forth of their respective members on a rotating,
reciprocal basis. Men devoted one day each week to
cooperative labor organized by the kumi. Then, as
today, membership in the groups was not based on kinship
principles, although they performed many joint activities which in other societies often are carried out by
kin or residential groupings. (Lewis 1949)

In the next few years following Lewis' study, the *kumi* apparently split into two organizations with separate functions, which I shall call "Office *kumi*" and "Church *kumi*." In the 1950s and into the 1960s, the Office *kumi* functioned in public works projects, such as the maintenance of public buildings and the construction and repair of village roads and sea walls. All men of the village aged 18 to 55 were required to devote Monday of each week to these public works tasks, under the direction of the elected village chief. The chief, who was then a more influential figure than he is today, decided what tasks most needed to be accomplished during a particular week and divided up the tasks among the groups. The Office *kumi* appears to have been completely separate from the Church *kumi*, for a man might belong to *itsi kumi* for purposes of public works and to *sang kumi* in the church organization.

By the time of my fieldwork, the Office *kumi* were defunct as a basis for acquiring and organizing labor for public works projects, although they still existed on paper (Peoples 1977). Their functions now are performed by temporary day laborers, whose wages in 1975 were paid by grants from the Ponape District Legislature and from the Congress of Micronesia, and from the Public Works Tax ($1 monthly for all adult males). In 1975, for example, the Ponape District Legislature appropriated $12,000 to Kosrae for the repair of municipal government office buildings in the four villages. Additional grants were made for sea wall repair and village road maintenance, which employed about 20 men for two or three weeks at a time during several periods in 1975. These grants are a source of income for those men who are not in the government's or some business' regular employment. Besides making the island further dependent on outside resources for public works tasks, which were formerly organized communally and performed as a part of public duty, this change has usurped many of the powers and functions of the village chiefs (Peoples n.d.).

The Church *kumi*, however, remain enormously important institutions in Kosrae, for they organize many of the church-related ceremonial events. The *kumi* may be conceptualized as the "arms" of the church into the village, for it is largely through their membership in *kumi* that those outside the church participate in its many activities. Because the Church *kumi* are the organizational channels through which many resources used in church-related activities and events are funneled, and because competition between the four of them makes the groups enormously effective organizationally, I shall give two examples of how the groups functioned in 1975.

As the first example, I return to the dedication feast of the Sharon Inn. In July, 1975, the Etawi Committee decided that the new building could be

completed by early September, so they set September 6 as
the day on which members of the other three villages
would be invited to Lelu for an enormous feast and dedication service. The monetary resources that the Adult
and Youth Etawi had collected through the mechanisms
outlined in the previous section were judged inadequate
to feed the estimated 2,000 guests expected from other
villages. Therefore, the Adult Etawi held a meeting in
the last week in July to decide how the additional rice,
flour, plates, cold liquids, fish, and chickens needed
for the feast were to be raised. It was decided that
the fastest way to acquire the needed foods was to allow
the four kumi to organize the collection and preparation. Etawi leaders knew that if they gave the responsibility to the kumi, the task would be accomplished
speedily and fully, for no group wanted to be outdone by
the others. As it happened, this strategy worked admi-
rably: all four groups contributed the large quantities
of goods (see chapter 10 for the totals) requested in
time for the event, in spite of the fact that the ship
carrying the imported chickens that were ordered arrived
barely in time. Lelu people judged the dedication quite
successful, for it rivalled in scale the feast that
Malem village had sponsored for its own new building
earlier in the year. In effect, the Etawi leaders had
capitalized effectively on the spirit of friendly
(usually) competition between the village's four kumi.
Aside from revealing the rivalry, this example shows
very well the time and commitment that Kosraens devote
to culturally meaningful tasks, especially when such
tasks are accomplished using organizational forms familiar to them.

The second example is the competitive singing and
marching that the four groups organize for several holiday celebrations that occur near the end of each year.
For example, each group invents elaborate marches and
writes impressive songs that are performed in front of
the whole village in the church building on Christmas
day. Each kumi selects two or more members to write
lyrics, match them to appropriate music from old
American hymnals, lead the singing, and make up the
marching formations. These are important, although
temporary, leadership roles, and those who are chosen
are generally considered to be the individuals who are
most skilled at their respective tasks. Each group
attempts to have the best possible lyrics attached to
the catchiest tunes that are sung while performing the
most elaborate marches. I happened to be good friends
of the couple chosen by the group I joined to write the
lyrics for its songs. Night after night they spent
hours looking through old American song books to find
pleasing music, and more hours writing words that
matched the notes and harmony.

Adequate performance in this good-natured rivalry
between the _kumi_ requires long hours of practice at
singing and marching. In 1975, the practicing began in
October. Each night (except Sunday), most of the members of each group met in one of the church buildings or
the Municipal Office building for two or three hours.
The practicing went on for six nights a week for about
ten weeks prior to Christmas. I observed (and also was
told) that most church members who were not too elderly
attended at least four times per week. Everyone took
great interest in the practices not only of their own
group, but in those of other groups as well, frequently
hanging around after their own session was completed to
listen and observe the members of other _kumi_.

As these two examples reveal, in 1975 the _kumi_
functioned mainly in the organization of church-related
ceremonial events. The specific mechanisms used by the
groups to acquire the material resources needed for such
events are detailed in chapter 10. Here I wish to
emphasize the competitive ethos that permeates most
social activity organized by the four _kumi_.

KINSHIP

A thorough discussion of Kosraen kinship is beyond
the scope of this work. Wilson (1969) discusses the
kinship rights and duties of modern Kosrae from an ethnoscientific perspective, and Ritter (1978) summarizes
the major categories and groupings of relatives and the
contexts in which kin relationships are activated.

In modern Kosrae, there are no longer any matri-
clans, subclans, nor any other kind of unilineal descent
group that anthropologists are so fond of investigating.
The clan structure already was virtually obsolete by
Sarfert's 1905 visit and Kosraens now show little interest in their historical clan affiliations. Instead of
sruf ("clan"), Kosraens now are interested in _sucu_
("family," "kinsperson," "consanguineal relative"). The
word _sucu_ not only is the generic term for "relative,"
but also may be applied to designate groupings of kin
from the range of nuclear family up to all persons
descended bilaterally from a common ancestor. It also
commonly refers to residential groupings, such as households or clusters of related households who live contiguously on a section of land. For example, the adult
children of a deceased man who reside at the place
called Finnem on Lelu island are called "_sucu_ Finnem"
when one wishes to designate the sibling set that lives
contiguously at Finnem.

The fact that the kinship system of modern Kosrae is
no longer especially exotic does not mean that its effects on patterns of economic behavior are unimportant.

Two aspects of Kosraen kinship are especially relevant for this study.

The first influence was discussed in chapter 5. The two main factors of agricultural production, land and labor, usually are acquired through activation of genealogical ties. Most land is acquired through inheritance, although normatively it also may be purchased or traded. At present, the preferred practice is to leave land to all of one's sons and, if circumstances warrant, to daughters as well. The fortunate effect of this preference is that no Lelu household lacks access to land for subsistence cultivation. Labor used in agriculture and fishing ordinarily is drawn from one's own household or, far less commonly, from genealogically related households. As discussed in chapters 5 and 7, the fact that most land and labor is acquired through kinship principles has important implications for how Lelu jobholders have responded to recent wage labor opportunities: it allows employees and their families to continue to participate in subsistence cultivation, and thus to avoid the status of a fully proletariat labor force.

Second, the relations established by kinship are important to the economy of the island because of their continued "strength" and "breadth." By "strength," I mean that most Kosraens feel more of a normative obligation to help and honor requests from their kin than do most Americans. "Breadth" refers to the fact that, in some contexts, kinship obligations are more wideranging, that is, they extend to a greater number of people, than in most industrialized societies.

With regard to "strength," moral norms specify the ideal relations that should characterize specific ties of kinship. For example, younger siblings should respect older ones, siblings should give one another mutual aid, and siblings should not quarrel among themselves. However, actual practices frequently vary from the ideal. Thus, the norm for land inheritance is that a father should divide his holding equitably (if not equally) among his male children, which often results in quarrels between brothers over land ownership and use (chapter 5). Ideologies of mutual aid between brothers also are breached. I do not believe, for example, that an employed man usually shares much of his income with his unemployed brothers, although a major deficiency of my study was the failure to acquire specific information on this point. One obligation that usually is honored in practice is that of sons to give financial assistance and labor to their elderly parents. This takes the form of outright gifts of money and imported food and of devoting a portion of one's own and one's children's labor to the support of one's parents. It is quite common for a well-to-do son, or a group of sons, to finance the construction of a new house for their parents. This practice is not free of self-interest, of course, for it is considered normal for a man to leave the most or best land to those sons who have given the greatest support to he and his wife during their old age. Thus, kinship obligations have a "social security" dimension, resulting in the redistribution of some cash income and consumer goods to the village's elderly.

The contexts in which the "breadth" factor exerts its economic influences are largely ceremonial, especially in various life crisis events. People regularly, although selectively, associate with their kin up to the range of first or second cousin, but beyond this range kinship relationships, as such, lie largely dormant in everyday life. But at funerals, distant kin ties are activated and many visitors and enormous quantities of food pour into the household of the deceased. In fact, it is probably accurate to say, as Ritter (1978:134) also believes, that the only occasion upon which an entire sucu (here meaning "kindred") cooperates and associates is at the time of a person's death. Similar remarks apply to many marriages, although some of these are quite small affairs. The large quantities of food provided for funerals and of gifts presented at the larger weddings have important economic effects. As shown in the next chapter, the wide "breadth" of contemporary kinship obligations tends to increase the quantities of goods contributed to such events, and therefore has important economic consequences.

9
Ceremonial Consumption:
Life Crisis Events

Like people everywhere, Kosraens as individuals and as members of families participate in a network of social relationships, many of which they activate mainly in the context of ceremonial events. Because most of these events involve a feast and/or an interindividual or intergroup exchange of goods, the ceremonies have a material dimension. They therefore affect how Kosraens allocate their material resources, and it should be possible to describe and analyze the magnitude and direction of these effects. Although the specific occasions that are "ceremonialized" have altered from aboriginal times, feasting and exchanging goods at ceremonial events is an old tradition on the island. While Benjamin Snow was attempting to Christianize Kosraens in the 1850s and 1860s, he complained often about their penchant for ceremonial feasting, which he saw as a heathen custom that inhibited his efforts to spread the gospel (chapter 3). In spite of the other cultural changes that occurred as a result of Snow's eventual success, ceremonial feasts and exchanges are an important focus of suprafamilial religious, social, and recreational activity in modern Kosrae. Far from being "heathen," the church itself now participates in and even organizes many of them.

Modern Kosraen ceremonial occasions may be classified into two categories on the basis of their purposes and organizing principles. Life crisis events include a child's first birthday party, weddings, and funerals. All these normally are organized on the basis of kinship, by the heads of households or of nuclear families: the father of the infant for first birthday parties, the respective fathers of the bride and groom for weddings, and the closest surviving senior male relative of the deceased for funerals. The second category, holidays, include several celebrations that occur annually: Liberation Day (September 8, a commemoration of the day the Americans "saved" the island from the Japanese in 1945), Christmas, and New Year's. In 1975,

although a one-time event, the dedication day of the
Sharon Inn also classifies as a holiday. All holidays,
as described in chapter 10, are organized by church
leaders or by the kumi. In this chapter, I shall discuss only life crisis events.

The preceding ceremonial occasions are not exhaustive, for other minor ceremonial feasts and exchanges
also are organized. Although there is no formal birth
ceremony, sometimes relatives and friends give presents
informally to a newborn infant. Birthdays often are
celebrated by relatives and friends. The high school
students hold annual feasts, as when one class sponsors
a celebration to honor the graduating seniors. A man
sometimes honors a child, parent, or sibling who is
leaving the island or who has returned after a long
absence with a small feast. Finally, the church organizes several minor ceremonies throughout the year, such
as a feast held at the beginning of each year to honor
outgoing church officers. In spite of these small
affairs, the seven ceremonially marked occasions listed
above were overwhelmingly the most significant events at
which special feasts and exchanges occurred in 1975.

THEORETICAL FRAMEWORK

How do these feasts and exchanges affect economic
change under present conditions in Lelu village? Over
the past two or three decades, a large body of literature has accumulated in the social sciences on the
impact of ceremonial exchanges on economic "growth."
That part of this literature that is written from a
modernization perspective typically considers ceremonial
customs as one attribute of "traditional" societies that
impedes their modernization by negatively affecting consumption and accumulation. For example, ceremonial customs lead those with surplus income to dissipate their
resources by contributing to or sponsoring expensive
feasts and celebrations; this decreases the quantity of
resources available for investment in technical improvements. Ceremonies may promote the consumption of luxury
goods, such as liquor, costumes, and expensive exotic
foods; by encouraging expenditures on such "frivoli-
ties," aggregate levels of savings are lowered. Ceremonial customs may discourage investment in innovative
economic activities; would-be entrepreneurs are unlikely
to begin new enterprises if they anticipate that the
material benefits will be lost through socially obligatory distributions on ceremonial occasions. (Lambert
and Hoselitz 1963; Nash 1961; Smelser 1963) The general conclusions of such arguments are that ceremonial
expenditures encourage consumption at the expense of

savings and investment and inhibit the accumulation of resources in the hands of those likely to invest them.

Several ethnographic studies of economic change in Oceanic societies suggest that ceremonial customs might instead have neutral or favorable effects on consumption and facilitative effects on accumulation. With regard to consumption, from his work in village Fiji, Belshaw (1964) concluded that most goods used in Fijian ceremonies are ordinary and useful goods that are consumed on an everyday basis by villagers. Further, the exchange and consumption of other kinds of goods in ceremonial contexts increased the demand for those goods and therefore had the beneficial effect of stimulating the utilization of land and labor that otherwise would have been underemployed. (Belshaw 1964:149, 152-3; a similar argument for Samoa appears in Pitt 1970) Although his argument is challenged by Rutz (1978), Belshaw raises the possibility that consumption in ceremonial contexts is best treated as "normal consumption," which is "neutral with regard to economic growth." (Belshaw 1964: 152) Notice that, in order for ceremonial consumption to be totally "normal" and "neutral," either the goods used ceremonially must be of the same kinds and quantities that are consumed every day, or ceremonial events must be the occasions at which ordinary consumer goods are acquired by individuals and households for everyday use.

Other case studies in Oceania reveal how ceremonial exchanges might have positive effects on accumulation and investment. For the Tolai people of New Britain, Salisbury (1970) and Epstein (1964) show that participation in traditional ceremonies is a means used by enterprising men to acquire labor and capital for investment in new businesses and technical improvements. By sponsoring and contributing to various ceremonial events, Tolai entrepreneurs reaffirmed traditional ties of kinship and affinity and created new relations of indebtedness. In the long term, these social bonds allowed businessmen to acquire labor and capital at low cost, and thereby facilitated accumulation. Finney (1973) was led to a similar conclusion for a region in highland Papua New Guinea.

Such studies suggest that the impacts of ceremonial feasts and exchanges on consumption and accumulation in village communities at least are problematic. Under varying conditions, some arising from within the local village, others originating from the worldwide system and affecting the village "from the outside," ceremonial customs can have many consequences for the pattern of resource allocation. In other words, whatever their nature, local ceremonial practices interact with exogenous forces; this process of interaction may generate a variety of effects on consumption and accumulation. In specific villages, it is possible to describe the ceremonial practices and to analyze how they interact with impinging exogenous forces. I begin this task for Lelu by identifying two "material" dimensions of ceremonial exchanges.

Two Dimensions of Ceremonies

It is useful to isolate two aspects of ceremonial customs that most obviously involve material goods. These may be called the demand dimension and the distributive dimension. The demand dimension encompasses, first, the quantity of goods used and consumed in ceremonial contexts. Are a significant proportion of individual or group resources consumed or exchanged on ceremonial occasions? All else equal, the greater the proportion of time, money, and other resources that are expended in or otherwise devoted to ceremonial occasions, the greater their impacts on village consumption and accumulation. The demand dimension includes, second, the kinds and characteristics of goods that are consumed and/or exchanged at ceremonial events. For example, are the "ceremonial goods" (that is, the goods consumed and/or exchanged in ceremonial contexts) exclusively consumer goods, or are producer's goods also involved? If they are consumer goods, are they perishables or durables? Are they produced locally or imported? Are the ceremonial goods produced or purchased especially and exclusively for ceremonial uses, or are they ordinary consumer goods? As the neologism suggests, the demand dimension purports to encapsulate the effects of various ceremonial events on the aggregate demand for goods in the community.

Ceremonial events not only affect the quantities and kinds of goods in demand; because they require the expenditure of material resources, they also are likely to affect how income and/or goods are distributed. The net aggregate effect of ceremonial practices on the distribution of resources in the village is the distributive dimension of ceremonies. For example, do the sponsors or organizers receive a net material gain from the events, or do they suffer a loss in income or goods from their expenditures? Do ceremonial requirements remove income from the control of those individuals or groups who otherwise would use it more productively? Do people not themselves involved directly in the events have their resources increased or decreased? Does the burden of expense for a particular event fall disproportionately on a few participants, or are costs widely shared? Like the demand side, the distributive dimension varies widely between societies, and probably also across different kinds of ceremonies in the same society.

In distinguishing these two dimensions, no slight is intended against other aspects of ceremonial practices that might be important in specific cases. It seems likely, however, that most of the significant impacts of ceremonies on village economies may be classified under one of these two dimensions, which therefore have widespread comparative validity. It also should be noted that these two dimensions need not vary independently of one another. It might be the case, as indeed it is on Kosrae, that some aspect of the demand dimension affects some aspect of the distributive dimension, and vice-versa.

The demand and distributive dimensions of ceremonies interact with each other and with extralocal inputs to affect the patterning of village economic change. That is, the impacts depend jointly on the nature of local ceremonial practices themselves and on the exogenous forces affecting the community. A pertinent example illustrates this point. Much of the existing literature focuses on the alleged detrimental effects of ceremonial expenditures on savings and investment levels. This concern is appropriate for those areas with such low incomes that shortage of capital is a serious barrier to increased productivity. But, as shown in chapter 6, given American policy, such a capital shortage is not a serious obstacle to investment in modern Kosrae. Indeed, under current conditions, it is not the magnitude so much as the form of investment that is affected by ceremonial feasts and exchanges, a point pursued in this chapter and the next. To anticipate the major conclusion, ceremonial practices increase the demand for certain imported foods and consumer durables (mainly, clothing) and thereby not only further increase the village's dependency on imports but also contribute to the channelling of income earned from government jobs into the import/retail trade stores.

PRELIMINARIES

Before presenting the data that I believe support this conclusion, notice must be given of two special situations in 1975 that affected ceremonial demand. The first is the soft taro disease, mentioned in chapter 5, that began in 1971. Soft taro (Colocasia) is used in the preparation of a highly valued food, called fahfah, which is consumed almost exclusively in ceremonial contexts. The root of the plant is baked in the earth oven, pounded using a special stone implement, mixed with boiled coconut milk or bananas (depending on the kind of fahfah, of which there are many), and served on a traditional wooded tray or wrapped in special leaves. By 1975, the soft taro disease had begun to abate, but some informants stated that they were still reluctant to resume plantings. Normally, much of the soft taro cultivated in the village is planted in anticipation of ceremonial needs, and 1975 was no exception. However, my observation of the several church-sponsored holidays that occurred near the end of 1975 indicated that many Lelu men purchased their soft taro from another village. I believe, therefore, that Lelu people did not have enough soft taro to meet the village's ceremonial demand, due largely to the disease.

The second special circumstance was a hog cholera epidemic that began in April, 1975, in Utwe village and in the next weeks spread over the whole island. The administration had little choice but to eradicate all domestic pigs on the island and to trap as many wild ones as possible. Prior to the epidemic, a census taken by the Agriculture Department revealed that the 164 pig owners of Lelu had a total of 1481 pigs (a mean of 9 pigs/owner, with a range from 1 to 44). The effect on the ceremonial demand of the village was profound. Pigs sometimes are slaughtered for everyday use, but most are consumed in the context of funerals, holidays, and weddings. As shown later, the absence of domestic pigs by August, 1975, had dramatic effects on the kinds of foods consumed at funerals and year-end holidays. (see Peoples 1977 for further discussion of the hog cholera)

One final preliminary is necessary before describing Kosraen life crisis ceremonies as I observed them in 1975. As mentioned, kinship relations are the organizational basis for all life crisis events. It therefore is useful to distinguish between different categories of kin, for each may have different normative rights and obligations in ceremonial contexts. Close kin will refer to the statuses of the nuclear family: for first birthday parties, to the parents and parents' siblings of the infant; for weddings, to the siblings and children of both sets of parents of the couple; for funerals, to the parents (if alive), siblings, and children of the deceased. Distant kin will refer to other categories of consanguineal relatives of the principal participants, largely including first and second cousins. Affinal kin will include the spouses of the participants and the close kin of these spouses. Terms such as relative, kindred, or kin in the following discussion are intentionally vague, for the specific relationship activated or category of kin included is indefinite.

As discussed in the previous chapter, Kosraen kinship is extended bilaterally, so the range or boundary of an individual's active kinship network is indefinite. However, unless an individual has established personal relations with someone outside his or her own household or circle of close kin, distant kin ties, as such, largely are dormant in everyday life. It is primarily

in the context of life crisis ceremonies, especially
funerals and the larger marriages, that distant and
affinal ties are activated. On these occasions, many or
most of an individual's kindred will congregate and
bring or send material contributions on his or her
behalf.

FIRST BIRTHDAY PARTIES

On Kosrae, the equivalent of the birth ceremony
found in most Pacific populations is an optional party
on the infant's first birthday. The hog cholera epidemic adversely affected the occurrence of this ceremony: I knew personally several couples who might have
organized a party for their child, but only two did so.
One man specifically told me that he did not hold the
event for his year-old infant because of the absence of
pigs with which to feast the guests. As a result, I
have a complete record of expenses for only one party.
At this event, the infant's father was absent,
working in another district, but the mother decided to
sponsor the ceremony herself. The party involved many
hours of preparation, but was itself short, lasting
about four hours. Food was prepared by the mother,
helped by neighboring girls and by assorted relatives of
her husband and herself. The mother spent $117 on food,
including many imports: rice, turkey tails, cakes,
banana turnovers, and biscuits (the last three were
baked in the village, but all the materials were
imported, except the bananas). Indigenous foods
included 50 pounds of fish, four trays of fahfah purchased from a Malem villager, and two bundles of sugar
cane, all common feast foods. In spite of the absence
of domestic pigs, the mother was able to obtain, by
gift, one wild pig, caught by the only active wild pig
hunter in Lelu, who was a good friend of her father. Of
the total $117 expended by the child's mother on food,
all but the $46 spent on fish, fahfah, and sugar cane
was used to purchase the imported turkey tails, rice,
and materials used in the baked products. As usual,
some food was consumed at the party, and afterwards each
guest was given a woven coconut leaf plate filled with
food to take home for their families.
The guests who attended, and some other relatives
who did not actually go to the event, brought or sent
gifts, all imported, for the infant. These consisted
mainly of useful clothing articles: 11 trousers, 6
shirts, 3 towels, 7 undershirts, 7 briefs, and 12 yards
of cloth. The market value of these durables (at prices
at the consumer cooperative) was $136. In addition,
small items were given: candy, crackers, soap, gum, and
a few toys. These were worth roughly $75. Altogether

about $210 were expended on imports by the 16 assorted
kin of the mother and the 15 kin of the father who
brought or sent gifts. I was told that this party was
about average in size for these events.

As soon will become clear, first birthday parties
are small celebrations compared to many weddings and
funerals, both in terms of numbers of people attending
and of quantities of goods contributed. The durable
consumer goods that usually are given have everyday use
to the infant and also will become hand-me-downs to
younger siblings or other relatives in later years.
Because the quantities are small, and the gifts are
useful, most of the clothing probably would have been
purchased eventually by the parents or other close kin
of the infant. The events thus seem to have effects
much like baby showers in American society: they spread
the short-term expense of child rearing more widely
beyond the child's immediate family. Thus, at the only
1975 event I witnessed, the infant's mother received a
net "benefit" of $90 to $100 worth of contributions of
goods over her "cost" in food expenses (I do not mean to
imply that she calculated expenses against anticipated
returns, however). She therefore came out "ahead" at
this event, but because of her own obligations at past
and future parties held for her own and her husband's
relatives, in the long term her returns are roughly
balanced by her contributions. It is thus unlikely that
the distributive dimension of first birthday parties
results in significant net gains or losses across families. The demand dimension may slightly increase the
consumption of imported children's clothing in normal
years, but the incidence of the parties was too low in
1975 for this effect to be significant.

WEDDINGS

For present purposes, the most outstanding charac-
teristic of modern weddings is that large quantities of
goods may be exchanged between the respective kin of the
bride and groom. Significant changes have occurred in
this century in the kinds and quantities of goods given
reciprocally. Previously, the period of engagement was
very long, so that the fathers and families of the couple would have ample time to prepare for the event.
Acting separately, the two fathers and their close male
kin would plant taro and sugar cane and prepare preserved breadfruit. The close female kin would make hats
and sewn sleeping mats from pandanus leaves and manufacture fine belts from the dyed fibers of banana stalks.
The native foods listed, together with fahfah, pork,
fish, fresh breadfruit, and drinking coconuts, were prepared for a large feast. The woven goods made by women

were part of the marriage gifts that the two fathers
presented to one another. A male informant in his 70s
recalled that the woven goods listed above were the only
kinds of formal gifts presented, and that both fathers
presented the same kinds of goods to their counterparts.
Both of these practices have altered today. It seems
probable, although I was unable to acquire specific
information on this, that marital exchanges were the
"entry points" of such woven goods into the economic
system, and that the redistribution of these goods following the ceremony was the usual means by which these
commodities were acquired by consumers.

Previously, as today, there was no custom that dic-
tated how many goods were required for a wedding. There
was and is a great deal of choice about how large a presentation to make. A father might opt for a big ceremony, with a huge feast and a large quantity of goods to
be presented to the opposite father. In this case,
Kosraens say that the father has decided to oruh (literally, to "make" or "perform"), that is, to have a large
ceremony to honor the marriage of his child. Alternatively, a father might decide to have no feast or to
make no presentation to his counterpart. In this case,
Kosraens say that the father decided to tiyac oruh ("not
to perform" a large ceremony). There are also degrees
of oruh: a father might decide to have only a small
feast and to make a small presentation to his counterpart.

In the reciprocal wedding presentations, the father
of the bride and groom are aided by their many relatives
and friends. I received somewhat contradictory information on the role of the father in determining who among
his kin would help and how much help would be required.
Some said that the father could "ask" or "request" but
not "command," whereas others claimed that the father
would tell at least his close kin what to provide. In
the weddings I observed in 1975, the fathers asked their
other children and siblings to provide certain goods in
certain quantities, but these kin are free to provide
more goods than requested. Also, a wide range of consanguines and affines will learn of the event and a
great many of these will make voluntary, unsolicited
contributions either directly to the father or indirectly to him through one of his close relatives. In
any case, there is a dual structure of choice involved
in this aspect of the ceremony: the father has to make
a general decision on whether or not to oruh, and his
close relatives have to decide whether to give more than
requested. This structure contributes to a tendency for
reciprocal wedding presentations to swell above anticipated levels, a fact to which I return later.

As for the distribution, there is also no fixed
custom. Informants disagreed on how the marriage gifts

were distributed once they were delivered to the respective fathers by their close relatives. Sometimes both fathers aggregate the contributions of their relatives and friends and present them in toto to their counterparts. Alternatively, the fathers of the couple set aside some of the goods to be given to the bride and groom to help them get started, while other portions of the contributions are redistributed back to the donors and/or presented to the father on the opposite side. The decision on how to redistribute the presentations is largely or entirely "up to the father," who takes into account the anticipated size of the return presentation of his counterpart as well as how much specific individuals in his kindred have contributed in the past. In short, there is much flexibility in the redistribution of the marriage gifts that are given by the father's relatives and friends.

There does seem to be general agreement among Kosraens that the size of the contributions given by the two fathers to each other should be roughly equal. The groom's side may give slightly more because, in the words of one man, the woman's side is "weak." However, in no way does an unbalanced exchange represent bridewealth.

There was no agreement about whether the decisions of the two fathers as to whether or not to oruh were made independently of one another. One person told me that it was up to the father of the groom to decide: the bride's father could not oruh unless the groom's father also was planning a large ceremony. Another said that the two fathers would meet before the event and jointly decide. Others said the decisions were made independently, so that one man could decide to oruh while his counterpart might decide not to. In actuality, this latter alternative is probably rare: if one father decided to have a large feast and make a large presentation to his counterpart, while the counterpart had decided not to oruh, the situation would be embarrassing for both parties. Most likely, both fathers would meet and jointly decide whether to have a big event, with the groom's father perhaps having more influence over the decisions. But each father considers the situation of his counterpart: if one father is poor, for example, the other father may decide not to oruh even though he is rich and has a large number of relatives to help with the contributions.

I have used the term "side" to refer to the respective friends and relatives of the bride and groom. Kosraens themselves think of the structure of the exchanges in this way, using the terms "lacyen muhkul" ("man's side") and "lacyen muhtwacn" ("woman's side") to refer to those who make contributions to the fathers of the groom and bride, respectively. Ideologically, they apparently see the exchanges as establishing relations of mutual aid between the two families. Thus, at one wedding in 1975, the father of the groom made a short speech after the pastor had performed the ceremony proper, stating to the bride's father that he and his family were poor, but if they could help the bride's kinsmen in any way they would try to do so. The bride's father responded in kind: he too was a poor man, and his family lazy as well, but they would do everything they could to help the groom's family. As might be expected given this ideology, both fathers deprecated the size of their contributions, an action that is common in other gift-giving contexts as well.

While in Kosrae, I acquired quantitative data on contributions for three weddings. Two of these occurred in 1975 and were seen as relatively small affairs, whereas the third occurred in 1972. I made an effort to acquire data on the 1972 event because it was remembered as quite a large wedding, and may be taken as representing the high extreme in the size of contributions. It was possible to acquire information on the kinds and quantities of goods given by the groom's side in this wedding because, as is customary, the father wrote down what was contributed. Before presenting these data, notice must be taken of the changes that have occurred in the kinds of goods exchanged between the two sides.

Before Japanese times, I was told that the non-food contributions made by both sides were identical: both sets of relatives gave mats, hats, and woven belts. I cannot state even the approximate date at which the change occurred, but today each side contributes the kinds of goods that are useful to the sex of the spouse on the opposite side. The bride's side gives goods used by men, or "men's goods," including pants, shirts, undershirts, briefs, and sometimes sheets, towels, pomade, and handkerchiefs. The kin of the groom contribute "women's goods" such as three yard lengths of cloth, home made dresses, panties, slips, brassieres, and household utensils. Both sides continue to give sewn sleeping mats made by women from the leaves of the pandanus tree. Unless the wedding is very small, each father will hold a feast in his house prior to the ceremony in which members of his side who will attend come and eat. Relatives also help the fathers with these feast preparations by giving food items, both local and imported.

The close kin of the two sets of parents have the primary responsibility to help with the provision of marriage gifts and needed foodstuffs. It must be emphasized, however, that although the close kin do bear much of the expense, they are also "focal points" for the contributions of more distant consanguineal and affinal kin. As an example, in the enormous 1972 wedding, a

sister of the groom who was married to a wealthy man in
Utwe village gave 105 sewn mats and 411 pieces of cloth
as her help to her father. Obviously, she did not herself make or buy the mats or purchase the cloth; the
Utwe relatives of her husband gave most of the items to
aid their kinsman. This pattern of spreading expenses
results not only in some very distant kin making contributions, but also in individuals giving goods to the
wedding of someone to whom they themselves have no special ties.

Quantitative data on the kinds and quantities of
goods provided by the groom's side (only) for three weddings are given in Table 9.1, broken down by the major
items contributed. Because the brides in the 1972 and
1975 (B) events were from other villages, I have no data
on the size of their presentations.

In the large 1972 wedding, the groom's kin provided
about $16,000 worth of goods; with the exception of
mats, all were imports. Because four of the groom's
seven female siblings were married to men of other villages, and some of the siblings of his parents also
lived in other villages, the expenses for this event
were shared widely throughout the whole island. In
fact, in quantitative terms, almost half the total dollar value of the various "women's goods" contributed
represented the presentations of members of other villages linked to the close kin of the couple through
affinal ties. Undoubtedly, hundreds of people purchased
imported goods to contribute to this event.

I have no data on the contributions of the bride's
side for the 1972 wedding. However, like the groom, the
bride was a member of one of the most important and
wealthiest families in her village, so it is reasonable
to assume that her kin provided nearly as much as that
of the groom. I would say that the total expenses for
both sides were at least $25,000, and perhaps as much as
$30,000. As mentioned previously, this wedding was the
largest in the memory of my 1975 informants. Its size
is partly explained by the wealth and influence of the
fathers of the couple. Possibly, the fact that the
groom and his parents had an unusual number of siblings
married into other villages also contributed: each of
the affines in the three other villages might have seen
the size of their contributions in terms of intervillage
rivalry, and so increased them accordingly.

In the 1975 (A) wedding, the groom's side contributed "women's goods" worth $3,300 (Table 9.1). The
Lelu bride's side gave 44 mats, 70 trousers, 63 shirts,
48 undershirts, 42 briefs, and other smaller items.
Altogether, her kin gave about $1,700 worth of "men's
goods" to the father of the groom. (This latter figure
might represent under-reporting rather than reflect-
ing the norm of the bride's side making a smaller

TABLE 9.1
Marriage gifts provided by groom's side, three weddings

Event	Mats[a] (no.)	Cloth[b] (pcs.)	Dresses (no.)	Slips (no.)	Panties (no.)	Brassieres (no.)	Other ($ value)	Total ($ value)
1972	541	2,320	397	100	69	23		
$ value	$1,082	$10,440	$1,786	$600	$69	$46	$1,600	$15,623
1975 (A)	122	375	56	51	43	3		
$ value	$ 244	$ 1,969	$ 294	$458	$54	$ 6	$ 300	$ 3,325
1975 (B)[c]	?	90+	11+	10+	10+	9+		
$ value							$ 70	$ 800+

a sewn by island women from local pandanus leaves. Some mats presented at weddings are purchased, whereas others are made by the contributors. Market value is $2.

b pieces of cloth are purchased in three yard lengths, which is considered the proper amount for a dress. In 1975, an average price was about $1.75 per yard. I estimate $1.50 per yard for the 1972 event. Because most of the dresses are home made, their $ value is the same as pieces of cloth.

c I was unable to acquire a complete list of the women's goods provided for this event, so the quantities indicated are minimal.

presentation). Again, with the exception of the mats, all the goods provided by both sides were imports. Total expenses for both sides totalled between $5,000 and $6,000, spread widely throughout Lelu village due to consanguineal and affinal kinship ties. This wedding was considered somewhat smaller than normal.

The groom of the 1975 (B) wedding was a Lelu villager who was a student at the University of Guam and who was visiting Kosrae on the summer break. The bride was from another village. Their plan was to marry, then leave the island. The groom was to return to Guam, but his parents were to go to Ponape to live for a while, taking their son's new wife with them. The ceremony, then, was something of a "rush job," and in fact was not even announced until one week before the wedding was to occur. Obviously, the groom's father did not have time to make preparations for oruh, even had he wanted to have a large affair. Accordingly, he announced to his four married sons who lived in Lelu that he wanted them each to provide one full slip, one dress, and one panty. This would have cost each son about $12. This represents a modified form of tiyac oruh: there would be a very small presentation made by the close kin of the groom's father, with little food served. This was the father's original plan. What actually happened was that the small presentations that he initially requested from his four sons snowballed.

Due to unusual circumstances, I was unable to acquire a complete list of the goods contributed by the groom's side to this wedding, so the totals given in Table 9.1 are woefully incomplete. But because I knew this family quite well, I was able to observe how decisions were made about the size of one's presentation, and how the scale of the events often grow as a result of these choices.

The eldest brother of the groom tried to keep knowledge of the event from spreading. Viewing this through my own cultural lenses, I initially thought that the secrecy was because no one but the immediate family would attend, and the groom's brother did not want anyone else to know of it for fear of hurting their feelings. I later learned that he did not want word to get out because other people would make (unsolicited) contributions that eventually would have to be returned, and the affair would in the end be very expensive for everyone, himself included. His wife previously had told me that her family was "really broke" at the moment, and in fact their purchases for the wedding were made on credit.

Having said that they wanted to keep expenses down, the very next day the wife of the groom's eldest brother went to a local store with which the family had long-standing credit and purchased cloth with which to make

the dress for the bride. In fact, she returned with
nine yards of cloth in three different patterns and
colors (sufficient for three dresses), one pair of
panties, and some lace with which to trim the slip she
would make. In the end, this couple provided three
dresses, two slips, two panties, rice and curry, and one
chicken to be given to the pastor who would perform the
ceremony. The total cost came to about $40, almost a
week's pay for the brother of the groom, who worked with
Public Works. Despite the fact that his father had
asked for only one dress, slip, and panty, another
brother also decided to give more: two dresses, one
piece of cloth, one half-slip, and one pair of panties,
worth all together about $27, a burden for this family
since this brother was unemployed.

By the day of the wedding, the plans of the father
to have a very small event had gone awry. Much food was
to be served after all: four tubs of rice, two tubs of
curry, about 300 pieces of bread, one hind-quarter of a
wild pig (caught by the eldest son), and one chicken
given to the pastor. In addition to the gifts contributed by the close kin listed in Table 9.1, mats were
given as well, in unknown quantities. Excluding the
mats, the total value of these gifts was about $730, and
the list is far from complete. Added to the estimated
$70 food costs, the event cost the close kin (I believe
that no distant kin contributed) a minimum of $800.

As previously noted, custom does not dictate
any minimal quantities of goods automatically to be
exchanged at weddings. Invariably, Kosraens told me
that it is "up to the fathers" of the couple to decide
whether or not to "perform," and to tell their close kin
what to provide. I also was told explicitly that a
father takes into account the personal economic circumstances of his relatives when he asks them for help.
These statements suggest a "flexibility" that might
allow the scale of the wedding exchanges to be adjusted
to affordable and desired levels, as Belshaw (1964) and
Pitt (1970) believe is true in Fiji and Samoa, respectively. In fact, every villager I questioned claimed to
prefer that weddings, as well as some other ceremonial
occasions, did not cost so much. And in fact, as the
preceding example shows, a father's plans about the
scale of presentations frequently are exceeded by the
quantities of goods actually contributed by various
categories of relatives. The extent to which the presentations can snowball is indicated by the enormous
1972 event (Table 9.1): the groom's father told me that
originally he had chosen not to "perform," but that he
ultimately received so many contributions from his
affinal kin through his married children that the
wedding turned out to be among the largest anyone could
recall. What can explain this frequent discrepancy

between the planned (and desirable, from the point of view of villagers) and actual size of marital presentations?

Part of the answer lies in the <u>de facto</u> structure of decision making for the events. Normatively, the primary role of the fathers is to decide the degree of "performance," and then to organize the acquisition of the wedding gifts that their side presents. As shown, they do this by asking their close kin and perhaps some distant kin to provide certain kinds and quantities of men's or women's goods. However, as exemplified by the 1975 (B) wedding, the close kin are free to give more than requested, and frequently do so. Also, a wide range of distant and affinal kin are told or otherwise learn of the event and many of these will make (sometimes unsolicited) contributions either directly to the appropriate father or indirectly to him through one of the close kin, as happened at the huge 1972 wedding. Thus, although Kosraens say that the couple's fathers decide the scale of particular weddings, in fact a variety of categories of kin and friends must choose how much they, as individuals or nuclear families, will contribute.

Why do relatives so often give larger quantities than requested? One reason is that by doing so, the close and distant kin <u>ahkfuhlwact</u> ("show respect for," literally, "make higher") the bride/groom and her/his parents, for generosity on such occasions is a material manifestation of relations of respect and reciprocal aid between relatives. Also, to some extent the size of the presentation a father collects from all categories of kin is viewed as an indication of extended familial solidarity and economic well-being; generosity in marital contributions thus also raises the esteem in the community of those who contribute. With regard to the "help" provided by affinal kin, which may represent a considerable fraction of the total presentation, in part it is an expression of proper relations with their own close kin who have married into the kindred of one of the couple. However, affinal relations themselves imply a diffuse obligation to aid in supplying goods for one another's ceremonial events. Thus, at a present wedding, help may be forthcoming from individuals and households who are affinally related through past marriages to the parents of the couple. For example, the groom in the 1972 wedding had seven married sisters. Altogether, over half the total of all the women's goods contributed for this event originated from the kin and friends of the groom's sister's husbands. From the affinal relatives of the groom, through his seven sisters, came 346 mats, 1,369 pieces of cloth, 295 dresses, 76 slips, 46 panties, and 20 brassieres (compare with the totals in Table 9.1). The groom's sisters thus were focal points for the contributions of affines; through marriages, new potential contributors are added to the ceremonial exchange network of a family.

Another reason the scale of presentations tends to grow over intended and preferred levels is the internal dynamics of gift exchange itself, which allows individuals no easy escape from ceremonial obligations. Gregory's (1982) distinction between commodity and gift exchange is useful in this context. In commodity exchange, one party transfers ownership of an object to another in return for an object of equivalent value; once the transfer is complete, the accounts are considered balanced, and no further transactions need occur. In those gift exchanges governed by the principle of balanced reciprocity, one party gives the gift object to another, who reciprocates with another culturally appropriate gift object, perhaps at a later time. But the accounts are not closed by the act of reciprocation; the last giver always is socially superior to the last receiver, so that the latter is compelled to return the gift or suffer social losses. Thus, in gift exchange, "opting out" by paying off one's ceremonial obligations is difficult because such a payment itself breeds more contributions to oneself. Logically, this model of how balanced reciprocal gift-giving "reproduces" itself will operate if ledgers are kept of outstanding ceremonial debts and if individuals take into account the social losses suffered by failure to reciprocate. The more precise the ledgers, and the more serious the perceived social losses, the stronger will be the tendency for the exchanges to reproduce themselves, or even to grow in scale if increased availability of resources leads some individuals to feed greater quantities of ceremonial goods into the exchanges. As shown, in Kosrae fairly precise written records of outstanding ceremonial obligations usually are made and kept for some period, and individuals and families certainly consider the losses in solidarity with kin and social esteem in deciding how much to give at weddings. Gregory's analysis of the social reproduction of reciprocal giving thus helps to account for the contradiction between Kosraens' stated (and I believe genuine) preference for scaled-down exchanges and their actual contributions: no ego is socially free to choose to give less to others unless others first choose to give less to ego.

The conclusions drawn from the preceding description about the net effects of marital exchanges on the village's economy may be expressed in terms of the distributive and demand dimensions of weddings. Considering first the demand dimension, because the quantities of men's and women's goods purchased and distributed are large, and because all are imports (except for sleeping mats), it seems that the effect of weddings is to increase the consumption of imported clothing. Against this conclusion, however, stands Belshaw's (1964) main point about Fijian ceremonial customs. Because all the goods exchanged are consumption items, the effect of the events might be merely to alter the timing of purchase (all at once instead of little by little) and the distribution following the purchase (instead of buying the clothing for themselves, individuals make purchases for gifts to others, and receive equal quantities from these others, at least in the long term). If this very plausible objection holds, marital exchanges are merely the context in which useful consumption items (clothes) are acquired; they have no real effect on the demand for imported textile products.

In consideration of this possibility, I acquired data on two kinds of women's goods, cloth and dresses, which commonly are distributed in large quantities at weddings. I asked 21 women to report how many dresses and pieces (three yard lengths) of cloth they had in their possession and to recall the source of each item (because almost all the dresses were home made, most of them originally also were purchased as pieces of cloth). Evidence that Belshaw's position applies to Kosraen marital exchanges would exist if women acquire a large percentage of their stock of cloth and dresses from ceremonial distributions. The results of the survey are summarized in Table 9.2. The data appear to vindicate Belshaw: women did indeed acquire a high percentage of the dresses and cloth in their possession from distributions at weddings, or as gifts from other special occasions. In fact, only about one-third of the dresses and one-fourth of the cloth was purchased outside the context of some special occasion (information on other occasions appears in the next chapter). Possibly, then, women are acquiring their useful clothing articles on ceremonial occasions rather than purchasing them at a local store.

It is thus quite true that women acquire many of their dresses (and cloth, which ultimately will be made into dresses) from ceremonial occasions. It also is true that the dresses so acquired are used later for everyday wear, that is, that they become ordinary consumer goods. This, however, is not all that is claimed by Belshaw for Fiji; what is claimed is that the same quantities of consumer goods (in the present case, cloth and dresses) would be purchased even if they were not objects used in ceremonial exchanges. I believe this argument is fallacious, for the following reasons. First, the women possessed a mean of 18 dresses and 8 pieces of cloth per capita (range 4 to 45 and 0 to 23, respectively), a relatively high number. It seems unlikely to me that their husbands would have allowed

TABLE 9.2
Quantities of dresses and pieces of cloth possessed by
21 Lelu women, by source

| Source | Dresses | | Cloth | |
	No.	% of Total	Pcs.	% of Total
Ordinary purchase[a]	117	32	39	23
Christmas uniform[b]	104	28	3	2
Redistributed marriage gift	27	7	55	33
Other gift[c]	101	27	70	42
Other special purchase[d]	21	6	1	--
TOTAL	370	100	168	100

[a]Purchased by the woman or her husband in the absence of some special occasion, that is, for "everyday demand."

[b]Purchased by the woman or her kumi especially for Christmas marching or kumi singing for 1975 or some previous year (see chapter 10).

[c]Received as a gift at Christmas (1975 or previous) or informally.

[d]Bought for some other special occasion, such as choir presentations.

them to buy these quantities without some special event occasioning the purchase. Second, all people whom I questioned about the matter viewed the presentations made at weddings as a burden to them, indicating that they would not otherwise have made many of these purchases, either for themselves or as gifts to others. Third, it appears to be theoretically unsound to maintain that the goods would have been purchased "anyway." From the viewpoint of the actors, the men's and women's goods contributed to weddings were purchased especially for the event; to say that they would have been bought and consumed in the absence of the motivating event is to make an empirically unfalsifiable and hence scientifically unsound statement. Fourth, it seems unlikely, to say the least, that people would buy for their own consumption all the goods that are given to them on ceremonial occasions, whether they be Kosraens, Americans, or members of any other culture. Fifth, as shown earlier, the social dynamics of reciprocal gift-giving often leads to the snowballing of marital presentations; surely, these dynamics result in the purchase of larger quantities of men's and women's goods than would be the case if everyone's purchasing were motivated by the objects' use-value to themselves and their households. For these reasons, I conclude that marital exchanges in the village do result in the increased consumption of imported clothing articles. However, Belshaw's analysis of Fijian ceremonial practices does contain an important insight: some fraction of these consumer goods would have been purchased even without the demand generated by weddings. With the information I have, it is impossible to estimate what this fraction might be; indeed, it is likely to be difficult, and perhaps impossible, to make such an estimate even with far more complete data than my own. At least the <u>direction</u> of the impact, if not its <u>magnitude</u>, can be established.

With regard to the distributive dimension of weddings, one aspect is the effects of the exchanges on the distribution of resources (in the Kosraen case, consumer goods) among individuals and groups who contribute and receive goods. I am unable to reach a definite conclusion about this aspect with the data available. As shown, no rule exists about how the fathers of the couple should redistribute the items they receive from their side at specific events. Further, I discovered no expectation of balanced reciprocity at particular weddings; for example, distant and affinal kin who contribute to a wedding do not necessarily expect to receive items of equivalent value at the same event. There is, however, an expectation of reciprocity over the long term, at future weddings and on other ceremonial occasions. It is probably the case that contributors receive men's and women's goods at future events, if not at the immediate one, in rough proportion to the amounts they contribute. Certainly, there is no indication that weddings are occasions on which significant transfers of consumer goods are made from one economic category to another, as from rich to poor. I believe, then, that the distribution of consumer goods among the participants is not affected significantly by marital exchanges.

However, there is another aspect of the distributive dimension, namely, the effects on individuals who are not themselves participants in specific weddings.

Because with the exception of mats, all the men's and women's goods exchanged are imports, and because almost all these imports are bought from local stores, retailers in the village enjoy an increase in their sales as a result of the kinds and quantities of goods transacted at weddings. The owners of the three largest stores who regularly carry a large stock of men's and women's clothing especially benefit. (I do not believe that they in any way manipulate the kinds and quantities of ceremonial goods used.) Again, to estimate the magnitude of this impact would require information on what proportion of the goods purchased especially for weddings would have been bought for everyday consumption; such data probably are impossible to acquire.

FUNERALS

Of all Kosraen ceremonial occasions, funerals probably were most affected by the 1975 hog cholera, which affected both their demand and distributive dimensions. Before analyzing these effects, it is necessary to describe the organizing principles and normative rights and obligations accompanying the events.

When a death occurs, the body is carried to the house of a close kinsman, usually the eldest son, brother, or father of the deceased. However, another close kinsman's dwelling may be chosen if the house of the senior surviving male relative is not sufficiently large to host the many guests who arrive. Members of the deceased's kindred go to the house where the body lies, bringing massive quantities of food to help the householders feed the funeral visitors. As Ritter (1978:90,134) also believes, it is primarily at funerals that most of the relatives, both close and distant, of the deceased gather at one place on his or her behalf. Ideologically, the main purposes of this gathering are to pay respects and to keep the immediate family of the deceased from becoming too distraught over the death. Kosraens often say that the visits are to ahkpwacr the family, literally "to make them happy," or in this context, "to cheer them up."

A death is announced by the ringing of church bells in a certain pattern that everyone recognizes as signifying that mwet misac ("someone died"). The identity of the deceased is communicated remarkably quickly from house to house, and word similarly is passed about where the body is to be taken. Soon after, the funeral guests begin arriving with their food contributions. They bring only food; no other goods of any kind are consumed or exchanged at Kosraen funerals.

Before the hog cholera, I was told, the close kin of the deceased prepared an earth oven consisting of pork, breadfruit, taro, and perhaps yams and other favorite indigenous foods. Each of the close kin generally killed one or more pigs, whereas distant kin contributed locally produced or imported foods to aid in feeding themselves and others who attended. Two categories of visitors may be distinguished. The "short-term guests," generally numbering in the hundreds, appear intermittently during the next day or two after the death. They consist mainly of distant and affinal kin and friends of the family; typically, they stay a few hours and eat a meal or two, then depart, but may stop by again later. All must be fed. Besides these short-term visitors, a smaller core of many of the close relatives of the deceased (for example, the children and/or siblings) often spend most of their time in the next month or so at the house. They form, in effect, a temporary enlarged "pseudohousehold." At the two funerals I was able to witness, this pseudohousehold also subsisted entirely from the stocks of food brought by the guests; both funerals, however, occurred after the hog cholera, and I do not know what they ate in normal years.

Funerals have two phases. The first is the actual "death and burial." There is a peak of visitors a few hours after the death that lasts until the body is placed in the ground, usually a day later. The number of guests falls off after this, until the next phase, a few days later. This is the kuhlyuhk (which I translate as "the making of the grave"), in which men mix and pour cement over the burial, making an enclosed rectangular structure. Those who come to help with the labor also are feasted from the contributions brought after the death itself.

I have quantitative data on four Lelu funerals. Of these, two occurred in March, 1975, before the hog cholera epidemic. The other two were in late August and early September, after the slaughter of all the domestic pigs. A comparison of these funerals, in a "before and after" fashion, shows the effects of the hog cholera on both the demand and distributive dimensions of funerals. I did not attend either of the March funerals, having just arrived on the island, but Kosraens keep records of the contributions brought by individuals and families at funerals. Someone writes down the name of the contributor and the kinds and quantities of foods he or she brought to the event. I helped keep the record for the August funeral, and believe it to be absolutely accurate; I watched part of the recording for the September event, and did not see any items omitted; I cannot personally vouch for the accuracy of the two March records, but believe it unlikely that they are seriously in error.

In March an elderly woman died, followed by the death of her husband three days later. Although unable to attend either of the funerals, I later interviewed the wife of one of the sons of the deceased couple, who provided a record of the contributions. Quantitative data on the types and quantities of foodstuffs provided for these two funerals are given in Table 9.3 (first and second funerals). Both of them occurred before the hog cholera epidemic struck the island, and a total of 43 pigs were provided by the couple's close kin. Table 9.3 shows the aggregated quantities and dollar values of the foodstuffs contributed for both the "death and burial" and "making of the grave" phases of the two funerals. I have not included the dollar value of the pork consumed because I cannot estimate the total pounds of live pigs contributed with the data available and because, at any rate, probably most of the pigs were not purchased but came from a family's own stock. At the woman's (first) funeral, a total of 35 individual or family units were identified as contributors, so the average size of presentation (which generally may be taken as contributions of nuclear families) was about $58, not including the dollar value of the pigs given. In addition to the pigs and imported rice, ship's biscuits, sugar, mackerel, sardines, and other minor items, some of the guests at the woman's "making of the grave" brought small quantities of breadfruit and drinking coconuts.

Besides revealing the large quantities of local and imported foods consumed at these two funerals, the data in Table 9.3 show a sizeable difference in the dollar values of the imports contributed for the two events. Whereas over $2,000 worth of imports were presented for the wife's funeral, only about $300 worth of rice and mackerel were contributed to the husband's (second) funeral. The reason for the large difference is that many of the storeable imported foods given for the woman's funeral were left over to be used at that of her husband. Once I realized this, it became apparent that perhaps not all the imported foods (which can be stored indefinitely) would actually be used to feed the short-term guests, so that the household(s) of the close kin of the deceased actually received imported foods that could be consumed for a period after the funeral. By contrast, the indigenous foods provided for funerals would not keep for more than two or three days, so the local breadfruit, taro, and so forth would be consumed entirely or largely by the short-term guests. This means that, to the extent that more storeable imported foods are presented by kin and friends than can be consumed at the funeral itself by the large number of guests, the funeral will have the effect of concentrating large quantities of imported foods in the

TABLE 9.3
Contributions for four Lelu funerals, 1975

Event	Pigs[a] (no.)	Rice (bags)	Biscuits (tins)	Mackerel (tins)	Sardines (tins)	Sugar (bags)	Other ($ value)	Total ($ value)
first	25	50	59	232	119	48		
$ value		$ 750	$826	$104	$ 85	$144	$110	$2,019
second	18	16	0	42	0	0		
$ value		$ 240	0	$ 19	0	0	$ 35	$ 294
third	0	25	38	219	0	53		
$ value		$ 381	$530	$110	0	$167	$100	$1,288
fourth	0	86	17	428	41	29		
$ value		$1,333	$238	$214	$51	$ 91	$200	$2,127

[a]The dollar value of the pigs for the first and second funeral is not included because I cannot estimate the weight of the animals and because most of the pigs came from the household herd rather than market sale.

household(s) of the close kin for a period of time following the event.   Observation of two later funerals
confirmed this hypothesis.

    I have complete quantitative data on the funeral of
an elderly Lelu man who died in late August, 1975, after
the pigs were slaughtered. The man died while living in
Ponape, but a funeral service also was held for him on
Kosrae.   He had four married sons living in separate
households in Lelu village, and the service was held in
the large house of his eldest son. The latter received
a cable informing him of the death of his father at
about 9:00 A.M. By late morning, relatives and friends
already were arriving at his house bringing imported
foods to help the family (Table 9.3, third funeral).
The contributions poured in all day in what seemed to me
to be incredibly large quantities, although people present declared that if the man had died on Kosrae, even
more aid would have been provided.

    In the afternoon, I asked a man why everyone was
bringing imported foods. He replied that "before," the
children of the deceased would have killed pigs and made
an earth oven of breadfruit, but now there were no pigs
and it was much "easier" to buy foods from the stores.
Why was it easier? Because, he continued, many people
work now and have no time to go to the mainland to get
food for such events. Also, the eldest son himself had
to make a decision about what he wished people to contribute. A neighbor asked the man what he was going
to do for the event, and he replied by listing some
imported foods. Immediately after he heard the news of
his father's death, he sent one of his sons to the store
to purchase ship's biscuits, coffee, and sugar. The
death occurred on a Friday, a day in which food stocks
are typically low and a great many men are working at
their government jobs. Further, the hog cholera had
resulted in the eradication of all pigs a few weeks
before, and the breadfruit was almost all gone from the
trees. Previously, pits containing preserved breadfruit
would have been opened for the event, and taro harvested. But today few Kosraens make preserved breadfruit, and the soft taro disease had greatly reduced
taro plantings. Bananas are considered a low status
food, and generally would not be served to funeral
guests. In letting it be known that the imported foods
would be served to visitors, the eldest son then made
the only decision feasible.

    About 8:00 the same evening, the Lelu pastor
arrived and conducted a 45 minute service at which three
of the four village deacons also spoke briefly. This
was followed by hymns sung by the village choir and by
the kumi to which the deceased and three of his four
sons belonged. The estimated 200 people present (about
one-half of them children) were served ship's biscuits

together with sweetened coffee. The singing lasted about three hours, until 12:30 A.M., then most people went home. However, some stayed the night, including all of the sons of the deceased and their families, and some of the deceased's siblings.

The next day, Saturday, about 15 adults remained at the house of the eldest son of the deceased, and many others were at the neighboring houses of the deceased's brother and sister. A large number of visitors came and went all day long at one of these three houses. All were served rice and gravy and ship's biscuits, taken from the contributions of the relatives of the deceased. This continued for a week, with people dropping in for short periods to eat the imported foods and drink sweetened coffee. For their part, the four sons of the deceased, three of whom were employed with the government, hardly left the house of the eldest son during the next week (the three employed men took emergency leave from their jobs). For all of this period, all the four sons and their nuclear families ate only the imported foods brought to the event, and all the short-term guests also ate only the imports for the duration of their visit.

Table 9.3 (third funeral) presents data on the amounts of imported foods provided. No locally produced foodstuffs were presented, and none consumed in the funeral context. Altogether, the various categories of kin and friends spent almost $1,300 on imported rice, ship's biscuits, mackerel, sugar, coffee and minor items. The help of 38 individuals or family groups (generally, a "sibling group" or "nuclear family") appear on the record, so the average size of contribution was about $34 worth of imported foods. However, as at weddings, many of the individuals who contributed were helped by their own consanguines, affines, and friends, so did not bear the entire burden of expense from their own resources.

I also have complete quantitative data on another Lelu funeral, which occurred in early September, one week after the death just described. This event was larger than the previous one, both in terms of quantities of foodstuffs contributed and of numbers of guests attending. This is because, as mentioned, the one held in late August was below the statistical norm in size due to the fact that the man died on Ponape. The major items given are listed in Table 9.3 (fourth funeral). All the $2,100 worth of foods presented were imports, purchased at the consumer's cooperative or at one of the other 15 retail stores in the village. The pattern of short-term visiting by about 300 guests, and temporary formation of a pseudohousehold by some of the close kin of the deceased, also was evident.

From the preceding data, a conclusion may be offered about the effect of funeral practices on the consumption of imported goods. Because no indigenous valuables or imported durable consumer goods are used in funerals, they have no direct effects on the consumption of durable imported commodities, unlike the clothing required for wedding distributions. However, in 1975, funerals did increase the demand for imported rice, tinned meats and fish, ship's biscuits, sugar, coffee, and minor items. This effect occurs in two ways.

First, on an everyday basis most households consume a combination of local foods, mainly produced by their own members, and imported foods, especially rice and canned fish and meats (chapter 7). But for the duration of the third and fourth funerals of Table 9.3, the over 200 visitors to the house of the close kin of the deceased consumed only the imported rice, ship's biscuits, canned fish, and liquids provided for the events by themselves and others. With regard to their demand dimension, and given the absence of pigs, funerals increased the consumption of imported foods by providing culturally significant occasions on which large numbers of people consume more imports than normal for short periods.

The difficulties of determining the magnitude of this effect are apparent, and I am unable to do so with the information available. However, I can mention one incident that shows the probable quantitative significance of funerals and other ceremonial events on the demand for imports. As shown in Table 9.3, the third and fourth funerals together resulted in the purchase of 111 bags of rice, each weighing 50 pounds. In this same two week period (early September), an additional 40 bags of rice were required for the dedication of the Sharon Inn (see chapters 8 and 10). As a result of the demand for 151 bags of rice generated by these ceremonies, every store on the island (including those in other villages) ran out of rice. This incident not only is evidence of the likely quantitative impact of ceremonies on the consumption of imported foods; it also shows that another unintended consequence of funerals is to increase retail sales by channelling part of the income earned through government jobs into the hands of village storeowners.

Second, with regard to their distributive dimension, funerals have the unintended effect of concentrating large quantities of imported foods in the households of the deceased's close kin. This is because not all the food is consumed by the short-term guests. For example, at the third funeral of Table 9.3, five bags of rice, nine tins of ship's biscuits, and many cans of mackerel were left in the household of the eldest son of the deceased 12 days after the man had died. His own family consumed only the imported foods contributed for the funeral for the whole week following the event, and the families of his three brothers also consumed far more imported food than usual. Similarly, 18 days after the fourth funeral of Table 9.3, 22 of the 86 bags of rice still were unconsumed, as were 48 of the 428 cans of mackerel, plus an uncounted number of biscuit tins. I was told that these "leftovers" would be shared out between the households of the deceased's close kin, not redistributed back among the original contributors, as proved to be the case. So although that portion of the imported foods that is not consumed by the short-term visitors is not physically redistributed, it is concentrated in the few households of the close kin of the deceased. It is easy to see how the ready availability of large quantities of rice, canned fish, ship's biscuits, and so forth increases the consumption of these foods by these households for several weeks or months after the event.

However, I hasten to add that this consequence applies only to the funerals that occurred after the hog cholera epidemic. At the two funerals about which I was able to acquire data while pigs were still available, a total of 43 pigs were killed and consumed by the guests, and breadfruit and drinking coconuts presented as well. Probably, before the hog cholera, lesser quantities of imports were used in funerals, and greater quantities of local foods. Certainly, the only food that was "customarily required" for funerals was pork, provided mainly by the close kin of the deceased. Furthermore, it is the storeability of imported foods that results in the concentration effect, which is a major influence on the increased consumption of imported foods due to funerals. The pork, breadfruit, and taro that used to be eaten in the context of funerals would spoil after a few days, so the concentration effect must have been negligible.

10
Ceremonial Consumption: Holidays

In 1975, the September 6 dedication feast of the Sharon Inn (chapter 8), Christmas, and New Year's day were the major holidays at which large feasts and celebrations were held. In most years, the date on which the American Navy rescued the island from the Japanese (September 8, 1945) also is commemorated with a large feast and recreational events. In 1975, however, this Liberation Day was only a small celebration, due to the dedication feast that preceded it by only two days. In fact, because almost all the foods provided for the feast were left-overs from the dedication feast, I shall exclude Liberation Day from consideration. In this chapter, I summarize the organization, by means of the kumi, and material components, especially the demand dimension, of the three other 1975 holidays. I conclude with an overall evaluation of the effects of ceremonial occasions on the economy of Lelu village.

KUMI INCOME

As described in chapter 8, almost the entire adult village population belongs to one of four kumi, groups connected to the church whose main function is the organization of activities on several holidays. Most of the organized activities of the kumi are devoted to earning income that is expended on feast foods on Liberation Day (in most years) and on several celebrations held near the end of each calendar year. The year-end events include small feasts held when new church officers are installed for the upcoming year (chapter 8), and much larger feasts on Christmas and New Year's day. Most adults in the village participate in the joint activities of one or another of the groups.

Throughout the course of the year, the members of each kumi engage in activities to earn money that will be spent on foodstuffs to be consumed at the year-end feasts. At the first monthly meeting of each kumi held

159

in January, the members decide, with the advice of their leaders, how much money will be required for their various celebrations and how they will raise it. Each of the four kumi earns its own money, keeps its own financial records, and makes its own separate plan about what it will do to finance its activities. The most common means, which all the groups used in 1975 and in most other years as well, is for each member to make an initial contribution to his or her group, which varied in 1975 from $5 to $24. At the next and all subsequent meetings the money so collected is loaned out to the membership, to be repaid the following month at the interest rate of 10% monthly. Each succeeding month, the money paid back, plus the interest collected, again is loaned out to individual members, each member being free to borrow whatever amount he or she wishes. By this method, each group potentially could double the amount of its initial contributions at the end of seven months. Actually, this potential was not realized by any of the four groups in 1975, because some members failed to attend and pay back their loans each month, so that their outstanding loans were not placed into the common pool. In three of the groups, separate budgets were kept for the men and women, and each sex maintained its own pool of funds from which money was borrowed.

Other means also were used to finance the year-end events. The women of two of the groups contributed coconuts for a joint copra-making enterprise and gave the proceeds to the budgets of their kumi. Typically, each woman gave a specified number of husked coconuts (say, 25) at several times during the year. The women met to cut and dry the copra for sale to the Kosrae Island Cooperative Association, the local copra purchasing agent. For their part, the men of one group worked as stevedores, and similarly contributed their wages to the budget of their group's men.

Quantitative data on the amounts and sources of earnings for the four kumi for 1975 are presented in Table 10.1. The almost $13,000 earned is a mean contribution of only about $25 per year per kumi member, or about $100 per household. In normal years, each group organized its own separate feast and celebrations for Liberation Day and for the year-end feasts. The groups spent the money earned during the year on these events, to buy imported foods and locally raised pigs and perhaps fish. However, 1975 was an atypical year, for two reasons. First, the Lelu church dedicated its new building, the Sharon Inn, on September 6, so that the Liberation Day feast two days later was much smaller than usual. Second, all the domestic pigs were killed by August due to the hog cholera, so that only one of the groups was able to acquire pigs, and those were wild. Again, the hog cholera exerted an influence on

TABLE 10.1
Sources of earnings for year-end ceremonies by four kumi

Group	Number of Active Members	Contributions and Monthly Borrowing	Copra (women)	Stevedoring (men)	Left from 1974	Total Earned, 1975
first						
women	78	$2,155	$500		0	$2,655
men	50	$1,354		$390	0	$1,744
seconda						
women	73	$1,049	0		$125	$2,614
men	49	$1,440		0		
third						
women	92	$1,655	0		0	$1,655
men	54	$1,169		0	0	$1,169
fourth						
women	69	$1,056	$461		$272	$1,789
men	54	$1,038		0	$280	$1,318
TOTAL	519	$10,916	$961	$390	$677	$12,944

aThe second group did not segregate the sexes for purposes of financial accounting. However, the women did set up a special fund to purchase cloth with which to make new uniforms; the $1,049 figure refers to this pool, and the $1,440 and $2,614 refers to amounts earned by both sexes.

the ceremonial demand of the village: normally, the groups spent much or most of the money earned during the year on pigs, bought from other Kosraens. For 1972, for example, Schaefer (1976:114) reported that the group he joined spent $1,300 on nine large pigs consumed at the Christmas feast. In 1974, however, all four groups spent practically all their income on imported foods bought from a local retail store or special-ordered from off-island, and on women's uniforms.

KUMI EXPENDITURES

Table 10.2 shows how the four groups expended the $12,944 collected from their members throughout the year. The footnotes to this table give an idea of the variability in how different groups organized their expenditures and in how they chose to celebrate the New Year (see Peoples 1977 for a more detailed discussion). In 1975, the women of all four groups earned, mainly from monthly borrowing and copra-making, a total of $7,148 (Table 10.1); almost half this sum, or $3,409, was spent on cloth to be sewn into uniforms. In 1975, as in other years, the four groups competed in a friendly fashion by singing and marching in the church's worship building on installation day, Christmas, the Sunday after Christmas, and New Year's (see chapter 8). On these four occasions, each woman required four new dresses, plus lace and trimmings, each of a different color, each to be worn at a different event. The groups organized the purchase of the needed cloth and lace differently. The first group bought the materials necessary for all four dresses out of the kumi's accumulated women's money; the third group bought only materials needed for two of the four dresses and had its women purchase materials for the other two dresses individually; the fourth group purchased materials for only one dress out of its own funds. This explains most of the variability in the amounts expended by the women of the four groups on uniforms in Table 10.2. It also means that the amounts shown in the table do not represent the total sums expended on uniforms for the four events, since women in three of the groups bought some of the cloth and lace used in the dresses individually. The total amount spent on these uniforms was at least $7,000. Each woman wears one of the dresses of the appropriate color at one of the events. The dresses later become part of her stock of clothing used for everyday wear (see Table 9.2). Although men participate in the marching and singing at the events, no special clothing is required other than a white shirt, which most men need not purchase especially for the celebrations.

Imported foods were the largest single category of expenditures from the groups' accumulated funds. Of the $7,018 spent on imported foods, $4,124 (about 60%) went for the imported frozen chickens that all four groups consumed at the huge Christmas feast, and at a smaller feast on New Year's day. Due to the hog cholera, all four kumi substituted imported chickens for locally produced pork. As a result, in 1975, the four groups combined expended only about $600 on indigenous pork and fish, but in normal years I believe that over $5,000 would have been spent on pork consumed at the year-end feasts.

The over $7,000 spent by the groups on chickens, rice, salted turkey tails, sugar, and baking materials (flour, shortening, yeast, baking powder, and so forth) is only part of the story of these holidays. All the groups also provided and consumed locally produced foods at Christmas and at least some of the other events. Christmas was the largest single feast during my stay that included Kosraen foods (the dedication of the Sharon Inn, discussed below and in chapter 8, was even larger, but included only imported foodstuffs). Customarily, such large feasts include breadfruit, fahfah (of many varieties, most of which use some combination of taro, coconut cream, and bananas), sugar cane, drinking (unripe) coconuts, fish, and pork. With the exception of pork, the 1975 Christmas feast of each of the kumi included this complement of native foods. From the leaders of the four groups, I obtained a list of the amounts of each kind of local food provided by each man of the kumi. Summing these contributions (I am confident of the accuracy of these figures), altogether the following rounded quantities of local foods were provided: 900 breadfruit, 2,000 drinking coconuts, 1,100 stalks of sugar cane, and 1,300 fuhsranyac (wrapped servings) of fahfah. With less confidence, I estimate the number of fish at about 1,000.

I mention these quantities because some of the indigenous foods that should be included in a large feast are rarely consumed everyday. These include Colocasia ("soft") taro, sugar cane, and pork. Villagers planted a considerable proportion of the soft taro and sugar cane produced in the village in anticipation of the ceremonial demand for year-end events. Thus, at a meeting held in mid-January, 1976, of the group I joined, one of the leaders reminded the men of the group to plant their sugar cane and soft taro soon, since they would be required for the year-end events of 1976. Also, my informal questioning of people of various groups revealed that many men did not have sufficient taro or sugar cane planted for their contributions to their respective groups, and had to purchase them from another village. Although I cannot quantify the

TABLE 10.2
Expenditures of four kumi on holidays, Lelu village, 1975 ($)

Category of Expenditure	Itsi kumi W	Itsi kumi M	Ni kumi[a] W	Ni kumi[a] M	Sang kumi W	Sang kumi M	Yung kumi W	Yung kumi M	TOTAL
Uniforms (W)[b]	1917	0	518	0	599	0	375	0	3,409
Imported foods									
Chickens	0	1200	670		662	622	465	465	4,124
Other[c]	600	400	904		171	201	345	293	2,914
TOTAL	600	1600	1574		833	863	810	758	7,038
Native foods									
pig[d]	0	0	150	0	67	99	200	0	516
fish[e]	0	0	0		0	0	52	26	78
Other[f]	0	0	56		25	25	187	118	411
TOTAL EXPENDED	2517	1600[g]	2298		1524	987	1624	902	11,452
Left for 1976[h]	139	?	308		126	160	167	456	?
$ accounted for	2656	?	2606		1650	1147	1791	1358	?
$ earned, 1975[i]	2655	1744	2614		1655	1169	1789	1318	12,944
Discrepancy	1	?	8		5	22	2	40	

Key: W=women, M=men

aSee note a of Table 10.1. Of the $1,049 the women of the second group accumulated for uniforms, only $518 actually were expended out of kumi funds. The remaining $531 were donated to the food expenses.

bThe variability in amounts in this row is due mainly to differences in how the groups organized their purchases of cloth and lace (see text), not to significant differences in the amounts expended on uniforms by women of different groups.

cIncluding rice, flour, sugar, turkey tails, and miscellaneous baking materials.

dThe second and fourth groups purchased pigs from individuals for a special feast held early in 1975, before the hog cholera. The third group spent $166 for four wild pigs caught by one of its members; the pork was consumed at Christmas and at a feast held on January 10, 1976, to celebrate the ending of a successful year for the kumi.

eOnly the fourth group purchased fish out of its own funds. The others also consumed fish at the year-end feasts, but had their members catch or purchase them individually.

fIncludes various recreational activities, e.g., on New Year's Day two groups rented a movie for their members and the fourth group spent $98 on truck rental for visiting other villages.

gThe treasurer of itsi kumi was unable to give an exact accounting of the men's expenditures on the year-end feasts, but could only provide rounded totals. He also could not say how much of the men's money was carried forward into the 1976 pool of funds.

hMonies not expended in 1975. These funds were carried forward into the 1976 budget, and helped form the initial pool from which the members borrowed to raise money for the 1976 Liberation Day and year-end feasts. The amounts in this row are the sums actually reported to me by the treasurers of the various groups (that is, they are not my residuals).

iFrom Table 10.1.

production-stimulative effects of Christmas, other year-end events, and other ceremonies on soft taro and sugar cane, production of these local foods would be lowered significantly were it not for ceremonial demand. I also noticed an increase in fishing activity by both sexes during the days before the Christmas feast. In these days, when most households consume canned mackerel and/or sardines on an everyday basis, the production of fresh fish received a boost.

It is possible that the ceremonial demand for these local foods has no real impact on production and consumption, but merely provides the culturally determined occasions for the consumption of foods that otherwise would be eaten in everyday diet. (See my previous discussion of this objection in the context of weddings in chapter 9.) Despite the impossibility of knowing with certainty what villagers would consume if there were no ceremonial demand, I am convinced that this argument does not apply to the year-end feasts. Most households, and especially those with one or more employed male members, consume a mix of imported and local foods in their everyday diets. Loosely, a category of import substitutes for a category of indigenous foods: rice for bananas, plantains, breadfruit, and taro; canned mackerel and sardines for fresh fish; and soft drinks and highly sweetened beverages for coconuts and sugar cane (Kosraens chew the cane for the refreshing sweet liquid). As I argued in chapter 7, the increasing scarcity of men's time is a critical influence on the substitution of imported for local foods. Yet two of the indigenous cultigens, sugar cane and soft taro, require more labor to cultivate than other crops, and fresh fish also are more difficult to acquire, clean, and cook than their canned substitutes. It therefore is most unlikely that these foods would be produced in the same quantities were it not for ceremonial feasts that encourage the demand for them. In normal years, the same argument would apply to pork.

DEDICATION FEAST

The preparations for the year-end celebrations just described do not exhaust the kumi's organizational activities in providing food for feasts. In chapter 8, I described how the Etawi leaders of Lelu decided, for reasons of efficiency, to allocate to the kumi the task of organizing the acquisition and distribution of food for the dedication feast of the Sharon Inn. The largest (in terms of numbers of participants and quantities of food distributed) feast I witnessed occurred in the afternoon following the dedication service. Etawi leaders asked each group to contribute the following quantities of imported foodstuffs: ten 50-pound bags

of rice, ten 50-pound bags of flour, ten tubs of liquid
refreshment (mainly cold sweetened coffee, kool-aid, and
lemonade), 600 fish, and 165 chickens, each cut up into
four parts (or 2,640 "quarters" of chicken total for all
four kumi). Because each plate contained one quarter
chicken, the 2,640 pieces of chicken also represent the
total number of guests anticipated. Additional imports
were required for baking the several kinds of bread that
would be included: shortening, yeast, baking powder,
salt, sugar, and so forth. To acquire these baking
materials, the Etawi leaders asked the members of the
Youth and Adult Etawi Committee to give a $10 contribu-
tion in lieu of the one pig that each member of an Etawi
Committee provided in normal years for assorted church-
sponsored feasts. Those outside the church who wished
to help could give whatever amount they wished, either
through their kumi or directly to the president of the
Youth or Adult Etawi. By late August when the four
groups had completed their efforts, the kumi had raised
a total of $1,330 to be used mainly for the purchase of
baking materials for the dedication feast. All along,
the groups had competed to see which could raise the
most money (chapter 8). In addition, many individuals
contributed directly to the Youth and Adult Etawi, and
the Etawi organization of the Kosraen community on
Ponape island also helped. Altogether, the Etawi and
kumi together raised $1,728. These funds were redis-
tributed in equal shares back to the groups; in the
end, each kumi had $432 to spend on baking materials
and other miscellaneous expenses, in addition to the
chickens, flour, fish, beverages, and rice that the members of the four groups were to provide on a voluntary
basis.

The kumi to which I belonged acquired the rice,
flour, and chickens in the following way. The group
held a meeting on August 1 to announce the items that
the Etawi leaders had asked its members to provide and
to work out a means to acquire the goods requested. The
members decided that the leader of the kumi, a large
storeowner, would order the chickens and the members
would buy them from him on an individual basis, at one
or more chicken per person, and then contribute the
birds to the feast. The $432 allocated to the kumi by
the Etawi Committee would be adequate to buy the minor
items such as paper plates, beverages, and baking
materials. However, there was still the problem of
acquiring the needed rice and flour. The treasurer of
the group asked: "flao, rice ac tuhkuh yac me?" ("where
is the flour and rice coming from?"). He repeated the
question several times before someone finally responded
and called out "luhk sie bag" ("I'll give one bag").
After this breakthrough, the response from the members
was very rapid and 10 bags of rice and 14 bags of flour

quickly were volunteered. Significantly, the members provided all these goods for the dedication without dipping into the group's regular funds, which were reserved for the year-end celebrations. The contributions of the villagers, through their kumi, were an extra levy made by the church for the general aim of holding a very large dedication feast that would raise the prestige of the whole village by showing its commitment to Kosraen Christianity.

In addition to organizing the acquisition of most of the money spent on the dedication, the kumi also organized their women to bake the various kinds of breads, doughnuts, turnovers, pies, and sweetcakes to be consumed by the members and the visitors from other villages. If pigs had been available, many of the preparations would have been made by the men, who would have harvested taro and breadfruit, killed and cooked pigs, and pounded fahfah. But, except for fish, this feast was to have no Kosraen foods, only mongo paclahng ("foreign food"). Two factors explain this decision. First, the date was set only six weeks before the event, so there was little time to make the preparations that would have been required if Kosraen foods were served. Second, no domestic pigs were available and Colocasia taro was already in short supply due to the fungus disease. According to informants, in this feast rice substituted for breadfruit, chickens for pigs, and various kinds of sweet breads for fahfah. By serving imported foods, the supply of soft taro was conserved for the year-end events, as was the availability of men's time, nowadays an increasingly scarce resource.

The detailed record of expenses for three of the four kumi for the dedication day appears in Table 10.3. The record of the third group, which I joined, is absolutely correct to the best of my knowledge. I acquired the information on the first and second groups from their treasurers, who probably failed to include some of the baking materials. The total for each of the groups was more likely close to the $1,530 spent by the third group. About $6,000 then were expended on this feast, almost entirely on imported foodstuffs.

The construction of the Sharon Inn and the dedication feast accompanying it should be understood in terms of the cultural value that many Kosraens place on the spiritual aspects of their lives and in terms of intervillage rivalry. Early in 1975, the Malem village congregation completed a fine new church building, also complete with a dedication feast, and the Lelu church officers and members did not wish to be "outorganized." We thus see how the attachment of church members (and even of many outside the church) to Kosraen Christianity affects the economy of the village: when the $6,000 spent on the dedication feast is added to the cost of

TABLE 10.3
Expenditures of three kumi for the dedication feast of September 6, 1975

	Group					
	First		Second		Third	
Item purchased	No.	$ Value	No.	$ Value	No.	$ Value
Rice (50 lb. bag)	10	155	10	155	10	155
Flour (50 lb. bag)	10	150	10	150	14	210
Chickens (number)	150	563	195	697	197	653
Sugar (5 lb. bag)	39	123	36	126	48	146
Shortening	41	103	40	110	49	135
Baking powder (boxes)	50	50	20	20	31	31
Canned milk	10	5	48	22	33	17
Yeast	4	4	5	5	8	8
Cinnamon	2	3	6	8	8	10
Beverages		20		?		35
Firewood		33		?		52
Fish (pieces)a	675	(118)	630	(111)	410	(70)
Other		180		80		78
TOTAL $ Value		$1,389		$1,373		$1,530

aMost of the fish provided by the members were caught by themselves, not purchased.
The $ Value shown represents the market value, and is not included in the total $ value.

imported construction materials and of the food purchased to feed the workers who built the structure over
a two-year period, villagers contributed a total of
$30,000 to add a building to the three others already
standing.

CHRISTMAS EXCHANGES

In 1975, the organization for Christmas gift-giving
was along the following lines. Two major kinds of asso-
ciations organized the exchanges: school (both elementary and secondary) and the four kumi. In both associa-
tions, names were drawn, in much the same way as modern
offices. In the kumi to which I belonged, men's names
were put in a container, but only the women drew; the
man whose name each woman selected also gave a present
reciprocally to this woman. I was told that in the
past, these gifts had gotten somewhat out of hand: neither party wanted to be put in the embarrassing position
of giving significantly less than their counterpart, but
since neither knew what they would receive many people
felt compelled to give a little extra. In 1975, the
leader of the group urged everyone not to do the same in
that year, but just to get "something small." In recog-
nition of the problem, another group made a "rule" that
no one was to give gifts over $5 in value, but the data
I acquired on the gifts of several individuals in this
group indicate that few adhered to this decision.

The items purchased by adult women to give to various men of their kumi consisted mainly of the same kinds
of goods that would be given to the groom's side at weddings: pants, shirts, towels, briefs, pomade, and tee
shirts. Small items like candy, soap, cookies, combs,
and zories also were given. Men likewise gave women's
goods similar to those given at weddings: pieces of
cloth dominated the gifts, but also goods such as hand-
bags, sewing materials, and other small items similar to
those above. In the school drawings, high school students gave the same general kinds of goods as the adults
who gave in the kumi organization, whereas elementary
students gave in addition small candies, crackers, pen-
cils, gum, and so forth. Not all adults participated in
the kumi-organized giving; one of the groups decided
that they would give small presents to the elderly in
Lelu instead of exchanging among themselves, and another
never did organize their drawing. Most children, however, participated in the drawing at their school.
Because many parents did not themselves give Christmas
gifts to their own children, for many youngsters the
gifts received from their classmates were the only presents they received. Yet most households had members who
gave gifts to someone, even if only children.

I have data on the items and quantities given by 23 households; in many of these, the adult members belonged to <u>kumi</u> that did not draw names, or they chose not to participate in their group's drawing. But in all these households, children did participate, either through the elementary or high school. The sample households gave imported goods, most of which they purchased at one of the village's retail stores, worth a total of $1,100. Undoubtedly, some items given were not remembered when I interviewed members of the households, so the actual total was probably around $1,200. An average household then expended about $50 on Christmas gifts (range $5 to $110). Table 10.4 shows the variations in the amounts spent by these 23 households. The one household that spent $110 was an unusually large and extended one, with many children.

Assuming there were 150 households in the village, and that the mean amount spent per household was $50, the total village expense on Christmas gifts was around $7,500, excluding the dollar value of some small handicrafts made by the givers themselves. All this money was spent on imports such as clothing, personal items, and snack foods.

CEREMONIAL CONSUMPTION: THE AGGREGATE EFFECT

From the descriptions of the last two chapters, it seems that the major ceremonial feasts and exchanges resulted in increased consumption of imported goods. This conclusion is most clearly evident for weddings, which stimulate the purchase of imported clothing, and funerals, which increase demand for imported foods. My analysis for various holidays and funerals is complicated by the shortage of soft taro due to the disease and by the absence of domestic pigs after August due to the hog cholera. In normal years, pork would be consumed at funerals and on year-end holidays, and probably the production and consumption of soft taro, sugar cane, and fish also would be stimulated. In ordinary times, it is likely that funeral and year-end feasts provided cultural occasions on which villagers consumed indigenous foods in greater-than-everyday quantities. For 1975, however, the net effect was an increased consumption both of imported durables (men's and women's clothing) and foods (especially rice, canned meats and fish, baking materials, ship's biscuits, and fowl).

As Rutz (1978) has noted, one requirement of arguments concluding that ceremonial customs have important effects on economic change is a demonstration that the quantity of resources expended on ceremonial occasions is large relative to the total resources available. In terms of the present argument, this means that the

TABLE 10.4
Variations in $ amounts spent on Christmas gifts, 23
households

Value ($)	Number of households
1-20	3
21-40	6
41-60	7
61-80	5
81-100	1
101-120	1

ceremonial demand of Lelu in 1975 should have consumed
some significant fraction of the total cash income of
the village. Was this condition met?

I cannot be very precise in answering this question. Two or three weddings and funerals occurred
either before I arrived in March, 1975, or about which I
did not acquire information. Also, there were numerous
minor ceremonies such as birthdays, high school feasts,
and so forth, and I can only roughly estimate the amount
expended on these small events. However, fortunately,
the data need not be exact, for all that is required is
an estimate indicating whether expenditure in ceremonial
contexts is a "significant" (say, 20% or more) or
"insignificant" (say, 5% or less) percentage of total
income.

From figures presented in Table 10.5, which are
based on quantitative data given in the last three chapters, I estimate that Lelu people in 1975 spent around
$100,000 in various ceremonial contexts. This is 15% of
the $650,000 total estimated village income for 1975
(chapter 6). I believe that this must be considered
"significant." I also believe that Lelu people themselves were unaware that they were spending so much
money on life crisis rites, holidays, and other ceremonial occasions.

Because, in 1975, the demand dimension of ceremonial feasts and exchanges increased the consumption of
imported goods, they also affected the distribution of
income and the pattern of investment in the village. To
the extent that the events increased the demand for
imported clothing, foods, and building materials used in

TABLE 10.5
Estimated total expenditures on ceremonial demand, 1975

Occasion	$ Expended (thousands)	
Life crisis ceremonies		
Weddings[a]	$30	
Funerals[b]	15	
First birthday parties[c]	1	
Subtotal		$46
Holidays		
Church dedication[d]	20	
Year-end celebrations[e]	16.5	
Christmas gifts[f]	7.5	
Subtotal		44
Other		
Church contributions[g]	3	
Miscellaneous[h]	10	
Subtotal		13
GRAND TOTAL		$103

[a]Assuming the two sides spent $6,000 on men's and women's goods plus feast for an average-sized wedding, (chapter 9), and there were five weddings.

[b]Assuming contributors expended $2,500 on foods for an average funeral (chapter 9), and that there were six funerals in 1975.

[c]Assuming an average party costs $200 on food and gifts for the infant (chapter 9), and that five parties were sponsored during the year.

[d]The total cost of the Sharon Inn was $30,000. Church records show that a little less than $10,000 were spent in 1974 (chapter 8). The $20,000 expended in 1975 includes both construction costs and the dedication feast.

[e]From Tables 10.1 and 10.2. Only about half the dollar value of the uniforms bought by kumi women for the year-end marching and singing appears in Table 10.2, so I have added an additional $3,500 to give a more realistic estimate of total expenses on these events.

[f]See text of the previous section.

[g]See chapter 8.

[h]Numerous small ceremonial feasts occur on a variety of special occasions, such as birthdays, annual celebrations sponsored by high school students to honor graduating seniors, and minor church feasts. The $10,000 figure is only a ballpark estimate, and likely to be conservative.

the construction of the Sharon Inn, the village's storeowners enjoyed increased profits, and investment in the
retail industry probably was encouraged.   Ceremonies
thus were cultural practices that, under 1975 conditions, helped circulate income earned from wage labor
with the Trust Territory administration into profits and
wages of the retail industry.   (This effect probably is
fortuitous, for I have no evidence that storeowners
actually manipulate the kinds and quantities of goods
consumed and exchanged on ceremonial occasions; however,
it may not be coincidence that, of the six largest
storeowners, four also were leaders of the kumi.)
Besides "circulating" the cash earned from wage work,
the use of imported goods in ceremonial contexts also
"drains" income earned by villagers off the island, to
the foreign producers of the imported goods consumed and
exchanged.

11
Conclusions

To conclude this work, I return explicitly to two issues raised in chapter 1. First, in what specific ways are American policies towards Micronesia consistent with dependency theory and in what respects are they divergent? Second, what is the contribution of the findings of this case study of a small island to the dependency approach? I begin investigating these questions by distinguishing two broad dependency approaches. The first attempts to formulate a general theory of underdevelopment using the concepts of imperialism and dependency. I suggest that, however accurately this theory explains relationships between "metropoles" and "satellites" in other parts of the world (an issue I do not address), it does not portray accurately the interests of the United States in Micronesia. The second dependency approach temporarily eschews efforts to develop a universal theory; dependency is instead a methodology or frame of reference in terms of which social scientists analyze specific cases.

DEPENDENCY THEORY AND MICRONESIA

Those who work within the general framework of dependency are well aware that the forms of dependence in the world exhibit temporal and geographic variation, and hence are "historically specific." In attempting to summarize a unified dependency "theory" I do not mean to downplay this empirical diversity, nor to imply that the various dependency theorists all agree on issues of fact or interpretation. Nonetheless, dependency theorists tend to share certain views about the general nature of relationships between economic systems, geographic regions, and nations. I merely attempt here to summarize those views that seem widely shared, omitting many areas of disagreement and thus risking distortion. Even if the result is merely a caricature, it will suffice for my purpose, which is to suggest that although the

175

economic structure of Micronesia shares several features commonly attributed to "peripheral" or "satellite" regions, American policy towards the islands may not be conceptualized adequately or usefully as imperialistic.

Dependency theorists attempt to apply two major concepts to the understanding of relationships between the developed capitalist nations and the underdeveloped world. These concepts are imperialism and dependency. One dependency scholar offers the following definition of imperialism:

> Simply put, imperialism is a system of capital accumulation based on the export of capital from advanced countries to less developed regions (or more precisely, center capital's acquisition of control over the means of production in those regions) accompanied by the utilization of political and military resources to protect and maintain the means of production over which control has been acquired. (Evans 1979:16-17)

The basic rationale for imperialist expansion is therefore the attempt by "agents" of one economic system to accumulate capital by acquiring control over the means of production in another economic system. Notice that this definition is sufficiently broad to encompass many actions of the agents of capitalism, yet sufficiently narrow that not just any action by any agent of any capitalist nation can be called imperialistic, that is, this definition is useful scientifically. Imperialism exists because the capitalist economic system experiences certain internal contradictions and failures, which are inherent in the capitalist system itself. These contradictions and failures produce a need for capitalists (and hence capitalism) to expand on a world level in order to: obtain and/or lower the cost of acquisition of raw materials, lower domestic wage rates or obtain cheap labor abroad, search for new investment opportunities for accumulated capital, take over or create new markets for products, and, most generally, to counter the falling rate of profit at home.

Imperialist expansion by the dominant capitalist nations and dependency in subordinant regions are two aspects of the same worldwide process. As Bodenheimer (1971:335) writes on Latin America:

> By itself the dependency model provides a view "from below". It traces Latin American underdevelopment to that region's function in the world market and international system, which is governed by the interests of the dominant nations. The theory of imperialism provides a view "from above" --an explanation of the specific nature of the

international system and its roots in the dominant nations. Through it the principal force which has conditioned Latin development--the global expansion of capitalism, which is the engine of the international system--is personified.

Thus, imperialism and dependency are two dimensions of the normal operation of capitalism: imperialism is the form of expansion of the capitalist system, which seeks to control economic resources as it grows; dependency is the consequence of this expansion for the previously noncapitalist regions incorporated into the global system (see also Johnson 1972). Accordingly, in their empirical studies, dependency theorists use a procedure much like the following. The relevant dynamics of the international economic system are described for the time period under investigation, the study area is assigned a niche in this larger structure, its function in the perpetuation and/or evolution of the global system is analyzed, and how the normal functioning of the world capitalist system generates the underdevelopment of the area is explained. The well-known writings of Frank (1966, 1967) on Latin America and of Rodney (1972) on Africa are examples.

Like any generalized theory, such efforts direct attention to phenomena and events and to relationships between them that are considered likely to be important on a priori grounds. In the case of dependency theory, our emphasis rightly was directed away from the modernization fascination with the internal characteristics of "traditional societies" to the historic and present external relations of these societies with the developed world. Notwithstanding this very significant contribution, dependency theory is prone to two misuses. First is the danger of overgeneralization: as postulated relationships are transferred from one region to another, they become increasingly devoid of content. Case after case is fitted into the preconceived categories of the theory; the theory then appears to encompass many cases, but much of the power of its analytical concepts is sacrificed. It becomes, as we say, "stretched too far." As I attempt to show shortly, a mechanical application of the concept of imperialism to American actions in Micronesia overgeneralizes the concept, thus robbing it of the very content that allows it to enlighten other cases.

A second, and related, hazard in the theoretical literature of dependency is a tendency to consider the global expansion of capitalism as a universal explicandum. In correcting the former preoccupation with endogenous "barriers" to change, dependency theory runs the risk of viewing the "world capitalist system," or the interests of the "metropole," as forces that are so powerful and ubiquitous that conditions within local economies hardly matter. To the extent that research attention is drawn away from how impinging elements of the world system interact with endogenous forces in specific regions and times, our understanding of patterns of change is impeded. From an anthropological perspective, "what's inside" the small villages in the world-- their economic organization, the relations of their inhabitants with one another and with their environment, the culturally specific practices, norms, and values that they inherit from previous generations--does matter. I return to this issue in the next section.

In what ways do American interests in and actions towards Micronesia, and Micronesian's responses to these actions, fit the dependency theory? From the description of the economy of the whole territory in chapter 2, and my own information on one island in chapters 4 through 7, it is apparent that the term "dependency" accurately, indeed rather precisely, describes Micronesia's relationship with the United States. The people of Micronesia rely on American tax dollars for most of their employment and income. Islanders also depend on American expenditures for public capital improvements and on the world market for most consumer durables and for a large and increasing proportion of their food supply. Because Micronesians spend most of the money they earn from employment with the administration on imported goods, in effect much of the income transferred from American taxpayers is exchanged for commodities produced both in the United States and in other countries, and thereby aids the accumulation of capital by overseas companies (although the income and number of Micronesian consumers may mean that this effect is not significant quantitatively to these firms). The territory exports only one commodity, copra, in significant quantities. The trade balance is markedly negative. The expansion of private business activity since the mid-1960s is largely concentrated in the service sector of the economy. At any rate, this "growth," even if it may be so called, is not self-generating, for it occurs as a dependent by-product of the expansion in external subsidies. As people have gone to work for the administration, for various reasons they have decreased production for household subsistence uses; because it is largely imported foods that have taken up the slack, per capita levels of production of local subsistence foodstuffs almost certainly have declined. As the present case study exemplifies, these characteristics apply to the island as well as to the territorial level, although obviously not all islands share them to the same degree.

Despite these and other isomorphisms, the case of Micronesia does not fit neatly into dependency theory. The various reasons for this conclusion may be collapsed

into two categories. First, the policies of the United
States, and the actions resulting from these policies,
towards the islands themselves are not imperialistic, if
the term is defined in its limited and scientifically
useful sense as the attempt to remove capital and
acquire control over the economic resources of a region.
Since 1947, the primary interests of various American
administrations in the islands have been political and
military.   Specifically, the American government's
concerns and policies have focussed on four primary
"national defense needs":   (1) denial for the indefinite
future of access to Micronesian land for military purposes by any foreign nation; (2) continued guaranteed
American access to the Kwajelein missile range in the
Marshalls; (3) future utilization of certain islands,
notably, Belau (Palau), for training of American military forces;   and (4) potential use of unspecified
islands as a "fallback" in the event that present United
States military bases in Eastern Asia should be lost.
(Goodman and Moos 1981:83; see chapter 2)   Second, to
acquire these strategic goals, the administering authority clearly has contributed more capital, both public
and private, and other kinds of material resources than
it or American firms have removed, at least to date. As
a result of these contributions (i.e., the American
subsidy), and also of the territory's small population,
location, and scarcity of land, the form that dependency
takes in the whole of Micronesia and on specific islands
is somewhat atypical, as documented in the substantive
chapters of this book.
     This is not to deny that some American corpora-
tions have investments and extractive activities in
the islands.   For example, at the time of my work, an
American oil company had a contract with the trust
territory government to supply the gasoline for
Micronesia's increasing number of motor vehicles.   An
American airline supplies air transportation and owns
some hotels.   United States banks have branches in some
islands. The American fishing industry, along with that
of Japan, Korea, and Taiwan, exploits the one natural
resource that the islands have in plenty.   Because no
survey or analysis of United States corporate investments presently exists for the islands, it is unfortunately impossible to document the number of American
businesses active in the territory or the magnitude of
their investments or profits.   Despite this admittedly
serious data gap, the major point stands: the rationale
for the American government's actions towards Micronesia
is the islands' supposed military value, which derives
primarily from their fortuitous location. This is true
at the historical roots of American policy, and it
remains true today (Gale 1979; Goodman and Moos 1981;
McHenry 1975; Nevin 1977).   For this reason, and if my

earlier point that useful theoretical concepts must be limited in the range of phenomena to which they apply is accepted, the policies of the American government in Micronesia are not imperialistic.

Another interpretation, more consistent with a narrow conception of imperialism, is possible: the past American subsidy is paving the way for future activities by U.S. corporations in Micronesia. Some dependency scholars interpret Australian aid to another Pacific region, Papua New Guinea, in these terms. There, too, foreign subsidies are an important sector of the economy, providing public goods and services and employment for many Papua New Guinea people. This aid, however, does not represent Australian altruism:

> Australian aid represents, and has always repre-
> sented, primarily a means of fuelling and trans-
> forming peripheral capitalism in Papua New Guinea
> so that it may perform more adequately its role as
> a secure and profitable centre for the expansion of
> Australian commercial, agricultural and industrial
> capital. Asking whether the Australian government
> obtains equivalent returns for its subsidies is as
> misleading as asking whether it obtains an equiva-
> lent material return from the construction of
> ports, roads, and other infrastructure in Australia
> itself; in these respects, the state acts as the
> service agency and co-ordinator for the capitalist
> structures. The simple fact was that the colony
> could not be held or incorporated into the metro-
> politan economy on a scale demanded by the times
> without relatively high injections of 'aid'.
> (Amarshi, Good, and Mortimer 1979:38)

According to this interpretation, Australian aid to its former colony, which is now an independent nation, itself is a form of imperialist expansion. With its large land area and natural resources, Papua New Guinea serves the world market as a source of agricultural commodities (coffee, cocoa, copra) and of minerals (notably, copper and gold). It has for many decades provided cheap labor for Australian capitalists, first on foreign-owned plantations and more recently in mining and forestry. Papua New Guinea's three million people also provide a sizeable and growing market for industrial commodities produced in Australia, Japan, and elsewhere. Aid from the government of Australia thus helps to provide a favorable economic and political environment for the acquisition of the new nation's raw materials, labor, and markets (Amarshi, Good, and Mortimer 1979:76) by foreign capitalists.

American aid to some of its own territories can be interpreted in similar terms. An example is Puerto

Rico, an American possession since 1898 and a Commonwealth since 1952. When the Puerto Rican Popular
Democratic Party came into power in 1940, it instituted
a program of promoting rapid industrialization through
large investments of foreign capital. As a result of
the subsequent enormous increase in industrial investment by American-based firms, Puerto Rico soon began to
produce consumer durables, using relatively cheap labor,
sold almost entirely to the United States. As urban
employment expanded, so did the internal Puerto Rican
market for imported foods, textiles, autos, and other
goods; by the early 1970s Puerto Rico's two million people were the world's fifth largest customer for American
products. In 1975, almost 7% of all profits earned by
American corporations outside the United States originated in Puerto Rico. (PSP 1976:48, 53-54) In 1977,
direct foreign investment totalled over $9,000 million,
and $924 million of income on direct investment were
earned by foreign corporations (Dietz 1979:26). To the
extent that the shareholders of American corporations,
and American consumers, benefitted from the labor and
market provided by the Commonwealth of Puerto Rico, the
over $2,000 million transferred to the island by the
United States government was money well spent. (The
preceding description is distilled from Christopoulous
1974; Dietz 1976, 1979; Lopez 1974a, 1974b; Maldonado-
Denis 1972; Morley 1974)

If a similar interpretation applies to the monies
that the American government transfers to Micronesia,
then the U.S. agencies who formulate policy act in the
interests of American capitalists. The subsidy itself
is an imperialistic act: it is an attempt to provide a
favorable investment climate so that, in the future,
U.S. corporations can profit from the area's natural
resources, labor, and market. Indeed, some of the policies of the administering authority have this consequence: various capital improvements projects, the
ready availability of an American-style education, the
inculcation of a preference for wage labor over productive activities that in the future will tend to reproduce reliance on world market suppliers of consumer
goods, creation of a "taste" in the younger generation
for imported foods, and so forth. It might even be
argued that the imperialism is especially insidious,
because it is the American taxpayers who bear the
expense of "aid" to Micronesia, whereas it is commercial, financial, and perhaps industrial capitalists who
eventually will receive most of the ultimate benefits.
Thus, for the Micronesian case, a possible argument
entirely consistent with dependency theory is the
following. Although the islands have not yet become
the object of significant investments by American private enterprise, the large subsidies provided by U.S.

taxpayers are establishing the economic conditions under which American corporations eventually will profit.

Such interpretations of economic aid and other subsidies imply a macro-functionalism that should be suspect. Politically influential American multinationals might indeed some day reap benefits as a result of the subsidies provided to Micronesia by the U.S. government in the past, but this does not make subsidizing an imperialistic act. However, my present purpose is not to question the dependency interpretation of aid to other regions. Rather, I suggest that, however correct such an interpretation might be elsewhere, it probably does not apply to historic and present American subsidies to Micronesia.

Like so much else in Micronesia, the geographic and demographic conditions of the islands partly explain why the sums appropriated by the U.S. Congress are not simply, or even primarily, an effort to provide a suitable environment for capitalism in the area. What, concretely, are the resources that an American corporation might find it worthwhile to exploit in Micronesia? In a popular study of the actions and effects of multinational corporations on the world economy, Barnet and Muller (1974:125) note that corporate managers want to know the following about a foreign country:

> What vital raw materials do they have and how dependent is he on them?

> What kind of labor force do they possess, and for what wages will they work?

> How many customers are there (now and in the future) with money to buy his goods?

The geographic features of Micronesia render it relatively worthless to the United States as a source of raw materials. Its low population combined with its distance from the mainland make it unlikely that an American firm could reduce its costs by using Micronesian labor. The administration's practice of hiring many islanders might even reduce the opportunities for foreign investors to locate operations in Micronesia to reduce labor costs, since employment with the government has driven up wage rates and certainly competes with private sector jobs. With respect to the last question, an American-based firm is indeed more likely to find Micronesian consumers able to buy its products as a direct result of the growth in cash incomes resulting from annual Congressional appropriations and other federal programs. But so are corporations based in other countries--probably about half the dollar value of imports into the islands come from

Japan, Australia, and the Phillipines. At any rate, certainly most of the profits U.S. corporations derive from selling goods to Micronesians are an unintended consequence of the subsidies provided by various American administrations.

Speaking broadly, if we ask over what specifically the United States government has attempted to establish its "control" in Micronesia, the answer is continued and assured rights of access to selected islands for present and possibly future military uses, and for purposes of "strategic denial." If we ask how the American government has pursued this political objective, it has done so by expanding greatly the contributions of its own population to the territory. By doing so, it has created a dependence on an activity (wage labor) and on a resource (money) that it can and does control through annual appropriations and other federal grants. The Solomon report (chapter 2) suggests that the creation of this dependency on resources that could be controlled externally was a self-conscious policy, and not an unintended consequence. If we ask, finally, whether this policy has been effective, the answer is a qualified yes, although only after a series of events and prolonged negotiations that American policy makers could not have foreseen in the early 1960s. Thus, in the late 1970s, people in the Northern Marianas, Belau, and the Marshalls voted to separate politically from the central districts of Yap, Truk, Ponape, and Kosrae, which now form the Federated States of Micronesia. It is precisely in those three separated island groups that the United States has specific interests and plans for present and future military operations. The "yes," however, is qualified, first, because many Micronesians (notably the people of Belau and Ponape—see Petersen 1982, 1984a,b) have been less willing to sacrifice their cultural integrity and political independence than the American defense establishment anticipated; and, second, other Micronesians (notably the Marshallese) have made the "strategic rental" of their lands more expensive than hoped.

DEPENDENCY AS METHODOLOGY AND THE CONTRIBUTION OF ETHNOGRAPHY

In the previous section, I noted that an unfortunate tendency within the "theory" of dependency is to underestimate the importance of internal economic and sociocultural conditions in favor of impinging, global-level forces in the analysis of dependent regions (see also Long 1977, who seems to share my view). I also noted that this hazard is especially apparent to an ethnographic fieldworker attempting to make a uniquely anthropological contribution to the theory and practice of development in villages in the Third World. Inherent in the whole ethnographic enterprise is the assumption that there are things to be learned about such villages that only can be known through our traditional "microscopic" (the term is from Geertz 1973:21) methods of participant observation. Fortunately, few ethnographers now make the mistake of assuming, or writing as if they assume, that contemporary institutions are "aboriginal"--in Wolf's (1982) terms, that the societies we study are "without a history." But we insist that, although not "immemorial," conditions inside these villages--patterns of social behavior, relations with the natural environment, cultural norms and values, and the like--are powerful, albeit partial, determinants of the responses of indigenous populations to global forces.

From within the general framework of dependency, many scholars emphasize the importance of understanding the relations between these endogenous and exogenous forces. Cardoso and Faletto quite early (1969) championed the analysis of interactions between impinging international capitalist forces and internal factors:

> In the case of economically dependent countries, the explanation of structures of domination involves establishing the links that may exist between internal and external determinants. These links should not be understood in terms of a mechanical and immediate determination of the internal by the external: it is important to delineate the interconnections between these two levels, suggesting the ways through which external factors are interwoven with internal ones. (Cardoso and Faletto 1979:15, original 1969)

In this approach (see also Cardoso 1977), dependency is a "frame of reference" (Kahl 1976:176), a "methodology" (Palma 1978), or a "perspective" (Johnson 1981), rather than a general theory. Conceived as a methodology, dependency suggests that we focus on the particular elements of the world system that impact the societies we study. What are the interests of global powers in the study area, what specific steps have they taken to achieve their ends, and what concrete inputs have resulted? On the internal side, the dependency methodology suggests that we research the history of the area to discern the historic forces that shaped the economic and sociocultural conditions of the present, that we empirically discover which of these conditions interact most significantly with external inputs, and that we analyze how these forces combine to produce the patterns of economic change that we discover.

The reader will have already realized that this was precisely the procedure used in the preceding chapters. My approach to the "links between internal and external determinants" in Lelu village is diagrammed in Figure 11.1, which summarizes the book by showing how the various chapters relate to one another in a general scheme. The chapter numbers that describe in detail the forces schematized in the figure are shown in parentheses.

The figure should be interpreted as follows. The historic interaction between Kosrae's stratified aboriginal social, political, and economic system (A) and its early contact and later colonial history (B) formed the economic and sociocultural conditions of modern Kosrae (C). The overall strategic and military interests of the United States in Micronesia after World War II were influenced by the global-level tensions and conflicts (D) that Micronesians themselves had no role in creating, but which profoundly affected their societies, economies, and polities. Micronesia's small population, relative lack of natural resources, and distance from North America (E) make the islands of marginal economic importance to the United States, but its location gave it great perceived strategic value (F). Political pressure from the United Nations and the desire of the American government to maintain military rights over selected islands for the indefinite future resulted in the large subsidization of the trust territory in the 1960s and 1970s. The resulting expansion at the island level of government-funded services, public works, capital improvement projects, and employment opportunities are the main exogenous economic inputs into the Lelu village economy (G). But these inputs alone do not determine the choices that Lelu people make about production, consumption, investment, and exchange. Rather, they are a "conditioning situation" (Dos Santos 1970) and exert their influence in interaction with several endogenous conditions, themselves an historic creation. These conditions include: the organization of labor for household subsistence, and small labor requirements of the major crops, the fact that all villagers continue to have access to land for subsistence uses, the strength and breadth of kinship relations, the cultural importance of active participation in church affairs, and the nature and frequency of major ceremonial occasions (C). Combined with wage labor, these local-level conditions have resulted in a readjustment of household subsistence production rather than an end to it (an adjustment that until the present has prevented wage earners from becoming fully proletarian); a clustering of business activities in retail and entertainment services rather than in the production sector; and a diversion of much cash income into religious and ceremonial expenditures that, because they use a different mix of imported and

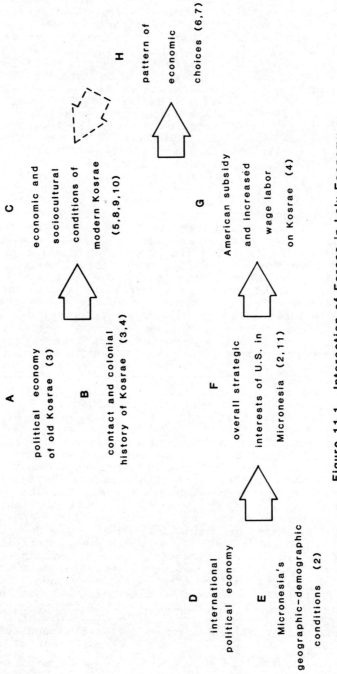

Figure 11.1. Interaction of Forces in Lelu Economy

A political economy of old Kosrae (3)

B contact and colonial history of Kosrae (3,4)

C economic and sociocultural conditions of modern Kosrae (5,8,9,10)

D international political economy

E Micronesia's geographic-demographic conditions (2)

F overall strategic interests of U.S. in Micronesia (2,11)

G American subsidy and increased wage labor on Kosrae (4)

H pattern of economic choices (6,7)

indigenous foodstuffs than everyday consumption and involve the purchase and exchange of textile products, increase the demand for certain imported goods (H). A more complete study than my own would show how the patterning of these choices in turn feeds back (the dotted arrow in the figure) to influence economic and sociocultural conditions. I have little information about this feedback, but have suggested one such effect elsewhere (Peoples 1984).

The key word in this summary is interaction. Dependency theory usefully corrected our previous distraction with the internal institutional framework of "traditional society" that so much of modernization theory uncritically assumed to be obstacles to desirable economic changes. Although this redirection generally is laudable, we must now resist the contrary temptation to underestimate the significance of the variability that anthropologists know exists across village societies. The anthropological predilection for the intensive first-hand case study dovetails with the suggestion of Palma (1978) that an analysis of more "concrete situations of dependency" is required. Our micro-studies can contribute both an empirical knowledge--otherwise often lacking--of internal conditions and a theoretical analysis--otherwise often impossible--of how internal and external forces interact to determine the structure and performance of village economies.

Appendix A:
Time Allocation

To determine how Lelu people allocate their time
across different activities, with the aid of a Kosraen
assistant I conducted a time budget survey among 17
households from October 27 to November 22, 1975. The
participating households were selected randomly with the
use of a random number table. Both male and female
working members (see below) of each household were
studied for one week. We surveyed four households six
days a week (excluding Sunday) for each of the first
three weeks, five for the fourth week. Neither I nor my
assistant attempted to accompany the individuals surveyed during their daily activities and record precisely
the time they spent in various pursuits. This method
would have yielded more detailed and precise data for
each individual, but only a few individuals of perhaps
only two households per week could have been studied.
Instead, I chose a more "extensive" method; I or the
assistant made at least two and sometimes three trips to
each house daily and asked about the activities of members since the last visit. Because of this method, the
data have limited uses; for example, data in Table A.3
cannot be used to conclude that men in the sample spent
8% of their total potential agricultural labor time
actually engaged in garden work. The figure means only
that they were away from their dwellings for purposes of
cultivation during 8% of the daylight hours; some of
this time was spent traveling, some resting and eating
at the garden site, and so forth.

I have data on the time allocation of 43 women and
girls and 44 men and boys of these 17 households, or
about five persons per household. Many of these individuals are young unmarried adults and children of high
school age. It was necessary to include these young
people in the study because boys do much of the garden
work in most households, and virtually all of it in
some, and children of both sexes participate in fishing
and copra making. To have included only adults would

189

have resulted in an artificially low proportion of time
shown as allocated to these activities.

I also included activities during the evening hours
in Tables A.1 and A.2, due to the facts that much fishing among men, much weaving among women, and most kumi
activities during the month of the survey, occurred
between sundown and bedtime. With regard to time devoted to kumi, special events occurred during the survey
that led to more hours spent in kumi activities than
during the rest of the year. This was the rehearsal of
songs and marches to be performed in competition with
other kumi at year-end church holidays (chapter 8).
Some members of all households participated in these
rehearsals, which occurred almost nightly (except
Sunday). To my knowledge, this is the only category of
activity that is "overevaluated" in the following data.

The main purpose of the study was to determine the
differences in time allocation between households in
which one or more members held a full-time job and those
in which no members had jobs. Therefore, I have par-
titioned the sample into "job" and "jobless" households.
This division is complicated by the chance appearance in
the survey of two households in which a total of three
male members had obtained part-time jobs. One worked as
a day laborer for a local storeowner, and two others
(brothers living in a single household) worked in stevedoring and sea wall repair, respectively. I include
these men in the "jobless" categories of Tables A.1 and
A.4, because all three together spent an average of only
14% of their time in wage-earning activities.

The column headings "job" and "jobless" in Tables
A.1 and A.2 refer to the presence or absence of a job
among one or more members of a studied household, rather
than to the employment situation of individuals; that
is, the household is the unit of analysis in these two
tables. Thus, in households with one or more employed
members, the male laborers (regardless of their personal
employment situation) spent 4% of their time in fishing;
male laborers in households with no employed members
spent 9% of their total time in fishing (see Table A.1).
Only males whom a household normally used in subsistence
cultivation were included in the survey. Their youngest
age varied from household to household, but averaged
around 12 or 13. Elderly or infirmed men are not considered potential workers, and so are excluded.

Table A.1 shows the total percentage of time allocated to various activities by the males in the survey,
and compares the time expenditures of men and boys of
job versus jobless households. Activities during evening hours are included in this table, which partly
explains the high percentage of "leisure." Notable differences between the two sets of households appear in
the categories of garden work, fishing, carpentry, and

TABLE A.1
Allocation of time, men and boys, by household

Activity	% of time spent		
	Job Households	Jobless Households	Total
Job (adult)	29	4	19
School (child)	17	20	18
Garden Work	5	10	7
Fishing	4	9	6
Carpentry, Housebuilding[a]	4	6	5
Copra[b]	4	7	5
Church, kumi[c]	5	3	4
"Helping"[d]	1	3	2
Leisure[e]	26	33	29
Miscellaneous[f]	5	5	5

[a]Includes also hauling sand, mixing and pouring cement, and other work connected to house building; figures in this row may be interpreted as time spent in constructing new dwellings.

[b]Collecting and husking coconuts for the sale of copra. Women ordinarily handle the cutting of the meat from the shell and drying.

[c]Includes maintenance of church buildings and grounds, preparation of studies, kumi practices, and so forth. This figure would be much higher for both categories of men if Sunday were included in the survey.

[d]Kosraen kuhlacnsap, meaning in this context aiding one's relatives and neighbors in small ways, such as visiting the sick, giving rides, and helping in household tasks.

[e]Time spent "resting" (mongle) and time devoted to various recreation and entertainment (sritacl), such as billiards, movies, and card games.

[f]Refers to various minor tasks, such as cutting firewood, making the earth oven, and repairs of houses, motor vehicles, and outboard engines.

copra, that is, in activities that transform "raw materials" into "goods," either for use or market sale. Except for most carpentry (largely, housebuilding), these activities produce goods using locally available materials. The male labor force of job households spent only 17% of their time in these four activities, or about half the proportion of time (32%) expended by their jobless counterparts.

The time allocation of women and girls appears in Table A.2. I cannot account for why the females in job households spent significantly more time in weaving and in activities connected to church, kumi, and school.

TABLE A.2
Allocation of time, women and girls, by household

Activity	% of time spent		
	Job Households	Jobless Households	Total
Housework[a]	33	33	33
Fishing	5	5	5
Weaving[b]	5	0	3
Garden work	1	0	0
Copra[c]	2	2	2
Church, kumi, school	17	8	14
"Helping"	3	6	4
Sick[d]	4	8	6
Business[e]	0	8	5
Leisure	28	27	27
Miscellaneous	2	3	2

[a]Cooking, washing dishes and clothing, sewing, sweeping and cleaning, child care, and so forth.

[b]Refers to weaving mats for household use and to making purses, fans, and other goods to be sold in the Women's Club.

[c]Cutting the meat of the coconut out of the husked shell (taktak), and subsequent drying.

[d]One woman in a jobless household was sick due to pregnancy during the whole period of the survey, accounting for most of the difference between the two sets of households.

[e]Baking of bread for retail or wholesale sale (four women); see text.

One difference closely related to government employment is the time spent in business. The women of two jobless households in the sample baked bread, turnovers, and doughnuts for retail in their families' own bakeries; women of two other jobless households sold baked goods wholesale to two of the village's private stores.

For maximum accuracy (given the methodology chosen), the data of Tables A.1 and A.2 necessarily include evening hours, because kumi rehearsals were occurring at the time of the survey and because much fishing by males --notably all gas lamp fishing and most spear-fishing-- occurs at night. Redefining an "activity day" as sunup to sundown, the allocation of male time appears in Table A.3. The table includes both men and boys, but is not broken down into job and jobless households. Those activities that occur almost exclusively during daylight--job, school, garden work, carpentry, copra, "miscellaneous"--naturally show a higher proportion of time devoted to them compared to Table A.1. I present the figures in Table A.3 mainly to show the relatively small amount of time spent in subsistence and copra production. Notice, in addition, that about one-fourth of the aggregate adult male labor time in the village is devoted to wage labor.

Finally, Table A.4 compares adult men with and without jobs, regardless of the employment status of their households (thus, some men in the "jobless" column live in "job" households of Tables A.1 and A.2). For purposes of this table, "adult" is defined as a man over 18 years of age. All but four of these men are married; the four single men lived in the household of their parents, and thus were part of their father's household labor force. Figures in the table, in which the employment status of individuals is the criterion for

TABLE A.3
Allocation of time, men and boys, for daylight hours only

Activity	% of time spent
Job (adult)	25
School (child)	24
Garden Work	8
Fishing	4
Carpentry, Housebuilding	6
Copra	6
Church, kumi	0
"Helping"	2
Leisure	17
Miscellaneous	9

TABLE A.4
Allocation of time, adult men only, by individual

Activity	% of time spent	
	Men with Jobs[a]	Men without Jobs[b]
Job	77	6
Garden Work	5	10
Fishing	5	11
Carpentry, Housebuilding	4	16
Copra	0	17
Church, kumi	0	1
"Helping"	0	5
Leisure	6	20
Miscellaneous	3	14

[a] 13 men in the sample had jobs.

[b] 12 men in the sample were jobless. The 6% figure spent on the job for "jobless" men reflects part-time work (see text).

assigning them to the job or jobless category, should be compared to those in Table A.1, in which the criterion is the employment status of an individual's household. Such a comparison documents a point made in the text, namely, that to some extent other members of the male labor pool of job households compensate for the large amount of time that employed members devote to their jobs. This "taking up the labor slack" especially is apparent in carpentry, copra, and miscellaneous activities, but seems to make little difference in garden work and fishing. Notice the large difference in leisure between job and jobless adult men. Notice, finally, that job-holding men spent only 17% of their time in garden work, fishing, carpentry, copra, and miscellaneous activities, compared to 68% of jobless men; that is, jobless men spent 400% more time in work that an (ethnocentric) economist might call "productive" or "useful."

Appendix B:
Variations in
Agricultural Production

To determine the variability in production and consumption between households, I surveyed 15 households over a four week period from November 24-December 21, 1975. I or an assistant visited each household daily to interview members about labor hours devoted to subsistence agriculture and fishing, food purchases made by the households, and meals. In addition, we weighed and recorded harvested produce; estimated weights were used if a family already had consumed the day's harvest, although this did not happen often.

A primary aim of the survey was to determine the effect of government employment on production and consumption decisions made by the various households. These decisions also are influenced by the composition of the household (among other factors): households with many mouths to feed but few male workers would be expected to work longer hours per worker than households with fewer consumers, all else equal. To control for this factor, I calculated a ratio of consumers to workers for each household (Sahlins 1972). In general, as the ratio of consumers to workers (C/W) rises, each worker would be expected to (1) work longer hours in subsistence and (2) produce more agricultural goods, if all other influences on the households are equal. In calculating the C/W ratio, adult males over the age of 15 were counted as one worker; male children under 15 were counted as .5 workers, if they did garden labor. To determine the number of consumers in each household, FAO (1950) figures for caloric requirements were used. Taking a male between the ages of 13 and 50 as one consumption unit (C.U.), children, women, and elderly persons represent the following fractions of one C.U.:

Children under 12	.5 C.U.
Women, aged 13-59	.8 C.U.
Elderly men, over 50	.8 C.U.
Elderly women, over 50	.5 C.U.

195

In the 15 household sample, there were a total of 117.5
C.U. and 40.6 workers, so the average household's con-
sumer/worker ratio was 2.9.
     Tables B.1 and B.2 give the results of the survey.
Table B.1 shows the composition (c/w ratio), the total
hours spent in agricultural labor, and the total hours
per worker, for each household.   Table B.2 shows the
pounds of each kind of produce harvested during the four
week period and the total pounds harvested per worker.
Grand totals are provided where relevant in both tables.
     The tables document several statements in the text.
First, Table B.2 reveals the overwhelming importance of
bananas (here including plantains) and breadfruit in
the everyday diet.   It also documents the relative in-
significance of both Colocasia and Cyrtosperma taro in
1975; only three households consumed significant quantities of taro.   Second, the low labor intense character
of Kosraen staples is apparent from Table B.1.   An average household spent 58 hours in agricultural labor, an
average worker spent 21 hours in subsistence cultivation, and each consumer (C.U.) required only 7.4 hours
of labor for subsistence during the four week period of
the survey.   Third, Table B.3 aggregates the labor hours

TABLE B.1
Hours spent in subsistence cultivation by 15 households
over a four week period

House- hold No.	No. of Consumers	No. of Workers	C/W Ratio	Total Hours	Hours/ Worker
1	3.6	2.5	1.44	81	32.4
* 2	1.5	1	1.5	10	10
3	3.8	2	1.9	63	31.5
* 4	9.2	4.5	2.04	103	22.9
* 5	11.6	4.8	2.42	46	9.6
* 6	10.2	4	2.55	104	26
* 7	8.8	3.3	2.67	76	23
* 8	12.2	4.5	2.71	45	10
* 9	9.1	3	3.03	35	11.7
10	7.9	2.5	3.16	53	21.2
*11	6.6	2	3.3	42	21
12	9.3	2.5	3.72	65	26
13	9.5	2	4.75	91	45.5
*14	5.9	1	5.9	20	20
15	8.3	1	8.3	32	32
	117.5	40.6	2.9	866	21.3

*Households in which one or more adult male members were
 employed.

TABLE B.2
Quantities of produce harvested by 15 households over a four week period

House-hold No.	Banana	Bread-fruit	Taro	Yam	Total	Lbs./Worker
			total pounds harvested			
1	338	167	181		686	274
* 2	65	56			121	121
3	141	215			356	178
* 4	413	446		16	875	194
* 5	550	69			619	129
* 6	688	171	139		998	250
* 7	516	211	181		908	275
* 8	385	276			661	147
* 9	78	363			441	147
10	604	277			881	352
*11	180	238	20		438	219
12	213	357			570	228
13	673	423	30	16	1142	571
*14	46	469	61		576	576
15	124	300			424	424
	5014	4038	612	32	9696	239

*Households in which one or more adult male members were employed.

and harvested produce figures of the previous two tables, for purposes of comparing the subsistence performance of job and jobless households. The figures in the table are arithmetic means of the nine job and six jobless households in the sample. Had the participating households been chosen randomly, a statistical test could give a confidence interval for these means; however, the month-long survey demanded substantial time from members of the households, which I felt I could only ask of families I knew well.

198

TABLE B.3
Mean subsistence performance, job and jobless households

	Job households		Jobless households	
	per worker	per consumer	per worker	per consumer
Hours	17	6	31	9
Harvest	201	75	323	109

Appendix C:
Dollar Evaluation of
the Subsistence Sector

In a mixed cash/subsistence economy, the usual means of estimating the contribution of the subsistence sector (foods produced for use by the households of the producers) to total income is to (1) estimate the quantities of the major foods produced for household consumption and (2) assign to these quantities the average price at which the foods are sold at nearby markets. Using this method, the dollar value of the subsistence sector of Lelu is estimated in Table C.1. The quantities produced of bananas, breadfruit, and taro are calculated in Appendix D. I assume, from repeated casual observation, that each of the approximately 150 households in the village consumed an average of two pounds of fresh fish daily. With far less confidence, I assume that each household consumed one pound of pork daily. The latter estimate is complicated by the fact that most consumption of pork occurs on ceremonial occasions, and also, of course, by the hog cholera. The "Others" category is merely a ballpark minimum estimate of the dollar value of the minor foods produced, such as tapioca, yams, citrus, coconuts, pineapple, papaya, mango, crabs, lobsters, and so forth. This latter figure is probably too conservative, but I do not wish to overestimate the value of the subsistence sector, for reasons apparent in chapter 6.

TABLE C.1
Dollar value of subsistence contribution to total income

Food	Quantity (lb.)	Price	Value
Bananas	727,000	$ .08	$ 58,000
Breadfruit	332,000	.10	33,000
Taro	96,000	.20	19,000
Fish	110,000	.40	44,000
Pork	55,000	.85	47,000
Others			50,000
TOTAL $			$251,000

Appendix D:
Demand for
Indigenous Foodstuffs

The level of demand for locally produced agricultural goods in 1975 may be estimated roughly from
data given in Appendix B. This quantitative analysis
involves the following simplifying assumptions:

1. The 1,500 people of Lelu village are equivalent
    to 1,016 Consumption Units (C.U.), taking an
    average adult male as equal to one C.U. This
    figure is obtained by assuming that elderly
    persons, women, and children represent the
    fractions of one C.U. stated in Appendix B, and
    multiplying these fractions by the number of
    individuals in the village of each age-sex
    category (an age pyramid for Lelu in 1975
    appears in Peoples 1977:165).
2. The consumption/production survey summarized
    in Appendix B occurred during November and
    December, during which breadfruit was in full
    production. Therefore, a straightforward cal-
    culation obtained by multiplying the mean pro-
    duction per C.U. per month by 12 months would
    both overestimate the annual production of
    breadfruit and underestimate the annual produc-
    tion of bananas and taro, because villagers
    consume more of the latter during the approxi-
    mately four months in which few or no bread-
    fruit are available. I assume that production
    and consumption of bananas increased by 50%, of
    taro by 100%, during the months of few or no
    breadfruit. I make these percentages larger
    than I believe them to be in actuality; for
    reasons apparent in chapters 5 through 7, I do
    not wish to underestimate the total annual
    production.
3. A great range in consumption of indigenous
    foodstuffs occurred among the 15 households
    surveyed, from 51 pounds of produce/C.U./month
    to 191 pounds/C.U./month, with a mean of 83

201

pounds/C.U./month. I simply assume that these 15 households are representative of the production performance of all households.

4. To calculate the numbers of calories that Lelu people produced from their own gardens, I assume that 100 grams of each foodstuff contains the following number of calories: bananas and plantains, 103 calories; breadfruit, 105 calories; taro, 104 calories (FAO 1949; Massal and Barrau 1956).

5. So far as I am aware, the actual daily intake of calories per C.U. is unknown for Kosrae or any other Micronesian island. I assume 2,500 calories/C.U./day, which should be considered an absolute minimum. For the whole population of Lelu, the total annual caloric intake is assumed to be 2,500 calories/day/C.U. X 1,016 C.U. X 365 days = 927,100,000 calories/year.

With these assumptions, the total annual production in Lelu village in 1975 of bananas (including plantains), breadfruit (of all varieties) and taro (both Colocasia and Cyrtosperma) may be calculated as follows. Using data in Appendix B, the production of the whole village during the four week period for each crop is estimated:

Crop	Mean Production/ C.U./ four weeks		Total C.U. in village		Estimated Total Production/ four weeks
Bananas	43 lbs.	X	1,016	=	43,688
Breadfruit	34 lbs.	X	1,016	=	34,544
Taro	5 lbs.	X	1,016	=	5,080

The above figures refer to the "as harvested" totals, including the inedible portions of each crop--the rough skin and interior of breadfruit, the skin and stalk of bananas, and the dirty surface of taro. The edible portions are calculated later.

Using the assumed percentages for the increase in production of taro and bananas during the approximately 17 weeks in which few or no breadfruit are available, the Estimated Total Production (E.T.P.) of the three crops for the whole year is:

Crop	E.T.P. for Breadfruit Season	E.T.P., no Breadfruit	E.T.P.
Bananas	382,270 lbs +	278,511 lbs =	660,781 lbs
Breadfruit	302,260 lbs +	0 =	320,260 lbs
Taro	44,450 lbs +	43,180 lbs =	87,630 lbs

The quantities in the E.T.P. column above were calculated from the amounts actually harvested by the 15
households in the sample. However, the amounts consumed
by these households were somewhat greater than this.
This is because three of the households in the sample
received frequent food gifts from the children of the
head, thus making them underproductive in the sense that
some other household was helping them obtain food for
their subsistence requirements. To allow for this discrepancy, I add 10% to the above figures to estimate the
village's total consumption of the three major subsistence crops. This final, rounded estimate of the total
production in 1975 of the main crops are: banana and
plantain, 727,000 lbs.; breadfruit, 332,000 lbs.; taro,
96,000 lbs.

Taking wastage into account, the caloric values of
the edible portion of these crops are:

Crop	E.T.P. (lbs.)	Edible Portion		Pounds Consumed	Number of Calories
Banana	727,000	X .50	=	364,000	170,600,000
Breadfruit	332,000	X .70	=	232,000	110,500,000
Taro	96,000	X .85	=	82,000	38,700,000
TOTAL CALORIES CONSUMED IN 1975					319,800,000

By these rough calculations, the three locally produced
staples of major importance in the everyday diet account
for only 320 million of the estimated 927 million calories of foods consumed by the village in 1975. However,
this figure underestimates the proportion of local foods
consumed, because other crops (coconuts, yams, citrus,
tapioca, papaya, cucumber, chinese cabbage, and so
forth) and animals (pigs, fresh fish, chickens) also are
eaten. Even taking these into account, it is most
unlikely that the village's own land and sea resources
produce more than two-thirds of the annual caloric
intake of Lelu people, and I believe that one-half is a
more reasonable estimate. Despite the simplifying
assumptions and potential sources of error in the preceding calculations, the data are sufficient to demonstrate that a significant fraction of the village's food
supply is imported.

Appendix E:
Lelu Village
Cash Income

     Cash income comes from so many sources that it is impossible to estimate its total confidently. However, I was able to obtain precise figures for several of the largest sources (Table E.1).   Amounts earned through employment with the trust territory administration were obtained from the personnel office on Kosrae.   The social security office provided data on earnings of some private sector employees. (Neither the personnel officer nor the social security officer violated the privacy of individual employees; they gave me only general information) Through municipal office records and conversations with the village chief and island treasurer, I acquired information on wages earned by short-term laborers in village road and sea wall repair and renovation of the Municipal Office Building and the Farmer's Market.   Financing of these latter activities came from one-time grants from the Ponape District Legislature and the Congress of Micronesia. The data on wages and salaries paid by the Kosrae Island Cooperative Association (K.I.C.A.), the Kosrae Island Credit Union (K.I.C.U.), the Kosrae Terminal and Stevedoring Company, and the Kosrae Island Fuel Transportation Company (K.I.F.T.) were obtained from records kept by those organizations. Data on sales of fish by members to the Kosrae Island Fishing Cooperative Association (K.I.F.C.A.) were obtained from the head of the co-op.

     Additional sources of cash income must be estimated, including copra sales, profits of the private sector, small-scale sale of fish, pork, and a few local foods on the farmer's market, other governmental agencies, and miscellaneous activities.   The figures on income earned from these sources are only approximate, and so are denoted by parentheses ( ).   The bases for these estimates are described in the footnotes to the table.

205

TABLE E.1
Income by source, Lelu village, 1975

Source	$ earned (thousands)	% of total
Public sources wages and salaries		
T.T. government	343	
Municipal government[a]	21	
Other government sources[b]	(30)	
SUBTOTAL	$394,000	61%
Private sources through services		
Wages and salaries		
K.I.C.A.	37	
K.I.C.U.	4.5	
K.I.F.T.	2.6	
Retail store[c]	11.7	
Stevedoring[d]	10.3	
Maids[e]	1.7	
Returns on investment (profits)		
Theaters, Billiard halls[f]	(13)	
Retail stores[g]	(66)	
Baking, wholesale and retail[h]	(10)	
SUBTOTAL	$156,800	24%
Private sources through production		
Copra sales[i]	(60)	
Sales to K.I.F.C.A. (fish)	12	
Private fish sales[j]	(10)	
Miscellaneous[k]	(15)	
SUBTOTAL	$ 97,000	15%
ESTIMATED TOTAL, ALL SOURCES	$647,800	100%

( ) denotes estimated income

[a]Includes salaries of members of Lelu village council ($1,100), salaries of the Lelu members of the Island Council ($2,400), and wages paid to short-term laborers on village and farm roads, sea wall repair, and renovation of the Farmer's Market and Municipal Office Building ($17,500).

[b]Other sources of public sector employment are the Post Office, the Ponape District Legislature, the Congress of Micronesia, and the judiciary. I also include the wages of the Lelu employees of the Philippine-owned Micronesian Construction Company, which had a contract with the T.T. government to construct a new health, educational, and administrative complex at Tofol.

cOne village storeowner employed a few girls to bake bread and other baked goods for retail in the store. The same man also provided jobs for five or six men (two full-time) as clerks, banana plantation workers, and day-laborers. Other stores used family labor only in 1975; their estimated remuneration is included in the category of profits.

dIncludes wages of permanent employees of the stevedoring terminal plus wages of men who work sporadically as stevedores for a day or two whenever a cargo-bearing ship arrives in Kosrae.

eTwo American employees of the administration hired two local girls part-time as maids in 1975.

fAssuming the village's two theaters made about $10,000 and the two billiard halls about $3,000 profit during 1975.

gAssuming the three largest stores had an average profit of $10,000 each, the four medium stores of $5,000 each, and the eight tiny stores of $2,000 each. These figures include also the wages (if any) of family members who worked as clerks.

hThere were four bakeries in operation by the end of 1975, two of which opened near the end of the year. I assume an average profit of $1,000. The female members of several households regularly baked bread for wholesale to one of the retail stores. I estimate that about $6,000 was earned by these women's households through this activity.

iThe amounts earned by copra producers for 1975 still were unavailable by the time I left the island in February, 1976. In 1974, Lelu people earned $51,000 through sales of copra. Although prices were high early in 1975, they had dropped to normal levels by the end of the year (see chapter 6), so I estimate that about $60,000 were earned during the year.

jAside from the sale of fish to the local market outlet run by the fishing cooperative (K.I.F.C.A.) some men occasionally sell fresh fish casually to other villagers.

kIncludes sales of mats woven from pandanus leaves and of other handicrafts, occasional sales of citrus fruits and a few other agricultural goods to the local Farmer's Market (which was closed for most of 1975), sales of pigs or pork, and small quantities sold of other locally produced goods.

208

The knowledgeable reader may notice that there is
no income category for remittances sent back to Lelu
from its many members who were employed in the
Marshalls, Ponape, Saipan, and Guam. I failed to
acquire any information on remittances, and so cannot
even estimate their magnitude. Therefore, they are
excluded altogether. This is another reason why the
total estimated village cash income of about $650,000
should be considered a minimal figure.

Appendix F:
Village Housing

The following data reveal the relatively high quality of houses in the village. I conducted a survey in January, 1976, of all houses occupied on Lelu island and of many on the mainland. The simplest way to present these data is to consider each major structural component of the population of total houses separately and subdivide each according to the kinds of materials used in its construction:

Walls		Windows	
Concrete	16%	Open-air	30%
Plywood	40%	Louver	37%
Sheet metal	30%	Screen	28%
Local wood	13%	Glass	5%
Masonite	1%		

Floor		Roof	
Concrete/Tile	81%	Galvanized iron	87%
Wood	19%	Thatch	13%

Obviously, the materials used in these components occur in definite combinations. Thus, walls of concrete, plywood, or sheet metal are combined with concrete or tile floors and galvanized iron roofs. Ordinarily, when walls made with these imported materials have open-air windows, it is because the owner has not yet put in screens or, better, louvers. Thatched roofs usually occur in houses with wooden floors, local wood walls, and open-air windows; together, these components define the "traditional" style house as this term is used in chapter 6. A modal "modern" style house usually has plywood or sheet metal walls, concrete floor, screened or louvered windows, and a galvanized iron roof. As the above percentages show, most of the private dwellings in Lelu village were made entirely with imported materials: cement, sheet metal, plywood, posts, beams, and studs, glass, screens, and galvanized iron.

Appendix G:
Food Purchases

    I acquired data on food purchases during two different periods. Household budgets were collected from 12 Lelu families for a two week period from October 8-16, 1975. Only nine of these are reliable, by my reckoning. In addition, I recorded information on purchases of foodstuffs by the 15 households who participated in the production/consumption survey (see Appendix B) on daily visits for a period of four weeks. I judge only 10 of these to be reasonably complete.

    During the two week period in October, the nine households purchased foodstuffs in the quantities and prices shown in Table G.1. The 10 households of the four week long survey purchased the quantities shown in Table G.2. If these data were complete, the participants in the October survey would have spent about $115 monthly on food, compared to about $86 monthly by the households in the November-December survey. To estimate the total amount spent on foods by the whole village, I take the mean difference between the two surveys ($100), and add 10% to account for probable underreporting. Lelu people then expended about $110 (per four weeks) X 150 households X 13 (number of four week periods in a year) = $215,000 total on food purchases. Only about $10,000-15,000 of this were spent on locally produced commodities. All these figures refer to foods purchased for everyday consumption; additional foods are bought for consumption on ceremonial occasions (chapters 8, 9, and 10).

211

TABLE G.1
Food purchases of nine households for two week period

Item	Quantity	Value	Mean per household Quantity	Value
Mackerel	84 tins	$ 49.40	9.3	$ 5.50
Sardine	17 tins	10.80	1.9	1.20
Tuna	14 tins	11.25	1.6	1.25
Other canned meats	7 tins	10.95	0.8	1.22
Rice	398 lbs.	153.88	44.2	17.10
Sugar	47 lbs.	28.75	5.2	3.19
Bread	318 pcs.	31.80	35.3	3.53
Fish, Local produce		36.84		4.09
Other Food		104.73		11.64
Gifts to other households		77.30		8.59
		$515.70		$57.30

TABLE G.2
Food purchases of ten households for four week period

Item	Quantity	Value	Mean per household Quantity	Value
Mackerel	221 tins	$118.20	22.1	$11.82
Sardine	24 tins	17.75	2.4	1.78
Other tin	28 tins	33.10	2.8	3.31
Rice	656 lbs.	204.38	65.6	20.44
Sugar	141 lbs.	85.56	14.1	8.56
Bread	639 pcs.	63.90	63.9	6.39
Fish, Local produce		52.25		5.23
Other Food		225.77		22.58
Gifts to other households		54.40		5.44
		$855.31		$85.50

Appendix H:
Household Goods

With the aid of an assistant, I conducted a survey of 22 households to determine the kinds and quantities of durable items in the possession of Lelu people. All households had a stock of the following items in various quantities: eating utensils (silverware, plates, glasses, and so forth), sheets, pillows, and pillow-cases, washtubs, teapots, frying pans, kitchen knives, machetes, miscellaneous hand tools, suitcases and/or trunks (in which clothing and personal items are kept), buckets, home-made cupboards, and various pieces of fur-niture in small quantities (such as a table and chair or two and perhaps one or two beds, usually all home-made). These kinds of items generally are necessary for the establishment of an independent household.

In addition, various households in the survey also had the quantities of items shown in Table H.1 in their possession. These data may not be totally complete, because some households undoubtedly owned some durable goods that were not reported to me nor to my assistant. But a relatively large inventory of household durable goods is apparent, especially considering that none of the families interviewed were among the most wealthy in the village.

TABLE H.1
Durable goods in possession of 22 Lelu households

Commodity	No. of Households in Possession	Total Number Possessed
Cooking Utensils		
Kerosene Stove	19	24
Table-top Electric Stove	7	7
Electric Coffeepot or Teapot	4	4
Electric Frying Pan	2	2
Electric Toaster	1	1
Major Appliances		
Washing Machine	1	1
Refrigerator or Freezer	8	8
Electric Stove	1	1
Tools		
Electric Drill	1	1
Electric Plane	1	1
Chain Saw	1	1
Sewing Machine	20	23
Fishing Equipment		
Traditional Canoe	9	11
Outboard	1	2
Surround Net	4	5
Throw Net	4	5
Spear	7	9
Gas Lamp	10	11
Miscellaneous Major Items		
Iron	9	11
Rifle	2	3
Camera	2	2
Electric Fan	10	16
Radio/Tape Player	14	17
Watch	14	19
Pandanus Mats	19	66
Imported Mats	19	42

Appendix I:
Food Preferences

To determine whether Lelu people prefer imported over locally produced foods, I conducted a food preference survey among 13 Lelu households. I asked all adults and young adults in these households to rank the most common foods in order of their "liking" of those foods. Only 10 of the households (with 34 respondents) provided data that I can utilize.

I included four "native" categories of foodstuffs, only two of which are considered here. "Staples" are the starchy foods that are eaten at almost every meal. "Protein" is the meat or fish that complements the staple dish at most meals except breakfast; Kosraens have encoded this concept linguistically, calling it acnuht. The results of the survey, along with the criteria I used to decide to which rank particular foods should be assigned, are given in Tables I.1 and I.2. The asterisk (*) denotes that a food is imported. The unfamiliar names in Table I.1 are all local recipes made with some combination of taro, bananas and plantains, and/or breadfruit; thus, they all are dishes made with locally produced foods (see table note b).

TABLE I.1
Preference ranking for 15 most common "staple" foods

Rank[a]	Food[b]	Criteria for ranking[c]
Highly preferred	yams breadfruit Colocasia taro	most rank in top 4, several rank 5-10, few or none rank 11-15.
Preferred	*rice tapioca Cyrtosperma taro	many rank in top 4, most rank 5-10, few rank 11-15.
Moderately preferred	aenpat pahsruhk kihriyacf aenpat mos aenpat usr pahsruhk usr	few rank in top 5, most rank 6-10, few rank 11-15.
Unpreferred	furoh ap tihpihr bananas, plantains	few rank in top 5, some rank 6-10, most rank 11-15.

*denotes imported food

[a]The four categories of rank were established using the criteria in the third column; the labels are my own.

[b]The unfamiliar terms in this column are Kosraen names for recipes made from a combination of locally produced ingredients, except furoh (preserved bread-fruit). For example, kihriyacf is pounded ripe banana, plantains, and coconut milk wrapped in banana leaves and baked in the earth oven; pahsruhk usr is Crytosperma pounded with bananas and baked; and so forth.

[c]Rank ordering of "staple" foods by preference was determined as follows. For each food, the number of individuals ranking it first, second, . . ., fifteenth was recorded. This yielded four categories that I labelled as indicated in the first column. The four levels of rank, then, are more or less "natural" categories, in that the ordering fell inductively into the labelled classes, the divisions between which were relatively sharp.

TABLE I.2
Preference ranking for 14 most common "proteins"

Ranking	Food	Criteria for ranking[a]
Highly preferred	*chicken wild pigeon *turkey tails	most rank in top 3, several rank 4-8, few or none rank 9-14.
Preferred	*beef eggs pork fish	many rank in top 3, most rank 4-9, few rank 10-14.
Moderately preferred	*corned beef lobster *spam mangrove crab *bread	few rank in top 5, most rank 6-11, few rank 12-14.
Low preference	*sardine mackerel	none rank in top 3, very few rank 4-9, most rank 10-14.

*denotes imported food (including baking materials for bread)

[a]The relative ranks were determined using the same methodology as for staple foods (see note c of Table I.1). Again, the categories in the first column are relatively unambiguous, that is, foods could be assigned with little difficulty to one or the other category. The exception is beef, which fell inductively between the highly preferred and preferred ranks, but seemed somewhat closer to preferred.

Bibliography

Aberle, David
  1962   "A Note on Relative Deprivation Theory as
           Applied to Millenarian and Other Cult Move-
           ments." In Sylvia L. Thrupp, ed., _Millenial_
           Dreams in Action. The Hague: Mouton and Com-
           pany, pp. 209-214.

Alkire, William H.
  1977   _An Introduction to the Peoples and Cultures of_
           Micronesia. Menlo Park, California: Cummings
           (second edition).

Amarshi, Azeem, Kenneth Good, and Rex Mortimer
  1979   _Development and Dependency: the Political_
           Economy of Papua New Guinea. Melbourne and
           New York: Oxford University Press.

American Board of Commissioners for Foreign Missions
(ABCFM)
  n.d.   _Letters_.

Amin, Samir
  1972   "Underdevelopment and Dependence in Black
           Africa--Origins and Contemporary Forms."
           Journal of Modern African Studies 10:503-524.

Barnet, Richard J. and Ronald E. Müller
  1974   _Global Reach: The Power of the Multinational_
           Corporations. New York: Simon and Schuster.

Bascom, W.R.
  1965   "Ponape: A Pacific Economy in Transition."
           University of California Anthropological
           Records, Number 22.

Bauer, Peter T., and Basil S. Yamey
  1957   _The Economics of Underdeveloped Countries_.
           Chicago: University of Chicago Press.

Benedict, Burton
1968   "Family Firms and Economic Development."
          Southwestern Journal of Anthropology 24:1-19.

Belshaw, Cyril S.
1964   Under the Ivi Tree. Berkeley and Los Angeles:
          University of California Press.

Bliss, Theodora Crosby
1906   Fifty Years in the Islands World. Boston:
          ABCFM.

Bodenheimer, Susanne
1971   "Dependency and Imperialism: The Roots of
          Latin American Underdevelopment." Politics
          and Society 1:327-358.

Boyd, David J.
1981   "Village Agriculture and Labor Migration:
          Interrelated Production Activities among the
          Ilakia Awa of Papua New Guinea." American
          Ethnologist 8:74-93.

Cardoso, Fernando Henrique
1977   "The Consumption of Dependency Theory in the
          United States." Latin American Research
          Review 12:7-24.

Cardoso, Fernando Henrique, and Enzo Faletto
1979   Dependency and Development in Latin America.
          Berkeley: University of California Press.
          (original 1969)

Christopoulos, Diane
1974   "Puerto Rico in the Twentieth Century: A
          Historical Survey." In Lopez and Petras 1974,
          pp. 123-163.

Cordy, Ross
1981   The Lelu Stone Ruins: Kosrae, Micronesia.
          Trust Territory Historic Preservation Office.

1982   "Lelu, The Stone City of Kosrae: 1978-1981
          Research." Journal of the Polynesian Society
          91:103-119.

Dannhaeuser, Norbert
1983   Contemporary Trade Strategies in the Philip-
          pines. New Brunswick, N.J.: Rutgers Uni-
          versity Press.

Dietz, James
1976   "The Puerto Rican Political Economy." Latin
          American Perspectives 3:3-16.

Dietz, James
  1979   "Imperialism and Underdevelopment: A Theo-
          retical Perspective and a Case Study of Puerto
          Rico." Review of Radical Political Economics
          11:16-32.

Dos Santos, Theotonio
  1970   "The Structure of Dependence." American
          Economic Review 60:231-236.

Dumont D'Urville, Jules Sébastien César
  1834   Voyage Pittoresque Autour du Monde. Tome
          Second. Paris: Furne.

Duperrey, Louis Isidore
  1828   "Memoire sur les Opérations Géographiques
          faites dans la Campagne de la Corvette de S.M.
          la Coquille, pendant les années 1822, 1823,
          1824 et 1825." Annales Maritimes et Colo-
          niales 1828 2e partie, tôme I:569-691.

Epstein, T. Scarlett
  1964   "Personal Capital Formation among the Tolai
          of New Britain." In Raymond Firth and B.S.
          Yamey, eds., Capital Saving and Credit in
          Peasant Societies. Chicago: Aldine, pp. 53-
          68.

  1968   Capitalism, Primitive and Modern. Michigan
          State University Press.

Evans, Peter
  1979   Dependent Development: The Alliance of Multi-
          national, State, and Local Capital in Brazil.
          Princeton, N.J.: Princeton University Press.

Finney, Ben R.
  1968   "Bigfellow Man Belong Business in New Guinea."
          Ethnology 7:394-410.

  1973   Big Men and Business. Honolulu: University
          Press of Hawaii.

Finsch, Otto
  1893   Ethnologische Erfahrungen und Belegstücke
          aus der Südsee: Kuschai. Annalen des K.K.
          Naturhistorischen Hofmuseums in Wein, Band
          III-VIII.

Firth, Raymond
  1954   "Social Organization and Social Change."
          Journal of the Royal Anthropological Institute
          84:1-20.

Firth, Stewart
1973   "German Firms in the Western Pacific Islands,
         1857-1914." Journal of Pacific History 8:10-
         28.

Food and Agriculture Organization of the United Nations
(FAO)
1950   F.A.O. Nutritional Studies No. 5: Calorie
         Requirements. United Nations.

Foster, George M.
1965   "Peasant Society and the Image of Limited
         Good." American Anthropologist 67:293-313.

Foster-Carter, Aidan
1978   "Can We Articulate 'Articulation'?" In John
         Clammer, ed., The New Economic Anthropology.
         New York: St. Martin's Press, pp. 210-249.

Frank, André Gunder
1966   "Sociology of Development and Underdevelopment
         of Sociology." Catalyst (summer):20-73.

1967   Capitalism and Underdevelopment in Latin
         America: Historical Studies of Chile and
         Brazil. New York: Monthly Review Press.

Gale, Roger W.
1979   The Americanization of Micronesia: A Study of
         the Consolidation of U.S. Rule in the Pacific.
         Washington, D.C.: University Press of America.

Geertz, Clifford
1973   The Interpretation of Cultures. New York:
         Basic Books, Inc.

Goodman, Grant K., and Felix Moos, eds.
1981   The United States and Japan in the Western
         Pacific: Micronesia and Papua New Guinea.
         Boulder: Westview Press.

Gregory, C.A.
1982   Gifts and Commodities. London and New York:
         Academic Press.

Hagen, Everett E.
1962   On the Theory of Social Change. Homewood,
         Illinois: The Dorsey Press, Inc.

Haley, Nelson Cole
1948   Whale Hunt. New York: Washburn.

Hammet, U.L.
  1854   "Narrative of the Voyage of H.M.S. Serpent
          from Hongkong to Sydney, etc." Nautical
          Magazine 1854:57-67.

Hernsheim, Franz
  1883   Südsee-Erinnerungen 1875 bis 1880. Berlin:
          A. Hofmann.

Hoselitz, Bert F.
  1960   Sociological Aspects of Economic Growth.
          Illinois: The Free Press of Glencoe.

Hutton, Caroline, and Robin Cohen
  1975   "African Peasants and Resistance to Change: A
          Reconsideration of Sociological Approaches."
          In Oxaal, Barnett, and Booth 1975, pp. 105-
          130.

Johnson, Dale L.
  1972   "Dependence and the International System." In
          James D. Cockcroft, Andre Gunder Frank, and
          Dale L. Johnson, Dependence and Underdevelop-
          ment: Latin America's Political Economy.
          Garden City, N.Y.: Anchor Books, pp. 71-111.

  1981   "Economism and Determinism in Dependency
          Theory." Latin American Perspectives 8:108-
          117.

Kahl, Joseph A.
  1976   Modernization, Exploitation and Dependency in
          Latin America. New Brunswick, N.J.: Trans-
          action Books.

Kittlitz, F.H.v.
  1858   Denkwürdigkeiten einer Reise nach dem russi-
          chen Amerika, nach Mikronesien und durch Kamt-
          schatka. Gotha: Perthes.

Kunkel, John H.
  1970   Society and Economic Growth. New York: Ox-
          ford University Press.

Laclau, Ernesto
  1971   "Feudalism and Capitalism in Latin America."
          New Left Review 67:19-38.

Lambert, Richard D.
  1966   "The Social and Psychological Determinants
          of Savings and Investment in Developing
          Societies." In Bert F. Hoselitz and Wilbert
          E. Moore, eds., Industrialization and
          Society. Mouton: UNESCO, pp. 116-132.

224

Lambert, Richard D., and Bert F. Hoselitz, eds.
1963   The Role of Savings and Wealth in Southern
        Asia and the West. Paris: UNESCO.

Lesson, René P.
1839   Voyage Autour du Monde sur la Corvette la
        Coquille. Tôme Second. Paris: Pourrat.

Levy, Marion J., Jr.
1966   Modernization and the Structure of Societies.
        Princeton, N.J.: Princeton University Press.

Lewis, James
1949   "Kusaien Acculturation." Coordinated Inves-
        tigation of Micronesian Anthropology Final
        Report No. 17.

n.d.   "Kusaien Acculturation, 1824-1949." Division
        of Land Management, Trust Territory of the
        Pacific Islands.

Lewis, W. Arthur
1955   The Theory of Economic Growth. Homewood,
        Illinois: Richard D. Irwin, Inc.

Linder, Staffan Burenstam
1970   The Harried Leisure Class. New York:
        Columbia.

Linton, Ralph
1943   "Nativistic Movements." American Anthropolo-
        gist 45:230-240.

Long, Norman
1975   "Structural Dependency, Modes of Production
        and Economic Brokerage in Rural Peru." In
        Oxaal, Barnett, and Booth 1975, pp. 253-282.

1977   An Introduction to the Sociology of Rural
        Development. Boulder, Colorado: Westview
        Press.

Lopez, Adalberto
1974a   "The Beginnings of Colonization: Puerto Rico,
        1493-1800." In Lopez and Petras 1974, pp. 12-
        41.

1974b   "Socio-Politico Developments in a Colonial
        Context: Puerto Rico in the Nineteenth
        Century." In Lopez and Petras 1974, pp.
        42-86.

Lopez, Adalberto, and James Petras
1974   Puerto Rico and Puerto Ricans: Studies in
        History and Society. New York: Halstead
        Press.

Lütke, Frederic
1971   Voyage Autour du Monde 1826-1829. New York:
        Da Capa Press (part of Bibliotheca Austra-
        liana, No. 58). (original 1835/6)

Maldonado-Denis, Manuel
1972   Puerto Rico: A Socio-Historic Interpretation.
        New York: Random House.

McClelland, David C.
1970   "The Achievement Motive in Economic Growth."
        In Gary D. Ness, ed., The Sociology of
        Economic Development. New York: Harper and
        Row, pp. 177-198.

McHenry, Donald F.
1975   Micronesia: Trust Betrayed. New York and
        Washington: Carnegie Endowment for Inter-
        national Peace.

Massal, Emile, and Jacques Barrau
1956   "Food Plants of the South Sea Islands." South
        Pacific Commission Technical Paper No. 94.

Morley, Morris
1974   "Dependence and Development in Puerto Rico."
        In Lopez and Petras 1974, pp. 214-254.

Müller, Ronald
1973   "The Multinational Corporation and the Under-
        development of the Third World." In Charles
        K. Wilber, ed., The Political Economy of
        Development and Underdevelopment. New York:
        Random House, pp. 124-151.

Nash, Manning
1968   "The Social Context of Economic Choice in a
        Small Society." In Edward E. LeClair and
        Harold K. Schneider, eds., Economic Anthro-
        pology. New York: Holt, Rinehart, and
        Winston, pp. 311-322. (original 1961)

Nevin, David
1977   The American Touch in Micronesia. New York:
        W.W. Norton and Company, Inc.

Nufer, Harold F.
  1978   Micronesia Under American Rule. Hicksville,
          New York: Exposition Press.

Nye, P.H., and D.J. Greenland
  1960   The Soil Under Shifting Cultivation. Techni-
          cal Communication No. 51, Commonwealth Bureau
          of Soils, Harpenden.

O'Brien, Philip J.
  1975   "A Critique of Latin American Theories of
          Dependency." In Oxaal, Barnett, and Booth,
          eds., pp. 7-27.

Oliver, Douglas
  1971   Planning Micronesia's Future. Honolulu:
          University of Hawaii Press. (original 1951)

OPNAV P22-5
  1944   Civil Affairs Handbook: East Caroline Islands.
          Office of the Chief of Naval Operations.

Oxaal, Ivar, Tony Barnett, and David Booth
  1975   Beyond the Sociology of Development. London:
          Routledge and Kegan Paul.

Palma, Gabriel
  1978   "Dependency: A Formal Theory of Underdevelop-
          ment or a Methodology for the Analysis of
          Concrete Situations of Underdevelopment?"
          World Development 6:881-924.

Peoples, James G.
  1977   Deculturation and Dependence in a Micronesian
          Community. (Doctoral Dissertation, University
          of California, Davis)

  1978   "Dependence in a Micronesian Economy." Amer-
          ican Ethnologist 5:535-552.

  n.d.   "Chiefs and Bureaucrats: Middlemen on Kosrae."
          Paper delivered to the Eighth Annual Meeting
          of the Association for Social Anthropology in
          Oceania, 1978.

  1984   "Material Affluence and Time Scarcity in
          a Newly Rich Society: Kosrae." In Richard
          F. Salisbury and Elizabeth Tooker, eds.,
          Affluence and Cultural Survival. Washington,
          D.C.: The American Ethnological Society, pp.
          105-118.

Peoples, James G.
1986   "Employment and Household Economy in a
        Micronesian Village." Pacific Studies.
        (forthcoming)

Petersen, Glenn
1982   "Ponape's Body Politic: Island and Nation."
        In The Politics of Evolving Cultures in the
        Pacific Islands. Institute for Polynesian
        Studies.

1984a   "The Ponapean Culture of Resistance." Radical
        History Review 28-30:347-366.

1984b   "A Moral Economy and an Immoral Trusteeship."
        In Catherine Lutz, ed., Micronesia as a
        Strategic Colony. Cambridge: Cultural
        Survival, Inc., pp. 89-96.

Pitt, David
1970   Tradition and Economic Progress in Samoa.
        Oxford: Clarendon Press.

Puerto Rican Socialist Party (PSP)
1976   "The Economic Importance of Puerto Rico for
        the United States." Latin American Perspec-
        tives 3:46-65.

Purcell, David C., Jr.
1976   "The Economics of Exploitation." Journal of
        Pacific History 11:189-211.

Richards, Dorothy
1957   United States Naval Administration of the
        Trust Territory of the Pacific Islands. (3
        volumes) Washington, D.C.: Office of the
        Chief of Naval Operations.

Richards, P.W.
1952   The Tropical Rain Forest. Cambridge: Cam-
        bridge University Press.

Ritter, Philip Lloyd
1978   The Repopulation of Kosrae: Population and
        Social Organization on a Micronesian High
        Island. (Doctoral Dissertation, Stanford
        University)

1980a   "Kosraen Circulation, Out-Marriage, and Migra-
        tion." Anthropological Forum 4:352-374.

228

Ritter, Philip Lloyd
  1980b "Social Organization, Incest, and Fertility in
          a Kosraen Village." American Ethnologist 7:
          759-773.

  1981a "The Population of Kosrae at Contact."
          Micronesica 17:11-28.

  1981b "Adoption on Kosrae Island: Solidarity and
          Sterility." Ethnology 20:45-61.

Ritter, Philip L., and Lynn T. Ritter
  1982   The European Discovery of Kosrae Island.
          Micronesian Archaeological Survey Report
          Number 13.

Rodney, Walter
  1972   How Europe Underdeveloped Africa. London and
          Dar es Salaam: Bogle-L'Ouverture and Tanzania
          Publishing House.

Rutz, Henry J.
  1978   "Ceremonial Exchange and Economic Development
          in Village Fiji." Economic Development and
          Cultural Change 26:777-805.

Sahlins, Marshall D.
  1958   Social Stratification in Polynesia. Seattle
          and London: University of Washington Press.

  1972   Stone Age Economics. New York: Aldine.

Salisbury, Richard
  1970   Vunamami. Berkeley: University of California
          Press.

Sarfert, E.
  1919-20 Kusae. (2 volumes) In G. Thilenius, ed.,
          Ergebnisse der Südsee-Expedition 1908-10.
          (Band 4 and 5) Hamburg: L. Frederichsen.

Schaefer, Paul Dufred
  1976   Confess Therefore Your Sins: Status and Sin
          on Kusaie. (Doctoral Dissertation, Univer-
          sity of Minnesota).

Schneider, David
  1968   "Abortion and Depopulation on a Pacific
          Island." In Andrew P. Vayda, ed., Peoples and
          Cultures of the Pacific. Garden City: The
          Natural History Press, pp. 383-406.

Smelser, Neil J.
  1963   The Sociology of Economic Life. Englewood
          Cliffs, N.J.: Prentice-Hall, Inc.

School of Naval Administration, Stanford University
  1948   Handbook on the Trust Territory of the Pacific
          Islands. Washington, D.C.: Navy Department.

Taylor, John G.
  1979   From Modernization to Modes of Production.
          Atlantic Highlands, N.J.: Humanities Press.

U.S. Department of State
  1948-77 Annual Reports to the United Nations on the
          Administration of the Trust Territory of the
          Pacific Islands.

Wallace, Anthony F.C.
  1956   "Revitalization Movements." American Anthro-
          pologist 58:264-281.

  1966   Religion: An Anthropological View. New York:
          Random House, Inc.

Wallerstein, Immanuel
  1974   "The Rist and Future Demise of the World
          Capitalist System: Concepts for Comparative
          Analysis." Comparative Studies in Society and
          History 16:387-415.

  1979   The Capitalist World-Economy. Cambridge:
          Cambridge University Press.

Wilson, Walter Scott
  1969   Land, Activity, and Social Organization of
          Lelu, Kusaie. (Doctoral Dissertation, Univer-
          sity of Pennsylvania)

  1976   "Household, Land, and Adoption on Kusaie." In
          Ivan Brady, ed., Transactions in Kinship:
          Adoption and Fosterage in Oceania. Honolulu:
          University Press of Hawaii, pp. 81-92.

Wolf, Eric R.
  1982   Europe and the People Without History.
          Berkeley: University of California Press.

Yanaihara, Tadao
  1940   Pacific Islands Under Japanese Mandate.
          London: Oxford University Press.

Index

231

United States Congress
(cont'd)
    61, 182, 183
    See also Exogenous
    forces; Subsidy;
    United States
United States Trust
    Territory of the
    Pacific Islands, 9
    See also Micronesia;
    Trust Territory
Utwe village, 32, 70, 87,
    90, 136, 142
    government jobs in
    62(table), 63

Wage labor, 12, 19,
    20(table), 21, 61,
    62(table), 67, 80, 84,
    85, 101, 104, 106,
    107, 110, 112, 113,
    114, 123, 128, 181,
    183, 185

Wage labor (con'd)
    See also Dependence;
    Employment; Exogenous
    forces; Government
    employment; Income;
    Labor; Labor time;
    Service industries
Weddings, 39, 129, 131,
    136, 138-151, 171
    snowballing of presen-
    tations at, 144-147
    See also Clothing; Ex-
    change; Gifts; Life
    crisis ceremonies;
    Mats, sleeping
Whalers, 43-46, 50
    See also Benjamin Snow;
    Depopulation; Mission-
    aries; Missionization
World War II, 12-13, 32,
    56-57, 185
    See also Japan